WHAT IS ISLAMIC STUDIES?

Based at the Aga Khan Centre in London, the Aga Khan University Institute for the Study of Muslim Civilisations is a higher education institution with a focus on research, publications, graduate studies and outreach. It promotes scholarship that opens up new perspectives on Muslim heritage, modernity, religion, culture and society. The Institute aims to create opportunities for interaction among academics and other professionals in an effort to deepen the understanding of pressing issues affecting Muslim societies today.

Exploring Muslim Contexts

Series Editor: Farouk Topan

This series seeks to address salient and urgent issues faced by Muslim societies as they evolve in a rapidly globalising world. It brings together the scholarship of leading specialists from various academic fields, representing a wide range of theoretical and practical perspectives.

Development Models in Muslim Contexts: Chinese, 'Islamic' and Neo-liberal Alternatives
Edited by Robert Springborg

The Challenge of Pluralism: Paradigms from Muslim Contexts
Edited by Abdou Filali-Ansary *and* Sikeena Karmali Ahmed

Cosmopolitanisms in Muslim Contexts: Perspectives from the Past
Edited by Derryl MacLean *and* Sikeena Karmali Ahmed

Ethnographies of Islam: Ritual Performances and Everyday Practices
Edited by Badouin Dupret, Thomas Pierret, Paulo Pinto *and* Kathryn Spellman Poots

Genealogy and Knowledge in Muslim Societies: Understanding the Past
Edited by Sarah Bowen Savant *and* Helena de Felipe

Contemporary Islamic Law in Indonesia: Sharia and Legal Pluralism
Arskal Salim

Shaping Global Islamic Discourses: The Role of al-Azhar, al-Madina and al-Mustafa
Edited by Masooda Bano *and* Keiko Sakurai

Gender, Governance and Islam
Edited by Deniz Kandiyoti, Nadje Al-Ali *and* Kathryn Spellman Poots

What is Islamic Studies?
European and North American Approaches to a Contested Field
Edited by Leif Stenberg *and* Philip Wood

edinburghuniversitypress.com/series/ecmc

What is Islamic Studies?

European and North American Approaches to a Contested Field

Edited by Leif Stenberg and Philip Wood

EDINBURGH
University Press

IN ASSOCIATION WITH

THE AGA KHAN UNIVERSITY

INSTITUTE FOR THE STUDY OF MUSLIM CIVILISATIONS

We publish academic books and journals in our selected subject areas across the humanities and social sciences, combining cutting-edge scholarship with high editorial and production values to produce academic works of lasting importance. For more information visit our website: edinburghuniversitypress.com

The opinions expressed in this volume are those of the authors and do not necessarily reflect those of the Aga Khan University Institute for the Study of Muslim Civilisations.

Edinburgh University Press Ltd
The Tun – Holyrood Road
12 (2f) Jackson's Entry
Edinburgh EH8 8PJ

Typeset in Goudy Oldstyle by Cheshire Typesetting

A CIP record for this book is available from the British Library

ISBN 978 1 3995 0000 5 (hardback)
ISBN 978 1 3995 0002 9 (webready PDF)
ISBN 978 1 3995 0003 6 (epub)

Contents

INTRODUCTION

What is Islamic Studies?
European and North American Approaches to a Contested Field

LEIF STENBERG AND PHILIP WOOD

This book examines how various disciplines and national academic traditions approach the field of Islamic studies. It emerges from a workshop held at Aga Khan University, Institute for the Study of Muslim Civilisations (AKU-ISMC) in February 2019. It aims to sketch the ways in which university scholarship might consider how actors, in their writing and practice, imagine Islam and how this relates to the behaviour and self-fashioning of Muslims. In particular, it considers how and why Islamic studies has been distanced from religious studies, and how the study of Islam and Muslims might benefit from a closer engagement with religious studies.

There is certainly no homogenous approach from 'the West' towards the study of Islam and Muslims. Distinct national approaches have evolved in response to the various ways in which Muslims and the 'Islamic or Muslim world' have been encountered and imagined, and in response to years of transnational migration. In this volume, scholars working in Sweden, France, the Netherlands, the United Kingdom and the United States discuss their scholarly understanding of Islamic studies in relation to their personal fields of study.[1]

Reflecting on national and scholarly traditions, and a tendency to dichotomise scholarship on Islam and Muslims by reference to a 'western' approach as opposed to an 'Islamic' scholarly tradition, we find three major axes by which to differentiate past and present attitudes in Islamic studies: the nation's place in geopolitics; attitudes towards religion; and the role of identity politics. We

---

[1] Daneshgar (2020) examines how 'Western' scholarship on Islamic studies, and on the Quran in particular, has been used in Muslim-majority contexts such as Iran and Malaysia. His work is further discussed in Daneshgar and Hughes (2020).

examine these before turning to two of the major watersheds in the study of Islam: 1979 and 2001.

We begin with geopolitics. Britain, France and the Netherlands have had a history of continuous involvement with Muslim-majority territories; this can be traced back to the formal imperialism of the nineteenth and early twentieth centuries. Here academic scholarship, the study of language, religion, culture, society and the environment, was often part of governmental attempts to classify and rule indigenous populations, to identify possible collaborators, and to produce laws that colonial populations themselves would acquiesce to. The issue of the extent to which all academic study of colonised peoples was linked to colonial governance, and how these academic interests continued to inspire neo-imperialism in the second half of the twentieth century, remains a matter of debate.[2]

However, it is important to note that not all European powers were engaged in imperialism in the sense of acquiring overseas colonies and extraterritorial jurisdiction. General conceptualisations of the term 'the West' often fail to note that we cannot attribute this kind of complicity to, for example, Islamic studies in Scandinavia, Switzerland or Poland. Indeed, we should be as reluctant to generalise about the so-called West as we are about forming stereotypes of Islam and Muslims. We can generalise more safely about the tendency of 'Islamicists' to be relatively uninterested in making the kinds of comparisons between religious traditions that are much more common for scholars of South Asia and East Asia. Traditionally, an emphasis on philological rigour meant that 'Islamicists' were more interested in comparative Semitic studies than in comparing Islam to (say) Buddhism, Hinduism or Zoroastrianism.[3]

In the second half of the twentieth century during its Cold War competition with the Soviet Union, the United States emerged as a significant imperial power. But its methods have tended towards co-option of regional states rather than settlement or formal agreements of extraterritoriality in the manner followed by nineteenth-century colonialists. European scholars such as H. A. R. Gibb, Josef Schacht and Gustave von Grunebaum played a role in founding academic lineages in the United States, but their students tended to operate in frameworks of area studies rather than academic traditions grounded in philology and the study of religion, as these were practised in Europe. After the Second World War a great deal of the study of Islam and Muslims took place in

---

[2] Said (2003) is the classic account. Note the comments of Hughes (2007: 27) on the distinct stance of German-speaking Jewish intellectuals like Geiger and Goldziher who are ignored by Said, as was scholarship in the Nordic countries and Russia. Marchand (2010) provides a detailed analysis of German orientalism before 1945. Waardenburg (2002: 2) describes how Islamic studies in the 1950s in the Netherlands came to adopt anti-colonial sympathies. The pivot away from empire seems to have been particularly rapid here compared to France and Britain. Also, see Bennett 2013: 11–19.

[3] Waardenburg 1995.

the rubric of Middle Eastern studies and the wish to inform Cold War foreign policy. In the 1950s and 1960s, the MA courses provided in area studies tended to offer interdisciplinary approaches to parts of the world seen as national priorities, sometimes to the exclusion of immersion in classical texts and language. This approach differed from European scholarly approaches in its commitment to the modernisation thesis, which in turn stimulated the American search for agents of change, who would bring Middle East countries closer to American values, defined as capitalism and democracy. This attitude has continued to be expressed by the neo-conservative architects of the second Iraq war.[4]

Foreign policy interventions in the Middle East by the United States and its European allies have increasingly stimulated a counter-reaction by Muslim-majority states in the region and elsewhere, and by Muslim diasporas. And this has given Islam a political salience that other religions like Hinduism or Buddhism have lacked. US support for Israel is a key example. The flashpoints of American intervention: the first and second Iraq wars, the 'Muslim' response to the 9/11 terrorist attack on American soil, and the declaration of the caliphate of the Islamic State in 2014, can all be related to the US–Israel axis, which has been exploited by hawks on both sides to generate conflict. Indeed, Cemal Aydin has observed how recently the notion of an Islamic world has begun to carry political weight. He argues that this only really began to emerge in the 1970s with the Iranian revolution, the Soviet invasion of Afghanistan, and Sadat's capitulation at Camp David; these events led to the realistic prospect of Islamist governments and discredited liberal or communist alternatives. Ongoing British and American support for Saudi Arabia and Pakistan, where 'Islam' was viewed as the appropriate tool of engagement for Arab countries or Muslim-majority states more broadly, has only served to consolidate this situation.[5]

Another difference in European and American experiences relates to the demographic changes of the later twentieth century, during which Muslim diasporas spread in western Europe and North America. Labour migration from Muslim-majority countries occurred in the 1950s and the 1960s, when migrants were sought to fill a vacuum in the post-war expansion of West Germany (from Turkey), France and Belgium (from North Africa), Britain (from Pakistan), and the Netherlands (from Indonesia and Morocco).[6] In many of these cases, migrants were poor and from rural backgrounds and often preserved connections with their villages of origin through marriage migration. In northern Europe,

---

[4] Bulliet 2020; Hughes 2007: 3, 35–50; Lockman 2016; Martin 1985: 12; Waardenburg 2002: 5. For a survey of anthropological approaches to Islam in the late twentieth century, see McLoughlin 2007.

[5] Aydin 2017. Cf. Cook 2014: 361–6 on the Soviet collapse and the American invasion of Afghanistan.

[6] Tribalat (1995) argues that French Algerians and Tunisians are unusual outliers among Muslim populations in Europe because they have markedly lower rates of cousin marriage and are much less likely to observe taboos on food and alcohol.

the migration of Muslims to Germany, Sweden and Denmark has also been coloured by conflicts and war that have generated refugees, such as in Lebanon, the persecution of Kurds in Turkey, the war between Iraq and Iran, the war in the former Yugoslavia, and the war in Syria.

In spite of attempts by governments and some Muslim leaders to create a French Islam or a British Islam, Muslim communities tend to worship in mosques linked to a specific ethnic group and, in terms of describing religious practice and networks, it makes more sense to write of a Kashmiri Islam, an Algerian Islam or a Turkish Islam. Nevertheless, Muslim diasporas are also important sites of small-scale experimentation in fields such as female leadership or LGBTQ+ inclusion.

Migration has definitely become more diverse since the mid 1970s, both in terms of sending and receiving countries. A marked pattern shows that recent migration to continental Europe has tended to be from Muslim-majority countries, whereas Britain and the United States have tended to receive migration that is more diverse in its origins.[7] In addition, Muslim migrants to the United States have tended to be fewer in number and more skilled than Muslim migrants to Europe and are also settled more diffusely in the United States, in contrast to the residential clusters found in several European migration sites.[8]

Attitudes towards the relationship between religion and the state also differ notably between the states of Europe and North America. Germany has state churches (*Landeskirchen*) that are paid for by taxing citizens according to religious affiliation. And German universities host departments of Protestant and Catholic theology, which are often restricted to ordained ministers of religion, and are paid for by the state.[9] These models have been extended to Islam as well, and confessional BAs in Islamic studies courses are often filled by Germans of Turkish origin, who are not obliged to take courses in other religious traditions.

The United Kingdom has an established church and many older universities are religious foundations with chapels. Many universities also host theology degrees, but these are frequently combined with religious studies that allow students to study multiple religious traditions and approach religious phenomena from both an emic and an etic perspective. The structure at British universities is also similar to that of the Nordic countries, in which the disciplines of the history of religions and religious studies grew out of theology.[10] The discipline of the history of religions was founded as a sort of auxiliary science studying

---

[7] Modood 2012.

[8] Uslaner (2005) compares segregation and trust across North America, the United Kingdom, Sweden and Australia. Peach (2006) charts the relative segregation of different religious populations in Britain.

[9] There is a useful summary in Ford 2015: 585.

[10] An overview of the relationship between the work of theology faculties and the anthropology of Islam in Scandinavia is given in Flaskerud and Leirvik (2018). Hoffmann (2019) reflects on the situation in Denmark.

religions other than Christianity, usually in its Protestant form, but with the axiom that Christianity was the word of God. According to this perspective, knowledge about Islam and other religions deepened the understanding of and truth claims ascribed to Christianity. Today the disciplines of the history of religions and religious studies have developed into non-denominational studies of religions. In Scandinavia the term 'religious studies' is now becoming dominant, especially at more recently established universities.

France's strongly secular constitution forbids religious instruction in schools and universities.[11] Religious phenomena are often approached through other disciplines like Arabic, literature, history, anthropology and political sciences. In the United States, while its population is much more likely to identify as 'religious' and its politics continues to use religious rhetoric (especially in the Republican party), the constitution forbids religious instruction in schools. However, 'religion' is taught in higher education in the United States, both as theology in seminaries and divinity schools and, more commonly, as the study of religion in universities and liberal arts colleges.[12]

A final variable that tends to set North America apart from Europe is the salience of so-called 'identity politics'. In the United States discussions on religious and ethnic diversity differ from those in most European states. For example, the Jewish population in the United States has been more numerous and politically salient than that in post-Second World War western Europe. In particular, American politicians sought to emphasise the United States' Judaeo-Christian culture as part of a Cold War response to the 'godless' Soviet Union. Jewish studies has been a trailblazer for the inclusion of histories that have been ignored by Christian America, and academics who identify as Jews are expected to celebrate Jewish religion and culture for a Jewish student body.[13] This has provided a model for other ethnic or religious minorities to find their own spaces in universities, whether these are other 'migrant' communities (Iranian or Armenian studies) or populations of much longer standing who have faced historical exclusion and discrimination (African American studies, Latino studies, Native American studies). In some cases, historically excluded populations have also demanded positive discrimination and affirmative action to give them a space in national institutions.

How far the model of identitarian politics is or ought to be applied directly

---

[11] Note the French government's own statements on *laïcité*: https://www.gouvernement.fr/qu-est-ce-que-la-laicite.
[12] See the special issue in *The Muslim World* 108, no. 2, 2018, on the challenges and opportunities of teaching Islam at theological seminaries.
[13] Goodman (2010) provides a critical overview of the twentieth century development of Jewish studies. He highlights how funders' interests in anti-Semitism and the Holocaust caused a loss of expertise in Hebrew and the rabbinic texts. He also criticises approaches in Jewish studies that ignore Jews' wider non-Jewish contexts. Cf. Shäfer 1995.

to Muslims is unclear, but some academics certainly expect a Muslim faculty to be peculiarly suited to communicate about Islam, especially in teaching environments where most students studying Islamic studies are from a Muslim background. In the 1990s, when Azim Nanji and Francis Sutton interviewed Jane McAuliffe, a Catholic expert on the Quran at the University of Toronto, she commented that her successor was unlikely to be like her. She stated that 'Islam in the future in North American universities will be taught mostly or exclusively by Muslims, just as Jewish studies are typically presented by a scholar with a commitment to Judaism.'[14]

Beyond the differences discussed above, there are certainly many elements shared between scholars in Islamic studies around the world. Today, discussions on theory and method are coloured by national contexts, but they are also transnational and available online. From many of the contributions in this volume it is clear that scholarship on Islam and Muslims is both local and global, and discussions may concern Islam and gender, music, knowledge, human rights, sexuality and politics.

The existence of a transnational Anglophone discussion on theory and method is sometimes used to claim that there is a specifically 'western' form of scholarship in the study of Islam and Muslims. However, in practice, scholars of Muslim origin are also part of university contexts in Europe and North America. Scholarly perspectives do not necessarily relate to ethnic or religious affiliation, but the presence of scholars with Muslim backgrounds teaching and researching Islam and Muslims at European and North American universities should make us guard against using terms like 'Islam' and 'the West' in a closed and mono-lithic fashion. As Eickelman and Piscatori state, essentialising the world into two, one called 'Islamic' and one called 'the West' 'deflects attention from their internal and historical variation and from the vigorous internal debate among their adherents'.[15]

EDWARD SAID'S *ORIENTALISM* AND ITS LEGACY

The philological roots of much scholarship on Islam and Muslims came under heavy attack in the late 1970s with the publication of Edward Said's hugely influential work *Orientalism*.[16] This was the first attempt to apply Foucauldian thinking to the European study of the Middle East. *Orientalism* drew attention

---

[14] Sutton and Nanji 1996: 79. For the assumption that the Jewish experience needs to be expressed by a Jewish professor, see Imhoff 2018: 131.

[15] Eickelman and Piscatori 1996: 162. Also cf. Bashir (2017) for the Eurocentrism of many attempts to critique 'the West'.

[16] There was a strand of (self-) criticism by some orientalists that precedes Said. Note Claude Cahen's scathing comments on philologists who know no history and historians who know no Arabic (Nanji 1997: xii).

to the links between the academic study of the Middle East and its imagination in literature, and the way in which the region was treated politically. Crucially, Said argued that Europeans' belief that they were equipped to govern the region more effectively than its current inhabitants was grounded in academic studies of the region's geography, history and languages. Superior knowledge of these domains allowed them to understand the region's inhabitants better than they understood themselves. Moreover, this intellectual manoeuvre was possible because (unlike Europeans) 'orientals' were unchanging and incapable of modernisation without outside intervention. Hence, one ambition of the present book is to discuss how we can study cultures without endorsing the interests of states and how we can eliminate the idea of an 'Orient' and an 'Occident' as ontological categories and classificatory concepts.

Said's work has been central in introducing an identitarian turn into Middle East studies. It draws attention to the contamination of the intellectual genealogies of American and European orientalists by those behind colonial projects. This accusation was especially damaging to an American foreign policy that represented itself as liberating the Third World from Communism rather than reproducing the evils of French or British colonialism. Said's argument threatened to undermine established academics in Middle East studies and Islamic studies and provided an empowering language for students and scholars with Arab or Muslim backgrounds to critique approaches that could be seen as Eurocentric or neocolonialist. Said's critique is perhaps also part of a process in which Islamic studies research drifted away from medieval texts and towards contemporary social contexts, using methods such as sociology, anthropology, and cultural studies that might evade Said's criticism of philology.[17]

But if Said was interested in countering the tendency of the academy to silence voices from the Middle East, *Orientalism* came to be applied to the ability of non-Muslims to comment on Islam. What began as a critique about Arab culture (in which stereotypes about religion were just one part), came to be employed as a critique about the treatment of Muslims.[18] The context of

---

[17] Waardenburg 2002: 7. He dates this phenomenon to the 1990s, but key pioneering works are Geertz (1968), which compares Indonesia and Morocco, and Geertz (1960), which treats religion as an open variable, to be named by its users and creators rather than etically described as 'Islam'. The varied output of Mohammed Arkoun is also an exception to Said's critique, with its interest in both medieval and modern manifestations of Islam that do not presume the significance of the Quran or hadith as anchoring texts.

[18] Al-Azm (1981) was an early critic of Said's, who noted that many of the stereotypes employed by 'orientalists' were also used by Arab nationalists and Islamists, partly because all of them had been schooled in similar medieval Arabic texts. Note the barbed letter exchanges between Said and al-Azm in 1980 that are published at http://pastandfuturepresents.blogspot.com/2016/12/edward-saidsadik-al-azm-1980.html. Al-Azm's approach was developed by Jung (2011). Varisco (2017) provides an important overview of critiques of Said (some of which were *ad hominem* attacks) as well as his own critique of how Said has been employed.

the 1980s and the growing salience of Muslim identity in the aftermath of the Iranian revolution must also be factored in. In the United Kingdom at least, the political turmoil that surrounded the publication of Salman Rushdie's *Satanic Verses* was a major watershed. Britons of Pakistani heritage began to identify as Muslim, rather than as black or Asian. And they came to identify blasphemy as a key site of their feelings of discrimination.[19] This was also the point at which British Pakistanis began to part ways with the wider anti-racist movement.

Nevertheless, we are not sure that Said necessarily approved of all the uses to which *Orientalism* was put. In particular, we think of the harder strands of postcolonial theory that adopted a positionalist epistemology that identified personal experience as foundational to all knowledge, which (for example) would prevent non-Jews engaging in Jewish studies or non-Muslims in the study of Muslims. Said's later book, *Culture and Imperialism*, is often ignored by those who invoke *Orientalism*, yet it both extends and adapts his earlier argument. In *Culture and Imperialism*, Said states that all scholars and all people have equal rights to comment on cultural production, even what comes from other cultures, and he observes that all empires generate stereotypes as part of their system of governance.[20] Here he extends his argument to the Ottomans, the Mughals, China, Japan and Russia. *Culture and Imperialism* retains the Foucauldian emphasis of *Orientalism*, but it allows for non-Europeans to create similar kinds of imperial systems of thought that he had described in *Orientalism* in relation to France and Britain.

It is also worth observing that *Orientalism* is not much concerned with religion, for all that European polemics against Muhammad are seen as examples of orientalism. Said has often been embraced as a critic of 'Islamophobia'. Our Muslim students at Aga Khan University are often very surprised that Said was not a Muslim. When he spoke in Cambridge in 2002 it was striking how anti-religious he was: he was adamant, for instance, that Judaism, Christianity and Islam had together caused political disaster in Palestine and that religion could not play a role in finding a peaceful solution. He had no time for interfaith dialogue as part of a peace process. Said's stance as a hard secularist has often been forgotten by later commentators on *Orientalism*.[21]

---

[19] Farrar 2002: 267; Birt 2009; Meer and Modood 2009. Note, however, that British Pakistanis were far from uniform in this turn to religious discourse. For instance, Pakistanis in Manchester did not participate widely in the protests against Rushdie that were so marked in mill towns like Bradford.

[20] Said 1994: xxviii, 300.

[21] Al-Azm (1981) sees Said as 'secular' in his approach.

FEMINISM, GENDER STUDIES AND ITS SIGNIFICANCE FOR THE FIELD

Around the same time that Said wrote *Orientalism*, scholarship also began to engage more complex commentary on the role of gender in politics and society, which also considered the role of religion in sustaining patriarchy. This moment in the history of scholarship also gave a voice to scholars from Middle Eastern universities: as we have already seen in the case of Edward Said, this was a moment when Middle Easterners acquired a much greater role in how the region was depicted.

The Moroccan professor of sociology Fatima Mernissi (d. 2015) is an example of this turn. She developed a critical stance towards the subordination of women in the interpretation and practices of Islam and in Midddle Eastern life in general. Mernissi studied the systems in society that establish power relationships and form notions on gender and sexuality that facilitated the control of women. Her scholarship critically discusses established understandings of the sources of Islam, primarily hadith and Quran, and reinterprets them to improve the life conditions and status of women. For instance, in her book *The Veil and the Male Elite: A Feminist Interpretation of Women's Right in Islam* (1991), Mernissi stated that the message of the Prophet Muhammad on gender equality had been misunderstood and misinterpreted by political and religious leaders. In her perspective, the Prophet strived to achieve gender equality and the foundational sources should be read with this in mind.

In the same generation of feminists as Mernissi, the Egyptian activist, author and medical doctor Nawal al-Saadawi (d. 2021) provides an example of a more secular perspective in the struggle for gender equality in Middle Eastern societies. Al-Saadawi's criticism of religion and political and religious leaders is strongly visible in her book *The Fall of the Imam* (1988). Here she combines her criticism of religion with a similarily strong criticism of the colonial, global and capitalist systems that she defines as racist and patriarchal. Her criticism of the practice of female genital mutilation contains an attack on religious clerics who justify the practice by reference to religion and asks questions about the underlying motives for the practice. She, like Mernissi, critically discuss systems of power and how they subordinate women, and considers the role of religion in relation to systems of power and subordination. But unlike Mernissi she does not hold out much hope for the possibility of reforming religion (and in this sense she bears comparison with Said). Mernissi and al-Saadawi have several followers today, including the Nobel prize laureate Shirin Ebadi (b. 1949), Ziba Mir-Hosseini (b. 1952) and Kecia Ali (b. 1972).

At the same time as Mernissi and al-Saadawi wrote, gender became a more widely used analytical tool in the scholarship on Middle East and Islam more generally. Over the years pioneering work has been carried out by scholars such as Leila Ahmed (b. 1940), Margot Badran (b. 1936) and Deniz Kandiyoti (b. 1944). In their scholarship women and gender have been an empirical focus as well as in their thinking on method and theory. A common statement Ahmed, Badran and Kandiyoti make is that a serious and contextual understanding of Middle Eastern societies, including theology and the practice of a religion, cannot be done in a comprehensive sense without an analytical framework that includes a gender perspective. Their ideas on gender as part of, or the entry point to, method and theory in the study of the Middle East and Islam have been further discussed and developed by later scholars, such as Farid Esack (b. 1955) and Saba Mahmood (d. 2018). Esack's work on equality and inter-faith relations and Mahmood's feminist anthropology are parts of a development in the study of Middle East and Islam that integrates broader social and political discussions with gender studies. To take gender into consideration while gathering empirical material has become natural parts of the method and theory of many disciplinary approaches today.

The World after 9/11

A second major watershed in relations between Muslim populations and the United States and Europe was the terrorist attacks of 9/11 and its aftermath: the bombings in London and Madrid, and later in Paris and Brussels; the invasions of Iraq and Afghanistan; and the creation of the Islamic State and the recruitment of European Muslims to fight in support of the caliphate that was proclaimed in 2014.

The events of 9/11 led to a burst of government funding for Islamic studies and an upsurge in the recruitment of faculty. Scholars from a variety of disciplines came to tackle Islamic topics and students of Islam and the Middle East increasingly took on roles as public commentators, sometimes in the contexts of states' interests in counter-extremism. Many more of these new faculty were from Muslim backgrounds than in the past and many had been trained in area studies but took up posts in the study of religion. Many of these new recruits were unfamiliar with the discussions in the discipline of religious studies and the distinctions made there between description and prescription. This unfamiliarity may be one reason they spoke of Islam in essentialised terms.[22] The extension of recruitment has meant that a greater number of disciplinary approaches have been brought to bear on Islamic studies. But the stimulus of a terrorist attack and its fallout has also meant that much of the research undertaken in the first decade of the twenty-first century prioritised the political significance of Islam

---

[22] Safi 2014; Bennett 2013: 22.

and the analysis of Muslims as a security threat. Sometimes this focus led to the neglect of the significance of Islam in everyday life.[23]

A second effect of 9/11 was that many academics with Islamic specialisms of any kind, often Arabists with expertise in the Middle Ages, were expected to account for recent events before a sometimes-hostile public. The immediate aftermath of 9/11 saw opportunistic attacks on Muslims (or people thought to be Muslims) in the United States and terrorist attacks by sympathisers. In addition, violent interpretations and practices of Islam against targets in Europe brought about responses by right-wing terrorists against Muslim diasporas in Britain, Norway and New Zealand. In this context there has been an understandable wish on the part of academics and politicians to exonerate Muslims from the behaviour of small numbers of individuals who claimed that their actions represented 'true Islam'.

In works such as *Situating Islam* and *The Tyranny of Authenticity*, Aaron Hughes has criticised the style of Islamic studies that emerged after 9/11. Hughes asserts that scholars have written in essentialist terms to present real Islam as peaceful and eternal, while the violence of terrorists (or the discourse of anti-secularist Islamists) can be dismissed as heterodoxy.[24] He argues that the work of scholars such as John Esposito, Seyyed Hossein Nasr or Omid Safi, who are (in part) responding to American Islamophobes like Robert Spencer, should really be treated as apologetics. Hughes suggests that we should read the work of Safi and others as primary data of how actors try to construct an Islam that is coherent with American values rather than as contributions to the scholarship about how Islam is constructed.[25] Hughes complains that truth claims in 'religious texts' are not interrogated for fear of showing insensitivity, and further, that scholars in Islamic studies are expected to over-identify with their objects of study to avoid accusations of orientalism.[26]

Several of Hughes' ideas can be seen as restatements of Bruce Lincoln's theses on method.[27] In particular, Lincoln demands that we ask irreverent questions of religious discourse: who speaks, to what audience, and with what interest when they claim that a religion has certain properties? Likewise, 'reverence is a religious, not a scholarly virtue', and there is no merit in failing to ask critical questions of the religious traditions 'of others', in the name of a misplaced cultural relativism. Above all, Lincoln asks that we differentiate the roles of advocate and scholar.

---

[23] Levine 2007.

[24] Hughes 2007: 7, 60; Hughes 2015: 2, 21.

[25] Hughes 2007: 53, 84–92; Hughes 2015: 58. For a study of the works of Seyyed Hossein Nasr as primary data in a construction of Islam, see Stenberg 1996.

[26] Hughes 2007: 6, 71–3; Hughes 2015: 15. Also, Martin 1985: 4; Lewinstein 2003: 47. Note the criticisms of Hughes in Stewart (2018), who calls for a return to philological training and knowledge of the classical texts.

[27] Lincoln 1996.

The position that true Islam is peaceful, and that it can be separated unprob-
lematically from culture and from false interpretation, is also commonplace for
many politicians and in school curricula.[28] Lynn Revell comments that religious
education in schools has a self-confirming bias that aims to affirm the validity
of all religions and that avoids tackling questions of religious authority.[29] In so
doing, issues of confessional disagreement are often ignored, and this has the
side effect of silencing minority positions.[30]

Revell and Panjwani note that it is not sufficient to simply endorse varieties
of essentialism that are politically expedient and read current values onto medieval scenarios. Such an approach has no guarantee of convincing an audience
that is willing to return to historical and scriptural sources that are often forged
in an environment of conflict with non-Muslims.[31]

Hughes and Lincoln are both clear that there is nothing wrong with advocacy, especially in an environment where Muslims are scapegoated for the
behaviour of a small number of terrorists. Their objection is to the confusion
between advocacy and scholarship. This is particularly marked in the study of
Islamic origins, where curricula at schools and universities commonly repeat
the narratives given in Muslim Arabic sources as fact, without considering the
later contexts in which these texts are written, the imperial vested interests they
seek to defend, or the confessional character of many sources. As Mohammed
Arkoun stated, 'research cannot proceed from the self-justifying discourses of
different faith communities'.[32] This is not to endorse any one revisionist version
of Islamic origins, but to insist that we need to foreground the problems associated with reading the sources straightforwardly and the existence of additional
and alternative bodies of evidence.

The work of Asma Afsaruddin, whose accounts of the Arab conquests
have been extensively criticised by Chase Robinson, is a striking example
of how modern apologetics can affect history writing.[33] For Afsarrudin, the
Companions of the Prophet are pious forebears, whose lives evoke an Islam
that 'empowers women, prescribes consultative government and fosters inclusion towards non-Muslims'.[34] She presents Islamists as simply ignorant of this

---

[28] Eickelman and Piscatori (1996: 38ff.) have described this type of thinking as the 'objectification of
Islam'. Also note the comments of Bolognani and Mellor (2012) on the self-confirming liberal bias in
ethnographic studies of British Pakistanis.

[29] Revell 2008.

[30] Panjwani 2005; Curtis 2006.

[31] Revell 2008; Panjwani 2005. Cf. Madhany 2008.

[32] Arkoun 2002: 2. Also, see the comments of Segovia (2018). Arkoun was key advocate for the
re-thinking of Islam in the contemporary world. In particular he argued that the whole of Islamic
tradition deserved engagement, including ideas and thinkers that had been ignored because of accusations of heterodoxy.

[33] Afsarrudin 2008.

[34] Robinson 2009: 208.

history, and condemns them as the intellectual heirs of minoritarian heterodox factions like the Kharijites and as cynical graspers for power. She builds her position by excavating proof texts from history sources that can be used to defend a 'liberal' Islam. Robinson observes that her case is highly problematic as a work of history: she endorses the anachronistic majoritarianism of Sunni texts written in a later era that purport to describe the seventh century; she believes that non-Muslims simply welcomed their Muslim conquerors and she claims that tenth-century compilations preserve the transcripts of seventh-century speeches. Here then, her purpose (of defending 'ordinary Muslims' and criticising Islamists) is presumed to excuse readings of history that are either naive or disingenuous.[35]

THE STUDY OF RELIGIONS

Participants in the workshop on which this volume is based were asked to consider theoretical developments in the field(s) of Islamic studies and exemplify this from their own field of study. These discussions went beyond exercises in mapping the field, but also extended into statements of what the field should evolve into and, in some cases, providing working, empirical examples of good practice.

Needless to say, not all the participants agreed. In France and Sweden in particular, scholars desired a non-confessional approach to religious subjects, framed in a methodological secularism. North Americans tended to stress scholars' positionality and be very sceptical about the possibility of objectivity. But it was not possible to generalise about a European approach to Islamic studies: the varied relations between religion and the state and the diverse migration histories of Muslim populations into Europe have made for very different scholarly milieux in Britain, France, Germany, the Netherlands and the Nordic countries. This workshop found a diversity of national intellectual approaches that is significant.

The work of Shahab Ahmed and Talal Asad were important points of engagement for many papers in this collection. Ahmed has produced a broad vision of Islam as a cultural complex from the Balkans to Bengal, a complex that is not centred on law-making or on Arabic. Ahmed responds to Marshall Hodgson's differentiation of 'religion' and 'culture' into two differentiated spheres of Islam and Islamicate. Ahmed observes that this leads to an unnecessary privileging of Quran, hadith and the legal tradition and that it invites an arbitrary separation between interior 'religion' and exterior culture – a separation that is rooted in

---

[35] A similar critique might also be levelled at Armstrong (2006).

Hodgson's own Quaker background.[36] Ahmed proposes a broader definition of Islam to encompass any situation in which people deploy the tradition to generate meaning. 'Islam', for Ahmed, is an etic term, albeit a very broad one.[37]

Asad imagines Islam as a discursive tradition, in which present practices by Muslims are related to a past Muslim context, where these practices were instituted, and to a Muslim future, in which it is hoped that these practices will continue.[38] Asad's conception has the advantage of allowing for constant change, while still recognising the primacy of a group of formative texts (the Quran and hadith) and the important sense of being part of an ongoing conversation about what it means for Muslims to practice Islam. In addition, Asad argues that Muslims are particularly committed to public manifestations of their religion, and that the prescriptions of secularism impinge on these obligations to such an extent that secularism cannot be seen as a neutral or equal system of government.[39] For both Ahmed and Asad, 'religion' is a concept loaded with (Protestant) Christian assumptions that make it unsuitable for use in describing Muslims, because of its assumption that religion can be privatised and distinguished from politics, society and/or from culture.

Nevertheless, a number of the papers presented in this workshop raise some important caveats. Asad's vision of tradition is still a Muslim tradition, which appears to be separate from other traditions. The conversation that he describes is one with other Muslims, past and present, rather than with members of other traditions. Aaron Hughes' paper for this volume warns against seeing Islam as an outgrowth from a single nucleus. Instead, Hughes states that we need to acknowledge the centripetal agency in which bottom-up expectations shape what Islam is in different localities, even as certain religious elites and institutions attempt to align these local 'Islams' with their own model of what Islam ought to be. Each of these Islams may present themselves as necessary outcomes of Muhammad's preaching.[40] But it is not the role of Islamic studies to select which of these is a real Islam, rather it is to highlight how each Islam is the product of its own varying circumstances, where ideas expressed in Arabic

---

[36] Ahmed 2016: 170–1. Ahmed suggests that Hodgson's division leaves Islamic discourse open to a Salafist-inspired differentiation of religion and culture.

[37] Ahmed 2016: 9.

[38] Asad 1993. Smith (1962) had already written of Islam as a cumulative tradition, rather than one that was simply established in the seventh century and found different political expressions. A comparison to Gibb (1949), with its one chapter on modern Islam, illustrates how novel Smith was in this regard. Cf. Waardenburg 2002: 4, 2007: 23.

[39] Asad 2003: esp. 8. Note the critique of Asad made by Jakobsen (2015), that he dismisses the voices of secular Muslims or those influenced by a European and North American discourse as inauthentic. Bangstad (2009) criticises Asad's use of a polarisation between 'West' and 'non-West', and identifies a strand of Romantic essentialism in Asad's thought. These and other critiques are assessed in Enayat (2016).

[40] For early studies on the plurality of definitions of religion and the impossibility of using 'Islam' as a term of analysis, see el-Zein 1977; al-Azmeh 1993.

in the seventh to ninth centuries might be reunderstood, translated, or even forgotten.

Hughes' paper asks if, how, and when we can talk of an ahistorical thing called Islam. When a Muslim does something, does it become Islamic? He takes the religious studies approach as a warning to recognise the genealogies of the categories that we use and take the formation and use of categories as our focus. He proposes that specialists of Islam should not merely use theory generated in religious studies more broadly, but also generate their own theories. One example he suggests is the investigation of small-scale cases in which assumed higher order categories fail to work, such as 'half-Muslims', 'occasional Muslims', or those who are both Jews and Muslims.

Carool Kersten's paper engages with the ideas of Shahab Ahmed and Hamid Dabashi. Kersten declares himself sympathetic to Ahmed's points of departure and criticism of defining Islam through Islamic law and Arabic texts, but he objects to his criticisms of other scholars as caricatures. In particular he high-lights Ahmed's criticism of Dabashi as 'locked into a religion–secular binary' as an unfair misrepresentation. For Kersten, Dabashi has blurred the lines between colonies and metropoles: there are no more easily located 'centres and peripheries' for cultural phenomena. Kersten sees Dabashi as a scholar who follows Mohammed Arkoun's conception of Islam as a 'civilization', rather than a narrowly conceived religious tradition; for Dabashi, *adab* and architecture are just as significant as *fiqh*. Indeed, Dabashi observes that Muslims in the past have been perfectly capable of distinguishing between religion, society and the state, in spite of claims to the contrary by both Muslims and non-Muslims.[41]

Hadi Enayat's paper turns to Talal Asad's treatment of secularism. Asad has stated that Islamic traditions encompass the whole of human society. Asad claims that this makes the secularist separation of politics and religion, in which religion is relegated to the private sphere, especially damaging for Islam. For Asad, secularism involves the fragmentation of social solidarity, because it strips away the connections between believers by denying religious belief any political space, and this then makes individuals vulnerable to exploitation by the state. Asad and his followers have represented secularism as an alien import into Islamic societies from Christianity. They see secularism as one of a number of colonial strategies that act in parallel to the colonial study of the history and language of the colonised as a tool of government. But Asad's followers go beyond Said in their defence of religion as a means of healing the anomie of the colonial or neocolonial industrial situation. Enayat's critique of this argu-ment rests on Asad's essentialisms. First, in imagining 'West' and 'non-West'

---

[41] On this point, note that Abbasi (2020) argues persuasively against Ahmed (2016) that pre-modern Muslims did make distinctions between the religious and the secular.

as uniform zones, where the latter is committed to religion as a form of social organisation, Enayat asserts that Asad fails to appreciate that secularism adopts different meanings in different places, and that borrowings between cultures are adapted to new situations. He observes that forms of secularist arguments are made by thinkers in Senegal, Indonesia and Iran and that the distinction between sharia and *siyāsa* justice have roots that go back to the Abbasid period: they cannot be dismissed outright, as alien imports. Second, Enayat follows Sami Zubaida in observing that Muslim societies have undergone functional differentiation in much the same way as Europe or North America, and that this proliferation of social roles, institutions and forms of expertise makes it hard for traditional religious authority to claim competence in all of these areas.[42]

Talal Asad's claim that the definition of 'religion' has been dominated by Protestant Christian conceptions of privatised, interior faith has been developed by scholarship in the study of religions that has problematised the genealogy of the term 'religion'. Tomoko Masuzawa and Brent Nongbri have both argued that Christian assumptions behind the term mean that belief systems like Buddhism, Islam or Hinduism end up being seen as inferior versions of Christianity. For Nongbri, this insight makes the scholarly use of the term religion intrinsically problematic. His solution is not to jettison it entirely, however, but to ask where we might substitute a word that is either more specific ('Quranic', for instance) or more general (custom, culture, worldview).

From an outlook grounded in the history of religions, the paper by Susanne Olsson and Leif Stenberg responds to this challenge in conceptualising the term 'religion' by observing that everything we write about inevitably involves acts of reduction or translation. In the words of J. Z. Smith, we are producing maps rather than replicas. Olsson and Stenberg state that comparison is such a routine cognitive activity that we cannot do without it, and that readers will inevitably use the category of religion since there are no clear-cut or shared definitions of the term and it can be utilised in a conditional, provisional and contextual sense to think about Islam or Christianity.[43] With these caveats in mind, we are better off using a familiar term, while being conscious that we are reconceptualising it. Therefore, 'religion' and 'Islam' are both terms that find many different forms of emic use, that depend on the context of the person making the classification and the (implied) body of ideas or practices with which she is trying to associate or disassociate her own ideas or practices.

---

[42] Zubaida 2011. Corm (2020) illustrates the different effects of non-religious worldviews in an Arab context.

[43] For a discussion of the definition of religion and the subject matter of religious studies, see Bergunder 2014.

WHO DEFINES ISLAM?

Individual Muslims may engage in their own interpretation of scripture, especially in response to problems that have no pre-modern precedent.[44] With
varying levels of formal religious education they may turn to the Quran and
hadith, or to the *Sira* (biography of Muhammad), the sayings of the imams, or
Islamic history, and generate solutions to queries that satisfy them as 'Islamic'.
It may be that the kind of discursive processes that Talal Asad has described, in
which non-Christian religion is reimagined along Christian lines, encourages
individual Muslims to generate personal exegeses, because of a broader shift in
Islam that emphasises the significance of scripture.

However, the direction that these personal exegeses take is still influenced by
models of what Islam in particular or religion in general ought to be, even when
the exegetes do not have access to formal religious education. One example is
the exegesis of the hidden meanings of numbers in the Quran, or the Quran's
'revelation' of scientific knowledge that remained unknown until the twenty-first
century. Both can be seen as responses to the challenge of 'modernity' in Muslim
societies, where Muslims trained in scientific or technical disciplines respond
to the apparent scientific superiority of Europe and North America by asserting
the priority of knowledge in the Quran. This is a process of eisegesis in which
current and personal notions about Islam is read into the text of the Quran.
The veracity of the divine revelation is therefore protected, and the exegete is
allowed to criticise traditional Muslim scholarship for failing to understand the
scientific knowledge embedded in scripture.[45]

Another area where Muslim thought has responded to global debates has been
the reception and development of feminism within Muslim societies. Women's
rights movements in Europe and North America have stimulated the creation of
feminist interpretations of Islam. The many different social contexts of Muslim
women make it difficult to generalise, but approaches founded on feminism and
gender equality have inspired Muslims creating new hermenutical approaches to
Islam, while rereading Scripture from a feminist perspective to justify the search
for female equality. A feminist approach founded on Islam and using Islamic
terminology to support gender equality goes against understandings in which
religion is seen as a patriarchal expression that supports the social and economic
suppression of women. For Islamic feminism, religion (properly understood)
is not to be rejected as a hinderance to gender equality. According to Amina
Wadud (b. 1952), for instance, patriarchal intepretations and structures in society have contributed to and influenced generations of male scholars in their

---

[44] One such area is bioethics; see Shaw 2011.
[45] Stenberg 1996.

work in Islamic jurisprudence on questions such as marriage, divorce, sexuality, and ritual aspects like the leadership of Friday prayers.

From an analytical point of view, Islamic feminism in its various forms contributes to the understanding of Islam as a developing phenomenon, in which interpretations and practices are formed in interaction with the surrounding society. Islamic feminism also illustrates how ideas and practices that are not explicitly connected to religion (in general) or to Islam (in particular) influence the way Islam is interpreted and practised and the questions that contemporary Muslim scholars have to address. Research on feminism has brought new perspectives to the study of Islam, including the question of how far scholarship can and should be involved in societal change (see Juliane Hammer's contribution in this book).

The definition of 'Islam' may also adapt to the self-definition of other religious traditions. One good example may be the discussion of male homosexuality. *Liwāṭ* (sodomy) is condemned in conceptualisations of the sharia that rely on the Quranic verses 29:28–31, but many Muslim-majority cultures exhibited a practical tolerance of sex between men, or only criticised the passive partner. This situation seems to have changed markedly in the nineteenth and twentieth centuries, partly in response to the definition of homosexuality as a condition of the personality.[46] Christian condemnation of homosexuality fits into this scientific context, but Daniel Boyarin comments that even highly isolated ultra-orthodox Jews started to escalate their criticism of homosexuality from being categorised as one sin of many (like breaking the Sabbath or missing prayers) to being the worst of all possible sins. A similar mirroring of Christian attitudes to homosexuality occurs in Muslim contexts: witness the support for the Islamic state in Mosul for its treatment of homosexuals, even from Iraqis who were otherwise highly critical of their interpretations and practices of Islam.

Papers by Leif Stenberg and Jonas Otterbeck explore the themes of the production of Islam by non-Muslims. Otterbeck tackles these problems from the perspective of social semiotics and cultural studies. He observes that 'Islam' functions as an overarching moral register for Muslims that depends on a cluster of common sources and symbols. He notes that these can be reorganised and 'shuffled' in many different ways, but they can also be used subversively or simply ignored. Samuli Schielke has proposed that there is too much Islam in the anthropology of Islam, meaning that anthropologists have devoted too much attention to religious elites (or sectarian entrepreneurs, to use Tobias Matthiesen's terminology)[47] who use theology to orchestrate Islam for others.[48]

---

[46] El-Rouayheb 2003.
[47] Matthiesen 2015.
[48] Schielke 2012, 2015.

In his analysis of the pop nashids of South African singer Zain Bhikha, Otterbeck follows Schielke in stating that we need to devote more time to the casual, inconsistent, or 'ignorant' deployment of Islamic semiotics by individuals who are not members of an organised Islamic institution. As he puts it, we should be just as interested in how children or madmen produce Islam as we are in 'religious scholars': Islam is a category we arrive at, rather than a point we depart from.[49] In this vein, Otterbeck follows Sindre Bangstad's critique of Talal Asad, in which he accuses Asad of being overly focused on foundational texts such as the Quran and the hadith. Likewise, no Muslim is just a Muslim,[50] and Otterbeck recognises this by writing of 'young adults with a Muslim background', in order to avoid any assumption that they consider all of their actions to be Islamic or that they are necessarily preoccupied with 'religion' to the exclusion of motivations such as masculine reputation, love or wealth.

Stenberg's paper considers the history of the contemporary discourse related to the confirmation of modern science by the Quran. Adopting a Foucauldian approach, he observes that, for some Muslim commentators, the 'identification' of scientific truths in scripture serves as a way of contesting the cognitive challenges of modernity. For others, like Muhammad Abdus Salam, the relationship between the Quran and modern science sets out a religious imperative for scientific discovery, and the failure to meet this imperative stands as a criticism of authoritarian regimes that neglect education. The constructions of these discourses are not merely responses to a static or abstract theology, but reflect how commentators produce different kinds of Islam in response to changing local environments and personal interests.

FORMATIVE ISLAM

Talal Asad's model of Islam as a discrete tradition is particularly vulnerable in Islam's formative period of the seventh to ninth centuries. The study of this period is especially important for highlighting the common origins of Muslim, Christian and Jewish thought. The quotation or paraphrasing of the Talmud or Christian apocryphal literature in the Quran is perhaps the most compelling example of how (sometimes peripheral) ideas produced in the milieu of one worldview may become anchored at the core of another worldview.[51]

Early Islam obviously carries a great significance for writers trying to assert

---

[49] Cf. Brubaker and Cooper (2000) who discuss how ethnicity is a discourse that is projected onto individuals and their practice, rather than an essential 'identity' that precedes discourse.

[50] Panjwani 2017.

[51] E.g. Quran 5:32 (Talmud); 19:22–6 (Gospel of Pseudo-Matthew); 3:37 and 19:16–26 (Protoevangelium of James). Andrae's is a classic study of the influence of Syriac narratives and ideas in the Quran (see Andrae 1932). More recently, see the studies in Amir-Moezzi and Dye (2019), which discuss the epigraphic background as well as texts in Syriac and Ethiopic.

their own forms of normative Islam. This is as true for contemporary Muslim feminists, defenders of 'Islamic' human rights, and proponents of a distinctively Islamic science as it is for Salafis. As individuals we may be sympathetic to progressive causes, but this does not absolve us of the need to read the sources of this period critically or to see Muhammad and his contemporaries, as well as the text of the Quran, as products of their age.[52] As Nicolai Sinai has observed, an advantage of a historical–critical approach is that it helps us to suspend our inherited presumptions about a text's origin, transmission and meaning and to avoid the danger that we affirm the truth of Scripture because we project onto it something that we happen to believe anyway.[53] Of course, the stakes for critical engagement with the Quran from within Muslim-majority contexts can be high, as witnessed in the case of Nasr Abu Zayd, who was subjected to accusations of blasphemy and divorced from his wife as an apostate because of his historicist approach to the study of the Quran.[54]

Contemporary Quranic studies is further complicated by the lack of consensus over what constitutes an appropriate context against which the Quran might be read (and the near-absence of the proper names of people and places in the Quran itself). The 'ulamā had traditionally clarified the Quran chiefly through the hadith.[55] This position of the hadith was heavily attacked in German-language scholarship in the twentieth century, in which the premier figure was the Hungarian Jewish scholar Ignaz Goldziher.[56] This scepticism was also influential for Muslim modernists such as the Pakistani Fazlur Rahman, the Syrian Muhammad Sharur, the Egyptian Nasr Abu Zayd and the Iranian Mohsen Kadivar all of whom advocate historicising the Quran without being bound by the hadith.[57] Nevertheless, the intertwining of Quran and hadith, and the methods employed by selected medieval 'ulamā have seen a strong defence by the American Muslim convert Jonathan Brown, who observes that the hadith as a whole tend to be dismissed with 'an air of supercilious moral disapproval'.[58] Needless to say, to read the Quran through the hadith remains the dominant approach in Muslim-majority contexts.

---

[52] Cf. Friedmann 2003: 8.

[53] Sinai 2017: 3–4.

[54] Also note the recent cases of a Malaysian academic, Mu'nim Sirry, who was charged with 'introducing deviant and liberal ideas' for stressing Mecca's connections to the late antique Near East (https://www.malaymail.com/news/malaysia/2017/08/26/called-deviant-muslim-scholar-says-was-just-challenging-orthodox-view-on-qu/1451327).

[55] Though note that medieval Muslim commentators drew freely on Christian and Jewish traditions to interpret the Quran, a process that began to slow from the tenth century but was still present in the thirteenth; Stewart 2017: 27.

[56] Goldziher 1920. Given the worldwide dominance of academic writing in English, the enduring importance of German in Quranic studies remains worth stressing.

[57] Brown 2014: 201–3.

[58] Brown 2014: 11.

Before the 1970s, the main approach taken by European Islamicists was to accept much of the narrative of the *Sira*, the Prophet's biography, and use this to situate the composition of the Quran. The orientalist Theodor Nöldeke used the framework given by the *Sira*, as well as his own understanding of the development of Quranic themes, to produce a relative chronology for the Quran (Early, Middle and Late Meccan and Medinan suras), and this continues to provide a starting point for studies of the Quran.[59] And histories of Muhammad as different as those by the Scottish clergyman Montgomery Watt (1961) and the French Marxist Maxime Rodinson (1971) employ the *Sira* in this way, without much detailed source criticism.[60] This *Sira*-and-Quran approach continues to typify semi-popular contemporary books on Muhammad and the Quran, such as those by Tariq Ramadan (2007), Karen Armstrong (2006) or Ingrid Matson (2008).[61] We should note, however, that when it is possible to test the *Sira* against epigraphic evidence, its testimony can often be disproved.[62] Sean Anthony's recent book (2020), which detects different authors and agendas within the *Sira*, offers a powerful way forward if we want to use the *Sira* to generate a context for the Quran.

Devin Stewart has suggested that many European scholars of the mid-twentieth century deliberately avoided the study of the Quran per se in favour of studying the commentarial tradition (the *tafsir*), in order to side-step the thorny issue of appearing to critique the Quran or the Prophet directly.[63] But since the 1970s some European scholars of the Quran have adopted a much deeper scepticism of the Arabic Muslim sources traditionally used to give the Quran context.[64] The work of John Wansborough in particular argued for the utility of the historical–critical methods used in biblical studies.[65] Wansborough aimed

---

[59] Nöldeke 1860. Nöldeke's work was informed by deep knowledge of the Arabic *tafsir* (as was Goldziher's). A revised version of Nöldeke 1860 was published by Friedrich Schwally, Gotthelf Bergsträsser and Otto Pretzl in 1909–38. Neuwirth (2014) and Chabbi (1997) both use Nöldeke's divisions. Sinai (2017, chap. 5) has used other methods to differentiate the layers of the Quran, most notably mean verse lengths and rhyme schemes. Also cf. the summary of scholarship on rhyme schemes in Stewart (2017: 38–44).

[60] Stewart (2017: 14–15) suggests that Watt was motivated to cleave close to the Muslim tradition to facilitate inter-religious dialogue.

[61] Ali (2014) surveys the different ways that Muhammad's biography has been re-told (in this context, note in particular chapter 1 on the historical Muhammad).

[62] Robin 2017: 293.

[63] Stewart 2017: 16.

[64] For a survey of other 'revisionist' approaches to the Quran, see Reynolds 2008. Reynolds also charts the remarkable story of how a critical edition to the Quran had been planned by Arthur Jeffreys of the American University in Cairo, together with Nöldeke's successors Bergsträsser and Pretzl, in the 1930s, but was prevented by their untimely deaths. A critical edition of the Quran is currently being pursued by the Berlin Corpus Coranicum, under the directorship of Angelika Neuwirth. Much of the source material derives from photographs taken in the 1930s by Bergsträsser and Pretzl.

[65] Wansborough 2004. Patricia Crone and Michael Cook were students of Wansborough. Their book, *Hagarism* (1977), avoided engaging with the Quran entirely and sought to reconstruct Muhammad's career purely on the basis of non-Muslim sources (especially pseudo-Sebeos and the *Doctrina Jacobi*).

to use the Arabic commentarial tradition to determine how, and how quickly, a fixed text of the Quran became established. He disagreed fundamentally with the Nöldekian paradigm and speculated that the Quran may have been a product of the same environment that produced the hadith (i.e. eighth- and ninth-century Iraq and Syria). However, Wansborough's re-dating of the Quran is now treated with scepticism in the light of the analysis of the earliest manuscripts. These show much less variation than biblical manuscripts, which may suggest that they were codified relatively early. Palaeography seems to confirm the narrative of a standard text that was disseminated by the caliph Uthman.[66]

Quranic studies has exploded over the last twenty years, and here we can only highlight a small number of exciting approaches. Angelika Neuwirth's model for Quranic studies rests on differentiating between the Quran as a dialogic text, produced in a relationship between prophet and listeners, rather than the monologic text that resulted from the process of canonisation. She lays great stress on the need to differentiate the Quran as a seventh-century literary arte-fact from the Quran of the later tradition that is read through the *tafsir*. And in recent work she has stressed the utility of pre-Islamic Arabic for understanding the Quran.[67]

Key points of departure within the sub-discipline are the Nöldekian paradigm for ordering the suras and the utility of the methods of biblical criticism and/or the canonisation of the Bible for studying the Quran.[68] One possibility is that earlier suras were revised according to later agendas.[69] Another is the identifi-cation of intertexts for the Quran, not just Jewish and Christian 'scripture', but the full range of rabbinic and patristic writing (especially in Syriac).[70] And yet another is the possibility of profiling multiple authors for different parts of the Quran, according to a passage's relationship to other parts of the Quran or to other religious traditions.[71]

Nicolai Sinai's comment on the Quran's attitude to previous religious tradi-tions is one of the stimuli for Philip Wood's paper in this volume. Sinai remarks that

---

[66] Van Putten 2019; cf. Déroche 2014. On the Sana'a Quran fragment, see Hilali 2017 and Cellard 2021.
[67] Neuwirth 2019: 35, 2007: 117–9. On the Quran and poetry, see Neuwirth 2019, chap. 12.
[68] Stewart 2017: 49–50; Dye 2015.
[69] E.g. Sinai 2017, chapter 5. Nagel 1995 is a good example.
[70] E.g. Andrae 1932; Witztum 2011, 2015; el-Badawi 2016; Segovia 2015; Hoyland 2018. Stewart (2017: 26) refers to this approach as 'the new Biblicists' and stresses their opposition to the use of the *tafsir* or the *Sira* to facilitate the understanding of the Quran in the seventh century. In time we hope that it will be possible to integrate these different approaches as studies on different source bases inform one another. Also note Sinai 2017, chap. 6.
[71] Pohlmann 2012; Dye 2019, and forthcoming. One aspect of this approach includes considering the authorship of some parts of the Quran outside the Hijaz. An earlier example of the multiple authorship approach is Lüling (2003). Important surveys of contemporary Quranic studies are given in Stewart 2017; Prieur and Mordillat 2015; and, in particular, Amir-Moezzi and Dye 2019.

> The Qur'an, not unlike other scriptures, grew out of a process of a community's successive appropriation of earlier traditions and thus forms a heterogeneous composition. . . [but unlike other scriptures], the Qur'an materialised in an environment familiar with pre-existent notions of sacred books, and consequently had to stake its own claim to authority in terms of these precedents. The Qur'anic consciousness of its own scripturality in turn shaped the kind of text that was evolving, and determined its literary and theological configuration.[72]

Wood's paper explores the significance of this 'consciousness', both with regards to exploring the environment in which the Quran was created and the development of Muslim assumptions about (and expectations of) non-Muslim religious traditions. The paper engages with the observation of Asad, Nongbri and others that the definition of 'religion' has been moulded in the nineteenth century around Protestant Christianity. Rather than focusing on the significance of this for contemporary scholars' own use of terminology, he sees the nineteenth century as but one example of the creation of a general paradigm for religion following the example of a single tradition. He goes on to explain the swift birth of Islam as a product of the Quran's production in a world that already had multiple religions based on or around books. He concludes by investigating how Islam, based on Muslim expectations of what a religion should look like, in turn influenced other religious traditions.

Shahzad Bashir's paper offers a critique of the notion of 'Islamic history', as a narrative that stretches from Muhammad to the present day, one that, by implication, treats Islam as a given constant that acts upon Muslims in different ways. Bashir stresses that 'Islam' is not an appropriate target for historical method: we cannot simply mine primary sources to determine the essence of Islam and then observe its changing effect over time. Instead, modern scholars must be attuned to the changing meaning of 'history' from the perspectives of the sources they use. Much of our 'clothes line' of Islamic history is actually the reproduction of a Sunni sectarian vision of the past that has been reproduced by 'orientalists' of the nineteenth and early twentieth century.[73] In response, he calls for a more nuanced reading of our sources, one that takes into account the different ways in which authors frame events, mark time, and defend their own authority. We must do this in order to see Islam as a discourse that is produced anew in each generation, by diverse groups of authors responding to their own priorities. As Bashir has stated elsewhere, in a critique of Ahmed's use of 'Islam' as an etic term of scholarly analysis,

---

[72] Unpublished paper quoted in Neuwirth 2007: 119.
[73] As Tolan (2019: 14) observes, 'The variety and historical malleability of what we call Judaism, Christianity and Islam give the lie to those who seek to reduce their religion to one sect.' For the suppression of Shii versions of history in contemporary Pakistan, see Abbas 2019.

Defining Islam as a coherent discourse is a normative concern that is the province of ideologues, to whom the term denotes a consequential system of thought and practice . . . it is better to presume that Islam is a field that is fundamentally incoherent across time and space.[74]

PUTTING IDEAS INTO PRACTICE

The 'Islamic studies' that is practised in these papers is complex. Scripture continues to anchor various traditions, but there are many different practices of interpretation and Muslim traditions overlap with and interact with other traditions too. Some of these are other religious traditions, but the discourses of human rights, socialism and scientism are also worldviews that are internalised by Muslims and create axioms with which they approach the medieval scriptures.[75]

Juliane Hammer's paper proposes that academic scholarship cannot be separated from the role of academics as activists. She observes that knowledge production is not just the description of the world, but also an attempt to make the world better. Hammer's work on domestic violence among Muslims in North America highlights how anti-Muslim hostility racialises Muslims as peculiarly disposed to violence and frames domestic violence in a discourse of honour killing, rather than analysing them as part of the broader trends in American domestic violence. Following Leila Ahmed, Hammer criticises 'western' feminists who have colluded in colonial projects by presenting Muslim women as submissive to Muslim patriarchy in a way that denies them agency.[76] Instead of rejecting religion *in toto* as a source of patriarchy, Hammer asks how religion can provide a basis for fighting patriarchal and racial injustice. At the same time, she notes that a sense of being observed and judged by wider society is used by those with relative power in Muslim communities to silence critiques of gender injustice.

For Hammer, scholarly objectivity is impossible, and many claims to objectivity from secularists or western feminists are actually embedded in colonial systems. Scholarship makes it possible to chart how forms of stereotypes and inequalities are perpetuated and raise the consciousness of the victims of oppression. However, she observes that this kind of normative stance has been unfashionable in American religious studies. Drawing on a feminist tradition of offering 'political prescriptions', she argues that objections to many Muslim scholars ignore the moral necessity of using scholarship to pursue political goals, of 'construction' rather than 'deconstruction'.

Hammer's arguments are provocative and interesting. However, we do not

---

[74] Bashir 2018.
[75] For the idea that 'worldviews' are an overarching category that includes religion and how this has become an important idea in British religious education, see Baumfield and Cush 2018.
[76] Ahmed 1992.

think scholarly objectivity is a goal that we should abandon, even if it is an ideal type that is extremely difficult to achieve.[77] We retain hope that discussions about different perspectives and reflections on our own experiences and formation can lead to greater insights in all of the humanities and social sciences. And if the thought of so-called 'western feminists' is embedded in forms of the knowledge that originated in nineteenth-century colonial systems, similar problems exist for thinkers engaged in Muslim traditions, whose foundational texts were redacted or composed by a slave-owning imperial elite who were beneficiaries of massive wars of conquest in the seventh to ninth centuries. Attempts to find a moral code in such texts must also acknowledge this context.

Nevertheless, we are sympathetic to Hammer's position that there should be a place for normative scholarship in traditions in the academy. We share the concern of Hughes and Robinson about the distortion of history through the retrojection of contemporary political concerns. But there may be a place for normative theology, and normative projects of other kinds, provided they are clearly distinct from and built upon the study of the past. As Hammer notes, it is possible to conduct theology in a way that does not essentialise and is built upon a historicised and source-critical understanding of how a religious tradition has developed.[78] Therefore, we would argue that disciplines that seek to describe societies in the past and the present in a critical fashion (such as sociology, anthropology or history) ought to strive to be pre-ethical, that is, they ought to provide a basis for the interventions of philosophers or theologians that is persuasive precisely because they avoid projecting idealised hopes for the future onto the present and the past. In this model, the study of religions and theology could enjoy a similar relationship to (for instance) the history of political thought and political philosophy, in which the first discipline provides an evidenced grounding for a normative project.

BIBLIOGRAPHY

Abbas, N. (2019), 'Politics of Religious Education in Schools in Pakistan: Education or Disintegration?' MA dissertation, Institute for the Study of Muslim Civilisations, London.

Abbasi, Rushain (2020), 'Did Premodern Muslims Distinguish the Religious and Secular? The Dīn–Dunyā Binary in Medieval Islamic Thought', Journal of Islamic Studies 31: 185–225.

---

[77] For a philosophical defence of objectivity, see Howes 2015. Howes' ideas have been applied in an Islamic studies context in Ahmad el-Shamsy's riposte to Chaudhury (2018) in https://islamiclaw. blog/2020/12/14/how-not-to-reform-the-study-of-islamic-law-a-response-to-ayesha-chaudhry/. El-Shamsy sees objectivity as 'a moral commitment to pursuing a reality that is not reducible to our preconceived notions and agendas'.

[78] Also, note Ford's (2015) call for a theology that is placed in dialogue with other disciplines.

Abu-Lughod, Lila (2014), *Do Muslim Women Really Need Saving? Anthropological Reflections on Cultural Relativism and its Others*, Cambridge, MA: Harvard University Press.

Afsaruddin, Asma (2008), *The First Muslims: History and Memory*, London: Oneworld.

Ahmed, Leila (1992), *Women and Gender in Islam: Historical Roots of a Modern Debate*, New Haven: Yale University Press.

Ahmed, Shahab (2016), *What is Islam? The Importance of Being Islamic*, Princeton, NJ: Princeton University Press.

Ali, Kecia (2014), *The Lives of Muhammad*, Cambridge, MA: Harvard University Press.

Amir-Moezzi, Mohammad Ali, and Guillaume Dye (2019), *Le coran des historiens*, 3 vols, Paris: Le Cerf.

Andrae, Tor (1932), *Mohammed: sein Leben und sein Glaube*, Göttingen: Vandenhoeck & Ruprecht.

Anthony, Sean (2020), *Muhammad and the Empires of Faith: The Making of the Prophet of Islam*, Oakland, CA: University of California Press.

Arkoun, Mohammed (2002), *The Unthought in Contemporary Islamic Thought*, London: Saqi Books.

Armstrong, Karen (2006), *Muhammad: A Prophet for Our Time*, New York: Harper Collins.

Asad, Talal (1993), *Genealogies of Religion: Discipline and Reasons of Power in Christianity and Islam*, Baltimore: Johns Hopkins University Press.

Asad, Talal (2003), *Formations of the Secular: Christianity, Islam, Modernity*, Stanford: Stanford University Press.

Aydin, Cemil (2017), *The Idea of the Muslim World: A Global Intellectual History*, Cambridge, MA: Harvard University Press.

Al-Azm, Sadik Jalal (1981), 'Orientalism and Orientalism in Reverse', *Khamsin* 8: 5–26.

Al-Azmeh, Aziz (1993), *Islams and Modernities*, London: Verso.

Bangstad, Sindre (2009), 'Secularism and Islam in the Work of Talal Asad', *Anthropological Theory* 9, no. 2: 188–208.

Bashir, Shahzad (2017), 'Eurocentrism, Islam and the Intellectual Politics of Civilizational Framing', *InterDisciplines. Journal of History and Sociology* 8, no. 2: 21–39.

Bashir, Shahzad (2018), 'Everlasting Doubt: Uncertainty in Islamic Representations of the Past', *Archiv für Religionsgeschichte* 20, no. 1: 25–44.

Baumfield, Vivienne Marie, and Denise Amelia Cush (2018), 'Religious Education: Time for a Change?' *British Journal of Religious Education* 41, no. 1: 1–7.

Bennett, Clinton (2013), 'Introduction', in Clinton Bennett (ed.), *Bloomsbury Companion to Islamic Studies*, London: Bloomsbury, pp. 1–29.

Bergunder, Michael (2014), 'What is Religion? The Unexplained Subject Matter of Religious Studies', *Method and Theory in the Study of Religion* 26, no. 3: 246–86.

Birt, Jonathan (2009), 'Islamophobia in the Construction of British Muslim Identity Politics', in P. Hopkins and R. Gale (eds), *Muslims in Britain: Race, Place and Identities*, Edinburgh: Edinburgh University Press, pp. 210–27.

Bolognani, Marta, and Jody Mellor (2012), 'British Pakistani Women's Use of the "Religion Versus Culture" Contrast: A Critical Analysis', *Culture and Religion: An Interdisciplinary Journal* 13, no. 2: 211–26.

Brown, Jonathan (2014), *Misquoting Muhammad. The Challenge and Choices of Interpreting the Prophet's Legacy*, London: Oneworld.

Brubaker, Rogers, and Frederick Cooper (2000), 'Beyond "Identity"', *Theory and Society* 29, no. 1: 1–47.

Bulliet, Richard W. (2017), 'Confessions of a Middle East Studies Specialist', *Middle East Law and Governance* 9, no. 2: 199–222.

Bulliet, Richard W. (2020), *Methodists and Muslims: My Life As An Orientalist*, Cambridge, MA: Harvard University Press.

Cellard, Éléonore (2021), 'The Ṣan'ā' Palimpsest: Materializing the Codices', *Journal of Near Eastern Studies* 80, 1–30.

Chabbi, Jacqueline (1997), *Le seigneur des tribus: l'islam de Mahomet*, Paris: Noêsis.

Chaudhry, A. (2018), 'Islamic Legal Studies: A Critical Historiography', in Anver Emon and Rumee Ahmed (eds), *The Oxford Handbook of Islamic Law*, Oxford: Oxford University Press, pp. 5–44.

Cook, Michael (2014), *Ancient Religion, Modern Politics: The Islamic Case in Comparative Perspective*, Princeton, NJ: Princeton University Press.

Corm, Georges (2020), *Arab Political Thought: Past and Present*, trans. P. Phillips-Batoma and A. Batoma, Edinburgh and London: Edinburgh University Press and Hurst.

Crone, Patricia, and Michael Cook (1977), *Hagarism: The Making of the Islamic World*, Cambridge: Cambridge University Press.

Curtis, Edward E. IV (2006), *Black Muslim Religion in the Nation of Islam, 1960–75*, Chapel Hill: University of North Carolina Press.

Daneshgar, M. (2020), *Studying the Qur'an in the Muslim Academy*, Oxford: Oxford University Press.

Daneshgar, M., and A. Hughes (eds) (2020), *Deconstructing Islamic Studies*, Cambridge, MA: ILEX and Harvard University Press.

Déroche, Francois (2014), *Qur'ans of the Umayyads. A First Overview*, Leiden: Brill.

Dye, Guillaume (2015), 'Pourquoi et comment se fait un texte canonique? Quelques réflexions sur l'histoire du Coran', in C. Brouwer, G. Dye and A. van Rompaey (eds), *Hérésies: une construction d'identités religieuses*, Brussels: Université Libre de Bruxelles, pp. 55–104.

Dye, Guillaume (2019), 'Ascetic and non-Ascetic Layers in the Qur'an: A Case Study', *Numen* 66: 589–97.

Dye, Guillaume (forthcoming), 'The Qur'anic Mary and the Chronology of the Qur'ān', in G. Dye (ed.), *Early Islam: The Sectarian Milieu of Late Antiquity?* Chicago: Oriental Institute.

Eickelman, Dale, and James Piscatori (1996), *Muslim Politics*, Princeton, NJ: Princeton University Press.

El-Badawi, Emran (2016), *The Qur'an and the Aramaic Gospel Traditions*, London: Routledge.

El-Rouayheb, Khaled (2003), *Before Homosexuality in the Arab-Islamic World, 1500–1800*, Chicago: University of Chicago Press.

El-Zein, Abdul Hamid (1977), 'Beyond Anthropology and Theology: The Search for the Anthropology of Islam', *Annual Review of Anthropology* 6: 227–54.

Enayat, Hadi (2016), *Islam and Secularism in Post-Colonial Thought: A Cartography of Asadian Genealogies*, Cham: Springer and Palgrave Macmillan.

Farrar, Max (2002), *The Struggle for 'Community' in a British Multi-Ethnic Inner-City Area: Paradise in the Making Lewiston*, New York: E. Mellen Press.

Flaskerud, Ingvild, and Oddbjørn Leirvik (2018), 'The Study of Islam Between University Theology and Lived Religion: Introductory Reflections', *Islam and Christian-Muslim Relations* 29, no. 4: 413–27.

Ford, David (2015), 'Christian Theology: Settings, Perspectives, Theology, Challenges', in A. Silverstein and G. Stroumsa (eds), *The Oxford Handbook of Abrahamic Religions*, Oxford: Oxford University Press, pp. 580–97.

Friedmann, Yohanan (2003), *Tolerance and Coercion in Islam: Interfaith Relations in the Muslim Tradition*, Cambridge: Cambridge University Press.

Geertz, Clifford (1960), *The Religion of Java*, Glencoe, IL: Free Press.

Geertz, Clifford (1968), *Islam Observed: Religious Development in Morocco and Indonesia*, Chicago: University of Chicago Press.

Gibb, H. A. R. (1949), *Mohammedanism: An Historical Survey*, Oxford: Oxford University Press.

Goldziher, Ignaz (1920), *Die Richtungen der islamischen Koranauslegung*, Leiden: Brill.

Goodman, Martin (2010), 'The Nature of Jewish Studies', in Martin Goodman (ed.), *Oxford Handbook of Jewish Studies*, Oxford: Oxford University Press, pp. 1–13.

Hilali, Asma (2017), *The Sanaa Palimpsest: The Transmission of the Qur'an in the First Centuries AH*, Oxford: Oxford University Press.

Hoffmann, Thomas (2019), 'Qur'anic Studies between University Theology and the Humanities: A Field Worth Cultivating?', *Islam and Christian-Muslim Relations* 29, no. 4: 429–43.

Howes, Moira (2015), 'Objectivity, Intellectual Virtue, and Community', in Flavia Padovani, Alan W. Richardson and Jonathan Y. Tsou (eds), *Objectivity in Science: New Perspectives from Science and Technology Studies*, Cham: Springer International, pp. 173–87.

Hoyland, Robert (2018), 'The Jewish-Christian Audience of the Qur'an', in Francisco del Rio Sanchez (ed.), *Jewish Christianity and the Origins of Islam. Papers Presented at the Colloquium Held at Washington, DC, October 29–31, 2015 (8th ASMEA Conference)*, Turnhout: Brepols, pp. 31–40.

Hughes, Aaron (2007), *Situating Islam: The Past and Future of an Academic Discipline*, London: Equinox.

Hughes, Aaron (2015), *Islam and the Tyranny of Authenticity. An Enquiry into Disciplinary Apologetics and Self-Deception*, Sheffield: Equinox.

Imhoff, Sarah (2018), 'Jews, Jewish Studies and the Study of Islam', in Matt Sheedy (ed.), *Identity, Politics and the Study of Islam: Current Dilemmas in the Study of Religions*, Sheffield: Equinox, pp. 121–37.

Jakobsen, Jonas (2015), 'Secularism, Liberal Democracy and Islam in Europe: A Habermasian Critique of Talal Asad', *Contrastes* 20, no. 3: 113–25.

Jung, Dietrich (2011), *Orientalists, Islamists and the Global Public Sphere: A Genealogy of the Modern Essentialist Image of Islam*, Sheffield: Equinox.

Levine, Mark (2007), *Why They Don't Hate Us. Lifting the Veil on the Axis of Evil*, Oxford: Oneworld.

Lewinstein, Keith (2003), 'Recent Scholarship and the Teaching of Islam', in Brannon M. Wheeler (ed.), *Teaching Islam*, Oxford: Oxford University Press, pp. 46–60.

Lincoln, Bruce (1996), 'Theses on Method', *Method and Theory in the Study of Religion* 8, no. 3: 225–7.

Lockman, Zachary (2016), *Field Notes. The Making of Middle East Studies in the United States*, Stanford: Stanford University Press.

Lüling, Gunther (2003), *A Challenge to Islam for Reformation: The Rediscovery and Reliable Reconstruction of a Comprehensive pre-Islamic Christian Hymnal Hidden in the Koran under the Earliest Islamic Reinterpretations*, Delhi: Motilal Banarsidass.

Madhany, al-Husein N. (2008), 'Pooh-Poohing Pluralism: Ijtihāding Ḥadith to Build a Theology of Exclusion', *Muslim World* 98, no. 4: 407–22.

Marchand, Suzanne (2010), *German Orientalism in the Age of Empire: Race, Religion and Scholarship*, Cambridge: Cambridge University Press.

Martin, Richard (1985), 'Introduction', in Richard Martin (ed.), *Approaches to Islam in Religious Studies*, Phoenix: University of Arizona Press.

Matson, I. (2008), *The Story of the Qur'an: Its History and Place in Muslim Life*, Oxford: Blackwell.

Matthiesen, Toby (2015), *Sectarian Gulf: Bahrain, Saudi Arabia and the Arab Spring that Wasn't*, Stanford: Stanford University Press.

McLoughlin, Sean (2007), 'Islam(s) in Context: Orientalism and the Anthropology of Muslim Societies and Cultures', *Journal of Beliefs and Values* 28, no. 3: 273–96.

Meer, Nasar, and Tariq Modood (2009), 'Refutations of Racism in the "Muslim Question"', *Patterns of Prejudice* 43, nos. 3–4: 335–54.

Modood, Tariq (2012), *Post-Immigration 'Difference' and Integration: The Case of Muslims in Western Europe*, London: British Academy Policy Centre.

Muslim World 108, issue 2 (2018), Special Issue: 'The Challenges and Opportunities of Teaching Islam at Theological Seminaries'.

Nagel, T. (1995), *Medinensische Einschübe in mekkanischen Suren*, Göttingen: Vandenhoeck & Ruprecht.

Nanji, Azim (ed.) (1997), *Mapping Islamic Studies: Genealogy, Continuity and Change*, Berlin: De Gruyter.

Neuwirth, Angelika (2007), 'Orientalism in Islamic Studies? Quranic Studies as a case in point', *Journal of Quranic Studies* 9: 115–27.

Neuwirth, Angelika (2014), *Scripture, Poetry, and the Making of a Community. Reading the Qur'an as a Literary Text*, Oxford: Oxford University Press.

Neuwirth, Angelika (2017), *Der Koran. Handkommentar mit Übersetzung*, 2 vols (of 5 projected), Berlin: Insel Verlag.

Neuwirth, Angelika (2019), *The Qur'an in Late Antiquity: A Shared Heritage*, trans. S. Wilder, New York: Oxford University Press.

Nöldeke, Theodore (1860), *Geschichte des Qorâns*, 3 vols, Göttingen: Verlag der Dieterichschen Buchhandlung. [Revised edition published with F. Schwally (vols 1–2), G. Bergsträsser and O. Pretzl (vol. 3) with translation by W. Behn, Leiden: Brill, 2013.]

Panjwani, Farid (2005), 'Agreed Syllabi and Un-agreed Values: Religious Education and Missed Opportunities for Fostering Social Cohesion', *British Journal of Educational Studies* 53, no. 3: 375–93.

Panjwani, Farid (2017), 'No Muslim is Just a Muslim: Implications for Education', *Oxford Review of Education* 43, no. 5: 596–611.

Peach, Ceri (2006), 'Islam, Ethnicity and South Asian Religion in the London 2001 Census', *Transactions of the Institute of British Geographers* 31, no. 3: 353–70.

Pohlmann, Karl-Friedrich (2012), *Die Entstehung des Korans: neue Erkenntnisse aus Sicht der historisch-kritischen Bibelwissenschaft*, Darmstadt: Wissenschaftliche Buchgesellschaft.

Prieur, Jérôme, and Gérard Mordillat (2015), *Jésus et l'Islam* (film by ARTÉ).

Ramadan, Tariq (2007), *In the Footsteps of the Prophet: Lessons from the Life of Muhammad*, Oxford: Oxford University Press.

Revell, Lynn (2008), 'Religious Education in England', *Numen* 55, nos. 2–3: 218–40.

Reynolds, Gabriel Said (ed.) (2008), *The Qur'an in its Historical Context*, London: Routledge.

Robin, Christian (2017), 'L'Arabie à la veille de l'islam dans l'ouvrage de Aziz al-Azmeh, *The Emergence of Islam in Late Antiquity*', *Topoi* 21: 291–320.

Robinson, Chase F. (2009), 'The Ideological Uses of Early Islam', *Past & Present* 203: 205–28.

Rodinson, Maxime (1971), *Mohammed*, trans. Anne Carter, New York: Vintage Books.

Safi, Omid (2014), 'Reflections on the State of Islamic Studies', *Jadaliyya*, https://www.jadaliyya.com/Details/30175.

Said, Edward (1994), *Culture and Imperialism*, London: Random House.

Said, Edward (2003), *Orientalism: Western Conceptions of the Orient*, London: Penguin.

Schielke, Samuli (2012), 'Being a Nonbeliever in a Time of Islamic Revival: Trajectories of Doubt and Certainty in Contemporary Egypt', *International Journal of Middle East Studies* 44, no. 2: 301–20.

Schielke, Samuli (2015), *Egypt in the Future Tense: Hope, Frustration and Ambivalence Before and After 9/11*, Bloomington: University of Indiana Press.

Segovia, Carlos (2015), *The Qur'anic Noah and the Making of an Islamic Prophet. A Study of Intertextuality and Religious Identity Formation in Late Antiquity*, Berlin: De Gruyter.

Segovia, Carlos A. (2018), 'Identity Politics and the Study of Islamic Origins: The Inscriptions of the Dome of the Rock as a Test Case', in Matt Sheedy (ed.), *Identity, Politics and the Study of Islam: Current Dilemmas in the Study of Religions*, Sheffield: Equinox, pp. 98–117.

Shäfer, Peter (1995), 'Jewish Studies in European Universities: Actual and Potential', in Moshe Davis (ed.), *Teaching Jewish Civilisation: A Global Approach to Higher Education*, London and New York: New York University Press, pp. 77–85.

Shaw, Alison (2011), '"They Say Islam Has an Answer for Everything, So Why Are There No Guidelines for This?" Ethical Dilemmas Associated with Births and Deaths of Infants with Fatal Abnormalities from a Small Sample of Pakistani Muslim Couples in Britain', *Bioethics* 26, no. 9: 485–92.

Sinai, N. (2017), *The Qur'an: A Historical-Critical Introduction*, Edinburgh: Edinburgh University Press.

Smith, Wilfred Cantwell (1962), *The Meaning and End of Religion: A New Approach to the Religious Traditions of Mankind*, New York: Mentor Books.

Stenberg, Leif (1996), *The Islamization of Science: Four Muslim Positions Developing an Islamic Modernity*, Stockholm: Almqvist and Wiksell International.

Stewart, Devin J. (2017), 'Reflections on the State of the Art in Western Qur'anic Studies', in Carol Bakhos and Michael Cook (eds), *Islam and its Past: Jahiliyya, Late Antiquity and the Qur'an*, Oxford: Oxford University Press, pp. 4–53.

Stewart, Devin J. (2018), 'A Modest Proposal for Islamic Studies', in Matt Sheedy (ed.), *Identity, Politics and the Study of Islam: Current Dilemmas in the Study of Religions*, Sheffield: Equinox, pp. 157–200.

Sutton, Francis X., and Azim Nanji (1996), *Report on a Survey of Research and Studies on Islam and Islamic Civilisations*, London: Aga Khan University.

Tolan, J. (ed.) (2019), *Geneses: A Comparative Study of the Historiographies of the Rise of Christianity, Rabbinic Judaism and Islam*, London: Routledge.

Tribalat, Michèle (1995), *Faire France: une grande enquête sur les immigrés et leurs enfants*, Paris: La Découverte.

Uslaner, Eric M. (2012), *Segregation and Mistrust: Diversity, Isolation and Social Cohesion*, Cambridge: Cambridge University Press.

Van Putten, Marijn (2019), '"The Grace of God" as evidence for a written Uthmanic archetype: the importance of shared orthographic idiosyncrasies', *Bulletin of the School of Oriental and African Studies* 82: 271–88.

Varisco, Daniel (2017), *Said and the Unsaid*, Seattle: University of Washington Press.

Waardenburg, Jacques (1995), 'Islamic Studies and the History of Religions: An Evaluation', in Azim Nanji (ed.), *Mapping Islamic Studies: Genealogy, Continuity and Change*, Berlin: De Gruyter, pp. 181–219.

Waardenburg, Jacques (2002), *Islam: Historical, Social and Political Perspectives*, Berlin: De Gruyter.

Waardenburg, Jacques (2007), *Muslims as Actors: Islamic Meanings and Muslim Interpretations*, Berlin: De Gruyter.

Wansborough, J. [1977] (2004), *Quranic Studies: Sources and Methods of Scriptural Interpretation*, trans., forward and expanded notes A. Rippin, Amherst: Prometheus Books.

Watt, Montgomery (1961), *Muhammad: Prophet and Statesman*, Oxford: Oxford University Press.

Witztum, Joseph (2011), 'The Syriac Milieu of the Qur'ān: The Recasting of Biblical Narratives', PhD thesis, Princeton University.

Witztum, Joseph (2015), 'Variant Traditions, Relative Chronology, and the Study of Intra-Quranic Parallels', in B. Sadeghi, A. Q. Ahmed, A. Silverstein and R. Hoyland (eds), *Islamic Cultures, Islamic Contexts: Essays in Honor of Professor Patricia Crone*, Leiden: Brill, pp. 1–50.

Zubaida, Sami (2011), *Beyond Islam: A New Understanding of the Middle East*, London: I. B. Tauris.

Chapter 1

There is No Data for Islam:
Testing the Utility of a Category

Aaron W. Hughes

In his review of Marshall G. S. Hodgson's *The Venture of Islam* in the *New York Review of Books*, the late Clifford Geertz asked the following set of questions,

> What is Islam? A religion? A civilization? A social order? A form of life? A strand of world history? A collection of spiritual attitudes connected only by a common reverence for Muhammad and the Quran? Any tradition which reaches from Senegal and Tanzania through Egypt and Turkey to Iran, India, and Indonesia, which extends from the seventh century to the twentieth, which has drawn on Judaism, Byzantine Christianity, Greek philosophy, Hinduism, Arabian paganism, Spanish intellectualism, and the mystery cults of ancient Persia, which has animated at least a half dozen empires from Abbasid to Ottoman, and which has been legalistic, mystical, rationalist, and hieratic by turns, is clearly not readily characterized, though it all too often has been.[1]

These words ring as true today as they did in the mid-1970s. This myriad of potential definitions of Islam has led, as Geertz subsequently elaborated, to all sorts of privileging. Islam is defined, dependent upon the time, place, and temperament of the interpreter as tantamount to Arabic culture, to 'Shariah-mindedness' (to use Hodgson's own locution), to Sufism, and, increasingly, to contemporary virtues such as ecumenicism and gender justice. The list goes on. Despite the partiality of all of these definitions, and what should by all accounts be a ready acknowledgement of this partiality, it has proved extremely difficult, even for leading scholars, to get around this impasse: much less is the general

---

[1] Geertz 1975.

public able to, bombarded as they are by attempts to define or, at the very least, reduce this impossibility of often contradictory or even mutually exclusive characteristics to neat slogans that reduce Islam to 'x', 'y', or 'z'.

Despite appeals to the contrary from the various agents involved – practitioner, scholar, scholar-practitioner, Islamophobe, to name but the most immediate that come to mind – Islam, like all religions, is not an ahistorical essence. It is, on the contrary, a site of contestation wherein various truth claims or, perhaps better, regimes of truth, make appeals to underdefined concepts, such as authenticity, authority or tradition.[2] Such concepts, and the groups who seek to appropriate them, are neither static nor eternal, but unstable and malleable. While this may be a theoretical claim, its repercussions are both practical and dangerous. Through a series of neat rhetorical moves, Muslim agents and their activities that do not fit into our preconceived model of what Islam is or should be are regarded as 'un-Islamic' or as 'inauthentic'. And, of course, those agents and acts that inspire us are labelled as 'universal' and then projected, often anachronistically, onto other times and places.

This collection, at least as I imagine it, seeks to provide a much-needed intervention to reflect on Islam as a scholarly and, by definition, critical category of analysis. What intellectual utility or payoff, in other words, does this term, as opposed to cognates (e.g. Arab, Islamicate or, more recently, 'Balkan to Bengals complex'), provide? Has it been so overdetermined, as Shahab Ahmed suggests, as to curtail certain forms of discourses by effectively putting them beyond the pale of that which is traditionally inscribed as normative or orthodox (to wit, legal)? Or, alternatively, as Wael Hallaq argues, does the term provide us with a lifeline, the Ockham's razor, as it were, to remove the detritus of the orientalist project so as to restructure modernity from a non-exclusionary point? Framed somewhat differently: 'Islam' as a category is simultaneously everywhere and nowhere, and it is as problematic as it is helpful. Despite their nuance – or perhaps because of it – both Ahmed and Hallaq, albeit for much different reasons, seek to use Islam as a category of analysis (Ahmed) or to reify it to the point of caricature and then hold it up as an antidote to western genocidal colonialism (Hallaq).

Having just set up a perhaps uncomfortable binary, I come at the issue from a slightly different angle. What if, to paraphrase, and admittedly provocatively, the words of the recently departed Jonathan Z. Smith, '*there is no data for [Islam]. [Islam] is solely the creation of the scholar's study.*'[3] Although I have put the word 'Islam' where Smith has 'religion', I would like to think the intent is similar, namely, we, as scholars marginalise certain features, emphasise others

---

[2] Here I am inspired by the language of Bruce Lincoln. See in particular thesis thirteen, Lincoln 1996.
[3] Smith 1982: xi.

and, in the process, create both our object of study and the discourses that structure it. I do not think I have the rigour, like Hallaq, to interrogate the entire
repertoire of western knowledge production, nor do I share Ahmed's desire to
redescribe the entire Islamic tradition to salvage, if not the over-determined
legal category, then at least the Muslim wine drinker. Nevertheless, I agree with
both that sufficient energy ought to be invested in interrogating the discourses
that produce Islam, while simultaneously highlighting the role of 'Islam' in
producing said discourses.

In what follows I want to steer between the Scylla of Hallaq and the Charybdis
of Ahmed with the aim of charting a way of talking about Islam in religious
studies. The latter, as I have pointed out in numerous contexts,[4] and indeed
as this workshop topic reinforces, would seem to be immune from the type of
more critical theorising of a certain strain of the larger field of religious studies.[5]
It strikes me, however, that this oversight – if this is, in fact, what we want to
call it – risks the health of the subfield of the study of Islam that takes place in
the context of religious studies. Not the least of these repercussions is the fact
that our data is simply regarded as self-evident and Islam then risks becoming
whatever we want it to be. There is, then, little higher order reflection on the
very category that brings everything we do into relief, namely 'Islam'.

This reflection is not meant to lead to solipsism. I am not interested, *pace* my
invocation of J. Z. Smith above, in asking whether or not 'Islam' exists. Such a
question would bring very few interesting reflections and ought to be confined
to a generic graduate seminar on theory and/or method. Instead, I think we
need to reflect on if, how, and when we can meaningfully talk about a coherent,
ahistorical thing called 'Islam' that causes or otherwise produces things in the
contingent, messy and mundane social worlds that Muslims inhabit.

Perhaps this is another way of saying that religions, and ostensibly we include
Islam under this rubric, do not simply exist all worked out in the ether, removed
from bodies, contexts and cultures. Islam, like the bodies that perform it and the
minds that imagine and produce it, is always contextual and always responsive.
Though we should, of course, be cautious of assuming that Islam, qua any
non-Protestant tradition or set of traditions, can be neatly categorised as a
religion or that it falls neatly along the lines of reification or the lies of essentialism. While we should know better, we nevertheless insist on isolating certain
expressions and actions as either 'Islam' or 'non-Islam' – or, alternatively, as
'good' Islam and 'bad' Islam – often decontextualising them in the process. We
would, however, do well to enquire into the various discourses, both western

---

[4] See, for example, Hughes 2012a, 2012b, and, most recently, Hughes 2015.
[5] Here I have in mind the likes of Jonathan Z. Smith, Bruce Lincoln, Daniel Dubuisson, Timothy
Fitzgerald, Tomoko Masuzawa and Russell McCutcheon.

and Islamic, that have manufactured such categories. I often find it problematic that whereas many Muslims in their various social worlds might not be quite so quick to isolate 'Islam' from 'non-Islam', we in the academy are often much more discriminating, if not selective (and, of course, I do not necessarily mean either of these positively).

Islam, like any religion, is not an essence. It exists neither as a slogan nor as a set of explicit dogmas and/or doctrines enshrined by centuries of theological accumulation or excrescence. Indeed, a huge percentage of Muslims do not even really know what the 'ulamā define and articulate as 'authentic', but, of course, if one were to ask them, they all too quickly play into the norms that said 'ulamā have articulated.[6] Yet, by invoking macro-terms like 'Islam' we miss or at least overlook this slippage. For some reason or reasons, we tend to think about a reified and doctrinal Islam that exists over and above local expressions and then present the latter in our scholarly and pedagogical lives. This causes real and fundamental problems. Not only, for example, does it posit 'Islam' in places it could not possibly exist – for example, in the seventh-century Hijaz, before it was worked out legally, doctrinally, and so on and so forth – but also implies a uniformity in those places that it did and does exist, where it is now made to appeal to some oddly constructed normativity or orthodoxy.[7] Moreover, it all too easily constructs a narrative that marginalises, if not actually excludes, those that are not imagined as fitting some narrowly constructed Sunni orthodoxy.

WRESTLING WITH AHMED'S *WHAT IS ISLAM?*

At the beginning of chapter 1 of his posthumously published *What is Islam?*, Shahab Ahmed makes the following bold statement,

> I am seeking to say the word 'Islam' in a manner that expresses the *histori-cal and human phenomenon* that is Islam in its plenitude and complexity of meaning. In conceptualizing Islam as a historical and human phenomenon, I am precisely *not* seeking to tell the reader what Islam is as a matter of Divine Command, and thus am *not* seeking to prescribe how Islam should be followed as the means to existential salvation. Rather, I seek to tell the reader what Islam has actually been as a matter of human fact in history.[8]

Ahmed subsequently tried to circumvent the usual definitions by arguing that, in our desire to define what is Islam and what it is not, what is Islamic and what

---

[6] I owe this insight to my colleague Amila Buturović at York University.
[7] Here it might be worth invoking Geertz's work, which offers an early iteration of this type of 'meta' studies. See, in particular, Geertz 1968.
[8] Ahmed 2016: 5.

is its inverse, we often lose sight of actual Muslim lives and the complex and often contradictory ways in which Muslims make sense of their worlds. While I certainly concur with such an assessment, the question then becomes: how do we theorise it? How, in other words, do we account for this inclusiveness in ways that avoid platitudes, such as 'Muslims, like all humans, are complex'?

Ahmed encourages us to suspend what we think we know about Islam, to unlearn that which we have learned, and instead imagine how, for example, the act of imbibing wine can be 'positively valued' using non-legal discourses or terms of reference. Islam, according to his reading, becomes more than simply a 'religion' and would seem to transcend a set of interlocking legal or cultural forms. What, then, is 'Islamic' about it, and then what sort of work does this so-called religious adjective signify? His analysis, then, upends a particular history of framing Islam – a history that has been constructed for various political and ideological purposes as much as anything we might label 'intellectual'. It is a history, moreover, that has always been predicated on an intricate system of inclusions and exclusions – and what gets to count and what does not is never just based on a natural or objective set of categories. The present is certainly no different than the past.

While ostensibly more quotidian and inclusive than that produced by many in religious studies, we now have the opposite problem: everything risks becoming 'Islamic' in Ahmed's reading! He is certainly correct in his assessment that to call something 'Islamic' is an act of authorisation, just as labelling something as 'un-Islamic' is an act of de-authorisation.[9] However, his subsequent desire to remove Islam from over-determined definitions (e.g. as law, as politics, and so on) paradoxically risks reifying something called 'Islam' that exists above all such expressions. If this were not the case, for example, then we could ostensibly dispense with the category altogether. But Ahmed wants to retain it. While Ahmed's inclusion moves far beyond the types of normativising discourses (e.g. Islam or Islamic is 'a', 'b', and 'c', but not 'x', 'y', or 'z') witnessed by many working in Islam in contemporary religious studies, his insistence that his interest is in Islam as a 'human and historical phenomenon', then, also seems to imply that, for him, Islam is also a trans-historical phenomenon.[10] His Kantian focus on the phenomenal nevertheless implies a noumenal, if historically inaccessible, realm that guides the entire apparatus. Ahmed thus would seem to ascribe – consciously or unconsciously, it is not entirely clear – to, what our invitation to this workshop called, 'a pure and unchanging belief system'. Indeed, this would seem to be captured in the tension of the terms 'Islam' and 'Islamic' in the very title. As Sajjad Rizvi reminds us, the two are not the same: if the former

---

[9] Ahmed 2016: 107.
[10] Ahmed 2016: 81–2.

is descriptive-analytical, the latter is proscriptive-judgmental.[11] In invoking Rizvi, we might also ask: where do minoritarian traditions (whether internal or external) – Ismailis, Twelvers, Jews, to name but a few – fit into this 'Islam'?

Ahmed's important work has the advantage of decentring the study of Islam, just as it removes traditional hegemonies implicit therein. But I want to go further than Ahmed here, much further. For ultimately Islam remains as a category that, while now greatly nuanced and expanded, nonetheless remains standing. An earlier obsession with Arabic and an Arabian Islam now gives way to a 'Balkans to Bengal complex', which, of course, risks replacing one orthodoxy with another. Despite this, we should be much further along in our collective musings about interrogating 'Islam' as a category of analysis than Ahmed's seemingly novel enterprise would have us believe.

ISLAM, AHISTORICITY AND EPISTEMOLOGICAL VIOLENCE

I would certainly not be so naive as to argue that our desire to resist essential-ising 'Islam', or any other concept for that matter, is tantamount to suggesting that 'Islam' does not exist. It certainly exists. Yet, it behoves us to ascertain, to repeat, just what intellectual or analytic work the term 'Islam' performs. Does it distort or clarify? Does it misrepresent or preserve? I would suggest the former of each of these two dyads, and then argue that we need to begin the process of nuancing our language with the aim of drawing attention to, and respecting, the great diversity – social, political, economic, material and intellectual, to name only some of the most obvious – that this category otherwise masks.

In a recent study, Jeffrey Guhin and Jonathan Wyrtzen draw on Said and other postcolonial theorists in order to propose a threefold typology of poten-tial violence associated with the production of knowledge: (1) the violence of essentialisation, (2) epistemic violence, and (3) the violence of apprehension.[12] These three types, the authors maintain, help to formulate authoritative struc-tures of knowledge that are, in turn, responsible for, among other things, the orientalist episteme.[13] While I certainly agree with their formulation, we must, of course, also be aware of the violence of essentialisation that goes on both in orientalist and Islamic discourses.[14] The deployment of ahistorical essentialised categories, to wit, 'Islam', regardless of those who use them, involves misrecog-nition and ultimately representational violence.[15] This is where Hallaq's recent work on orientalism tantalises, but ultimately disappoints. Scolding Said for

---

[11] Rizvi 2016.
[12] Guhin and Wyrtzen 2016
[13] Guhin and Wyrtzen 2016: 114.
[14] This became particularly acute for me in Hallaq's *Restating Orientlaism* (2018).
[15] Here I use, but go further than, the comments in Guhin and Wyrtzen 2016: 117–18.

simultaneously going too far and not far enough, he suggests, on the contrary, that *all* academic knowledge production – from history to philosophy, science and economics – has the same epistemic structure as orientalism – that devalues the structure of the Other. While I agree, the way he reifies '*the shar'i* subject' of medieval Islam as the antidote is as problematic as it is helpful.[16]

This translates, for me at least, into the fact that we – whether as Muslims or as non-Muslims – meaningfully deploy a coherent thing called 'Islam' that does not so much create phenomena in the world, but instead imagines 'Islam' as been actively created by them. The study of Islam should not be about finding and interpreting a set of meanings or symbols that transcend particular contexts. Islam is not something that has been worked out and to which Muslims either ascribe or from which they disassociate. On the contrary, 'Islam' is about how Muslims create worlds for themselves. The study of Islamic data, then, ought to be as much about constant reflection on our own choice and selection, including the various motivations and implications that attend to such choice and selection, as it is about the data. This is perhaps another way of saying that we, as scholars of religion, do not find Islam 'out there'; on the contrary, we conjure it into existence by the theoretical choices, methodological moves and rhetorical flourishes we choose.[17]

The study of Islam, in the pre-modern period as in the modern period, by insiders as well as outsiders – by practitioners, by '*ulamā*, by *fuquhā*, by orientalists – has always been about construction and subsequent projection. This, of course, is why the greatest charge that one can level at one's enemies is *bidā*, that one's interpretation is an innovation and has thus strayed from some kind of imagined normativity. These cumulative projections are, in turn, responsible for the creation of a transhistorical and transgeographic Islam, one that is imagined to transcend any one particular contextualisation or iteration. Whether in the writings of early Islamic historians concerned with the time of Muhammad or among modern academics speaking of Islam as a 'world religion', the structure of our knowledge about Islam is always produced and is always contingent.

ISLAM'S BLIND SPOTS

The greatest antidote to essentialisation is historical nuance. Here we must remember that the construction of Islam responds, or ought to respond, to the construction of other socio-historical traditions and concepts, not to mention recent trends in the humanities. If recent years, for example, have witnessed

---

[16] Hallaq 2018: 78–84.
[17] See my introduction to the forthcoming review symposium on the work of J. Z. Smith in the *Journal of the American Academy of Religion*.

the interrogation of phenomena that we have traditionally tended to treat as both transhistorical and transgeographic (e.g. religion, the secular), then surely we must equally interrogate something as large and as polysemantic as 'Islam'. Islam, it is assumed, emerged fully formed in the Arabian Peninsula in the seventh century and then began its gradual and inevitable spread outwards. This view 'from the center', in the words of Bulliet,

> portrays Islamic history as an outgrowth from a single nucleus, a spreading inkblot labeled 'the caliphate'. But what other than a political label held Islam together? And why did its political cohesion evaporate after little more than two centuries, never to reoccur?[18]

Whereas the view from the centre begins with political institutions and religious dogma, often overlooked is the fact that such phenomena are often of a much later provenance and the result of real intellectual skirmish and ideological struggle, all of which are kept out of view the moment we invoke monolithic categories such as 'Islam'. The view from the edge, however, is often the place where we can witness such skirmishes and struggles to which the 'centre' invariably responds and works out its own orthodoxies.[19] A centripetal as opposed to a centrifugal model thus has the distinct advantage of demonstrating how centres (e.g. 'Islam') are created, often in response to margins (e.g. 'islams'), as opposed to assuming that the latter exists de facto. In Bulliet's phraseology, a view from the edge 'starts with individuals and small communities scattered over a vast and poorly integrated realm, speaking over a dozen different languages, and steeped in religious and cultural traditions of great diversity'.[20] Doctrinal cohesion and theological proclamations only emerge slowly, the products of considerable political manipulation that respond to the dialectic that occurs between centre and margins. And even when such cohesion emerges, why should we assume that they are universal?

The view from the centre, we would also do well to remember, is defined by and from a retroactively projected Sunni-centrism, which is imagined normatively. Where do minoritarian traditions – for example, all those that are simply folded into the equally problematic and flattening rubric 'Shia' – fit into the category and the narrative that it structures, to say nothing of all those Jewish and Christian communities that Muslims encountered, both historically and geographically? Here the study of Islam in general and the category of 'Islam' in particular needs to determine how to think through issues of sectarian identity.

---

[18] Bulliet 1994: 8.
[19] Or, indeed, maybe this is even the wrong model, and instead of centres and margins, everything is imagined as its own centre.
[20] Bulliet 1994: 8.

To return briefly to Ahmed, for example, his rethinking of the category of Islam is unable to deal adequately with the Shia, with Judaism, with Christianity, and with other traditions that actively produced, by reacting to or against, what came to be defined as majoritarian Sunni traditions. Attention to such detail and such contestation further problematises the utility of a generic category such as 'Islam'.

Once we give 'Judaism' or 'Christianity', or even 'Shiism', for that matter, their own subfields and tools/methods of analysis, we miss out on the depth and breadth of the category 'Islam'. Shii interpretations, constructions, theologies and cosmologies, not unlike Jewish or Christian ones, tend to be cordoned off from other studies that tend to focus solely on Sunni discourses. Our paradigm for 'Islam', thus needs to move towards one in which we acknowledge that we cannot know about the Quran, hadith, kalām, and so on effectively without studying the various Shii, Ibadi, Jewish and Christian literatures. The category of (Sunni) Islam thus needs to be seen as a contingent development of Muhammad's preaching rather than as its necessary historical outcome, the way that it is most customarily portrayed.

CONCLUSIONS

It seems to me, in the final analysis, that the category of 'Islam' needs to be, perhaps paradoxically, both narrowed to include local expressions and expanded to bring it in line with critical discourses of the academic study of religion. In this paper I began with Geertz's critique of broad definitions and then segued into a paraphrase of Jonathan Z. Smith's claim that *'there is no data for [Islam]'*. By this I mean nothing more than that it is the category of 'Islam' that all too frequently structures, through an intricate system of privilege and denial, what we desire. Here it might be worth invoking another historian of religion, Donald S. Lopez Jr, who argues that we tend to see religions as vacuums, wherein complexities and competing histories are flattened into stereotypes.[21] Such stereotypes, he continues, 'operate through adjectives, which establish chosen characteristics as if they were eternal truths'.[22] Islam, for example, can now be made to coincide with any type of adjective – peaceful, bellicose, socially just, homophobic. 'With sufficient repetition', Lopez cautions us, 'these adjectives become innate qualities, immune from history'.[23] Once we remove Islam from the light of history, it becomes little more than a shell, an essence, and that which we want it to be.

---

[21] Lopez 1998.
[22] Lopez 1998: 10.
[23] Lopez 1998: 10.

BIBLIOGRAPHY

Ahmed, Shahab (2016), *What is Islam?: The Importance of Being Islamic*, Princeton, NJ: Princeton University Press.

Bulliet, Richard (1994), *Islam: The View from the Edge*, New York: Columbia University Press.

Geertz, Clifford (1968), *Islam Observed: Religious Development in Morocco and Indonesia*, Chicago: University of Chicago Press.

Geertz, Clifford (1975), 'Mysteries of Islam', *New York Review of Books*, 11 December, https://www.nybooks.com/articles/1975/12/11/mysteries-of-islam/.

Guhin, Jeffrey, and Jonathan Wyrtzen (2016), 'The Violences of Knowledge: Edward Said, Sociology, and Post-Orientalist Reflexivity', in Julian Go (ed.), *Postcolonial Sociologies: A Reader*, Bingley: Emerald Group Publishing Limited, pp. 113–44.

Hallaq, Wael B. (2018), *Restating Orientalism: A Critique of Modern Knowledge*, New York: Columbia University Press.

Hughes, Aaron W. (2012a), 'The Study of Islam Before and After September 11: A Provocation', *Method and Theory in the Study of Religion* 24, nos. 4–5: 314–36.

Hughes, Aaron W. (2012b), *Theorizing Islam: Disciplinary Deconstruction and Reconstruction*, Sheffield: Acumen.

Hughes, Aaron W. (2015), *Islam and the Tyranny of Authenticity: An Inquiry into Disciplinary Apologetics and Self-Deception*, Sheffield: Equinox.

Lincoln, Bruce (1996), 'Theses on Method', *Method and Theory in the Study of Religion* 8, no. 3: 225–7.

Lopez, Donald S., Jr (1998), *Prisoners of Shangri-La: Tibetan Buddhism and the West*, Chicago: University of Chicago Press.

Rizvi, Sajjad (2016), 'Reconceptualization, Pre-Text, and Con-Text', *Los Angeles Review of Books*, 25 August, https://marginalia.lareviewofbooks.org/reconceptualization-pre-text-con-text-sajjad-rizvi/.

Smith, Jonathan Z. (1982), *Imagining Religion: From Babylon to Jonestown*, Chicago: University of Chicago Press.

CHAPTER 2

Critics as Caretakers, Religion as Critique

CAROOL KERSTEN

INTRODUCTION

As a scholar of Islam specialising in the intellectual history of the contemporary Muslim world, I haven't taken a keen interest in questions around taxonomy. Reflections on how to characterise and experimentations with categorising different strands of thinking about religion, and Islam in particular, have remained a constant preoccupation. This issue is also relevant when dealing with Islamic studies as a field of academic inquiry and the involvement of scholars from Muslim backgrounds in that enterprise. When I examined Muslim intellectuals qua scholars of Islam for my book *Cosmopolitans and Heretics*, I used the taxonomy developed by Russell McCutcheon in *The Discipline of Religion*, because I found his categorisation of scholars of religion as either theologians, phenomenologists or 'critics not caretakers' (of this or that religious tradition) could be profitably applied to the selected case studies.[1]

After moving to the history of ideas in Indonesia and the different approaches taken by Muslim intellectuals in their engagement with Islam, I added a nuance, in the sense that I adopted Atalia Omer's suggestion that it is possible for a critic to also act as a caretaker.[2] Aside from engaging with McCutcheon's assertion that scholars of religion should operate as 'critics not caretakers', and Omer's suggestion that they can be both, I went on to develop a taxonomy of my own. In *Contemporary Thought in the Muslim World: Trends, Themes, and Issues*, I differentiate between traditional/conservative, reactionary and progres-

---

[1] Kersten 2011: 17–25; McCutcheon 2001, 2003.
[2] Kersten 2015; Omer 2011.

sive interpretations, with the caveat that these distinctions refer to ideas and strands of thought rather than individuals; people seldom fit snugly into a single category.[3]

More recently, I have wandered beyond Islamic studies, taking part in research projects on comparative philosophy and world philosophies in which yet other, but still comparable, interrogations of taxonomies present themselves.[4] As part of my involvement in these projects, I have developed an interest in the work of the historian of Islam and sociologist of knowledge Hamid Dabashi, in particular in what he calls the 'Hermeneutics of Alterity', which includes interrogations of 'religion' and 'Islam' as analytical categories. Originating from Iran, but educated and employed in US higher education, Dabashi matches the profile of that emerging new scholar of Islam signalled in the introduction, although I think it is important to correct Jane McAuliffe's assertion that Islam will be taught primarily by 'Muslims' to 'academics from Muslim backgrounds'. When discussing Islamic studies as a field of academic inquiry this distinction matters, because these scholars continue to negotiate the push and pull of both critique and caretaking.

In this chapter, I not only continue to investigate Dabashi's contributions to Islamic studies as a scholarly field, but I also return to examining the critic as caretaker by putting Dabashi in conversation with other scholars of Islam from Muslim backgrounds. The points of (re)departure for this are two recent books: Shahab Ahmed's *What is Islam?* and Irfan Ahmad's *Religion as Critique*.[5] Although the latter book has not received the same kind of exposure as Ahmed's, in spring 2019, the journal *Critical Research on Religion* (CRR) dedicated a symposium to *Religion as Critique*. In terms of similarity and comparability, we can see that both authors trained in the study of religion as a field of academic enquiry in North American and European universities, while – as Bruce Lawrence has noted – both publications are also invested with the scholars' South Asian Muslim backgrounds.[6] Because of these profiles, I treat them here as illustrations of critics who also act as caretakers of a religious tradition.

Hamid Dabashi fits into this examination because Shahab Ahmed included a lengthy critique of Dabashi's book *Being a Muslim in the World*.[7] As a fourth key interlocutor, I consider Gil Anidjar. Aside from taking part in the *Religion as*

---

[3] Kersten 2019.
[4] The Politics to Ethics Project of the Institute of Philosophical Studies at the Slovenian Science and Research Centre in Koper (2014–16); the World Philosophies Project initiated by Cosimo Zene at SOAS (2015); the Challenging Continental Philosophy of Religion Project of the Faculty of Catholic Theology at the University of Vienna and the Institute of Human Sciences (2017–present); and the Project on Philosophical Hermeneutics in the Islamicate Context, a joint initiative of the Catholic University of Louvain, the University of Bern and Mayis University in Istanbul (2018–present).
[5] Ahmed 2016; Ahmad 2017.
[6] Lawrence 2019.
[7] Dabashi 2013.

Critique symposium, he is also relevant for the present investigation because of Dabashi's references to Anidjar's other work, and because of their joint concern with semantics and the deconstruction of terms.[8] Both Dabashi and Anidjar have attracted criticism for the tone of their writings, the positions they have taken, and the theses they have put forward. But despite the controversies this has caused in some circles, I believe their work is, in the words of Claude Lévi-Strauss, 'good to think with' in relation to the subject of the present project.[9]

CRITICAL ISLAMIC STUDIES

Critical assessments of the study of Islam as a field of scholarly enquiry often include agenda-setting lists, consisting of themes and issues that need to be examined, or offering parameters for alternative approaches. For example, as part of his 'critique of Islamic reason' project, Mohammed Arkoun introduced a fourteen-point agenda for his 'Applied Islamology' project that consisted of researching and investigating:

> The inception of the Qur'an and embryonic Muslim community or what he calls the 'Medina experience'; the role of the Companions and the early Sunni Caliphate and Shi'i Imamate in transforming a living tradition into a traditionalisation of the *Sunna*; the emergence of academic disciplines in Islamic learning (foundational sciences, the synthesising of Hellenist *falsafa* and Eastern *hikma* into a philosophical tradition accommodating both reason (*logos*) and poetry (myth), the functioning of reason in the rational sciences, and – in combination with the imaginary – in historiography, geography, poetry, and oral literatures); as well as the transition from the 'practical sense' embodied in scholastic knowledge and empirical know-how into positivist reason flourishing in the early modernist experience of *Nahda*, followed by the revolutionary episode with its new social imaginaries, until the final con-frontation with the 'metamorphosis of meaning' at the end of the twentieth century.[10]

In *Theorizing Islam*, Aaron Hughes distils ten of Bruce Lincoln's original thirteen theses on method into a tool set to be applied in what he proposes to call 'new Islamic studies', which privileges examination and analysis instead of merely describing Islamic data.[11]

In the case of the two publications at the centre of this chapter, the authors

---

[8] Anidjar 2019.
[9] Knecht and Feuchter 2008: 11.
[10] Kersten 2011: 202, Arkoun 1984: 43–64.
[11] Hughes 2014: 118, 126.

have formulated their agendas interrogatively, producing lists of questions to be addressed. In *What is Islam?* Shahab Ahmed addresses 'six questions about Islam' to ask what makes philosophy, poetry, arts, law and medicine 'Islamic', and how does this affect the question of transcendence versus immanence, and the ultimate truth claim of Islam.[12] Ahmed aims to demonstrate three claims: (1) When talking about Islam, we are not so much 'conceptualizing unity in the face of diversity, but rather [talking] about conceptualizing unity in the face of *outright contradiction*'. (2) He notes that this is not done at the margins, but '*at the very social and political and intellectual center of Muslims' discourses about Islam*'. (3) And, instead of trying to understand these contradictions by 'separating them out as differences between the *religious* and *cultural* (or *religious* and *secular*) spheres of something called Islam', it is more profitable to

> call for – indeed, demand and require – a suspension of these received categories of distinction in order to reconceptualise Islam as a human and historical phenomenon in new terms which map meaningfully onto the import of the prolific scale and nature of the contradictory normative claims made in history by Muslims about what is Islam.[13]

In *Religion as Critique*, Irfan Ahmad also 'signals a research program', in which the following nine key questions need to be addressed:

> Why is critique being made? Who is making it and for what purposes? What is the condition which facilitates or hampers the practices of critique? What are the anthropological coordinates and power configurations – local, national, transnational, and global – under which practices of immanent critique, of this or that variety, are undertaken? What are the streams of critiques and how do they, with their respective ideologies, utopias, and social capital, interact with one another? How do they define and use tradition? How is the boundary drawn between 'self' and 'other'? How and why are networks of critics forged, maintained, or severed? To this end, what are the resources harnessed for dissemination, persuasion, and resistance?[14]

Of the other interlocutors, Hamid Dabashi also offers a set of characteristics pointing to an alternative way of engaging with religion, and Islam in particular. For Dabashi, our present-day decentred world is not only postcolonial and postmodern, but also post-Islamist, post-orientalist and post-western.[15] To that

---

[12] Ahmed 2016: 5–71.
[13] Ahmed 2016: 72–3.
[14] Telliel 2019: 4 n.3.
[15] Kersten 2016: 122–31.

end, a new hermeneutics is needed, conceived as a rhetorical device that is contrapuntal; not oppositional (there is not East and West) but appositional; centrifugal as opposed to the centripetal tendencies of an essentialised West and Islam; exhibiting cultural heteroglossia; and anthropocentric in orientation.[16]

HERMENEUTICS OF ALTERITY AND ITS DISCONTENTS

Before turning to Shahab Ahmed's sixteen-page criticism of Hamid Dabashi, first I must lay out the evolution of the latter's 'Hermeneutics of Alterity'. Dabashi's increasingly prolific output over the last fifteen years or so can be grouped in two sets of texts. The first set is a trilogy, in which he defines a research agenda and deals with relevant concepts; this trilogy is formed of *Islamic Liberation Theology*, *Post-Orientalism* and *Being a Muslim in the World*.[17] The other set of texts consists of political histories and engaged writings, including *Iran: A People Interrupted*; *Iran, the Green Movement and the USA*; *The Arab Spring: The End of Postcolonialism*; *Brown Skin White Masks*; and *Can Non-Europeans Think?*[18]

It is the first set that is of interest here because it forms the theory-laden and agenda-setting framework for Dabashi's 'Hermeneutics of Alterity'. *Islamic Liberation Theology* provides the central blueprint for both a critique and an emancipatory mission, but it is interconnected with *Post-Orientalism*, where Dabashi maps a new liberation geography for our decentred world. By contrast, *Being a Muslim in the World* proposes a new ethos, informed by a disposition he calls, alternately, worldly cosmopolitanism or cosmopolitan worldliness. This last book also contains a chapter with the telling title, 'Breaking the Binary'.[19] With a nod to Vattimo's notion of *pensiero debole* ('weak thought'"), Dabashi provides his propaedeutics for the 'Hermeneutics of Alterity' as a version of a 'number of weak strategies' designed to subvert an ontological remnant of the modern colonial world: the metaphysics of identity, featuring prominently in (western) sociological literature and characterised by essentialising categories of a religious Muslim world allegedly in opposition to a secular West.[20] It is predicated on a – in Hamid Dabashi's conviction – now obsolete opposition between Islam and the West as irreconcilable adversarial civilisational categories. From a historical perspective, this dichotomous worldview only functioned briefly during the Muslim world's colonial encounter with European modernity, in the sense that Muslim formulations of what Dabashi terms 'specifically

---

[16] Kersten, 'Anti-Foundationalism in Contemporary Muslim Thought', opening lecture at the workshop *Islamic Reformism in the West*, Institute of Arab and Islamic Studies, University of Exeter, 17 June 2015.
[17] Dabashi 2008, 2009, 2013.
[18] Dabashi 2007, 2010, 2011, 2012a, 2015a.
[19] Dabashi 2013: 19–41.
[20] Vattimo and Rovatti 2012; Dabashi 2013: 26.

"Islamic" manners of opposing this imperial upsurge', were fitted into a West versus Islam binary.[21]

As for Shahab Ahmed's criticism of Hamid Dabashi's hermeneutics, three observations are in order. First, Ahmed has only engaged with Dabashi's *Being a Muslim in the World*.[22] Second, while presenting his evaluation under the rubric of 'religion', Ahmed disregards the very chapter of *Being a Muslim in the World* entitled 'Religion – Quote, Unquote', in which Dabashi deals with religion as an analytical category.[23] Finally, one-third of Ahmed's critique consists of stringing together lengthy quotes from *Being a Muslim in the World*, rather than contextualising it and offering an in-depth critical engagement. Furthermore, a closer reading of Ahmed's criticisms of Dabashi demonstrates that there are actually more similarities than differences between them.

Ahmed presents Hamid Dabashi's 'Hermeneutics of Alterity' as a failed attempt to break away from the religious–secular binary. This is not the case at all. A large part of Dabashi's *oeuvre* is guided by his intention to overcome not just this specific binary, but the whole dichotomy of Islam versus the West.[24] Contrary to Shahab Ahmed's claims, Hamid Dabashi does not suggest that only Islam's 'doctrinal foundations' and 'juridical character' can be considered 'Islamic'. He says that Islam should not be limited to doctrine and law, but that it constitutes 'a vast and diversified heritage' encompassing 'discursive, institutional, and symbolic forms' as well.[25] In this sense, Dabashi's position is not dissimilar from the heritage thinkers (*turathiyyun*) I have studied on earlier occasions, including Mohammed Arkoun, Hasan Hanafi, Muhammad Abid al-Jabri and Nasr Hamid Abu Zayd. The accusation that Dabashi excludes the Quran from 'the vast range of symbolic, discursive, and institutional domains' also does not stand up to scrutiny. Instead, I suggest that Dabashi's position resembles Arkoun's distinction between Quranic fact and Islamic fact.[26] Dabashi is not reducing the role of the Quran to 'generating a fundament of *doctrinal absolutes*', nor is he denying that the Quran has given rise to 'a matrix of *semantic relativities*'.[27] Shahab Ahmed was also incorrect in equating Hamid Dabashi's advocacy for a re-appreciation of 'literary humanism' with Lenn Goodman's 'Islamic humanism', which Ahmed criticised earlier in the same chapter on religion (in *What is Islam?*).[28]

The fact that Dabashi's identification of 'cosmopolitanism' and 'worldliness'

---

[21] Dabashi 2008: 2.
[22] Ahmed 2016: 224–38.
[23] Dabashi 2013: 110–57.
[24] Kersten 2017: 81–96.
[25] Ahmed, 2016: 225, 227.
[26] Kersten 2011: 203, 206.
[27] Ahmed 2016: 226.
[28] Ahmed 2016: 229.

is not grounded in binary understandings of mundane/profane/secular versus sacred/religious, is also borne out by formulations like 'the existence of a continuous, almost uninterrupted, history in the multifaceted confrontation between the sacred and worldly imagination in the widest and most pervasive sense of the terms'.[29] The distinction Dabashi makes is appropriately characterised as heuristic rather than categorical. In fact, he considers the adjectives 'Islamic' and 'secular' categorically flawed – both epistemically and aesthetically – in relation to describing arts, poetry and sciences (Peter Adamson consistently makes a comparable point in regard to 'Islamic philosophy'). The fact that the distinctions might nevertheless work heuristically is affirmed by Dabashi's analogy with food (that is, what is called Chinese, Mexican or Lebanese food in New York, is just called 'food' in China, Mexico and Lebanon).[30]

Ahmed's claim that Dabashi does not accept that the poetry of Ḥāfiẓ or Ibn Sīnā's philosophy are also informed by their 'Muslimness' and being embedded in 'a "community of discourse" of Islam' is rather astonishing, because Dabashi has dedicated two monographs to Persian poets, in which he presents them as epigones of an Islamic variant of literary humanism, figures who have also exercised considerable influence on European literati and scholars of Islam.[31] It is also belied by a cautionary word included in yet another long direct quote from *Being a Muslim in the World,* in which Hamid Dabashi wonders 'whether the *totalizing* categorization of "Islamic" does justice to the internal and syncretic dynamics, forces of self-contradiction, and dialectical disposition that constitute these so-called Islamic societies'.[32] Islam/Islamic as a totalising categorisation would indeed make an accommodation of contradictions in society and culture problematic. But Shahab Ahmed does not attach sufficient importance to Hamid Dabashi's use of the qualification 'totalizing'. Moreover, in terms of Islamic versus worldly, Dabashi does not speak of binaries, but of bi-polarity. A sphere has two poles, but this does not undermine its integrity as a sphere. The same image can be applied to a culture.

Finally, Ahmed's doubts about the academic rigour of Dabashi's representations of Islam are much less persuasive when read in conjunction with the following statements he himself has made:

The intervention in the world of the Divine Author, Allah, has posed problems of reading and meaning on an order of conceptual complexity and

---

[29] Ahmed 2016: 230.
[30] Dabashi 2013: 25.
[31] Dabashi 2012b, 2015b.
[32] Ahmed 2016: 232.

socio-historical scale to which very few textual phenomena in human history can compare.[33]

Dabashi's axiomatic insistence on the 'bipolarity of the sacred and mundane imaginations' ... simply fails to take into account the existence – never mind the social and imaginal prolificness – in the history of Muslims of the Akbarian concept of the Perfect Man.[34]

These are faith-informed rather than scholarly or critical positions and are not very compelling as a metacritique of the twin terms religious/secular, sacred/profane, theocentric/anthropocentric.[35] In fact, such statements squarely position Shahab Ahmed in McCutcheon's category of 'theologians', rather than a critic who is also a caretaker.

Meanwhile, Ahmed's accusation that Dabashi axiomatically insists on bipolarity is also belied by another chapter called '*Din, Dowlat* and *Donya*'. In Dabashi's political theology, *dīn* and *dowlat* are part of the same 'modus operandi of the biopower and governmentality', and 'what was lost between "Islam and the West", between "tradition and modernity", "the religious and the secular" ... was *donya* – the world'.[36] Just as Anidjar's *The Jew, the Arab* illustrates how these interior-theological and exterior-political enemies could only be constituted in relation to a European political theology, so Dabashi also argues his case 'in patently European terms to underline the fact that this whole separation of din and dowlat business (or Church and State to be exact) is a European phenomenon at the capital end of Enlightenment modernity'.[37]

Here we enter into the domain of Dabashi's hypothetical suggestion of interjecting *dunya* between *dīn* and *dawla* as a way of dismantling the 'metaphysical binary of din and dowlat' and replacing it with a hermeneutics open to 'our lived polyvocal experiences'.[38] In the remainder of the chapter, Dabashi illustrates the cosmopolitanism of *dunya* by pointing to its resonance with the hopes hidden in seminal texts, such as Kierkegaard's *Fear and Trembling*; notions of the in-between and in-betwixt found in Gadamer's 'effective history'; the 'traveling theory' of Edward Said; and with Derrida's 'dangerous supplement' overcoming the 'evident hostility' of the 'debilitating binary' of *dīn* and *dawla*.[39] Again invoking Gadamer's observation that we live in language, Dabashi stresses that 'it is precisely that language that needs to be altered to be in tune with the world

---

[33] Ahmed 2016: 227.
[34] Ahmed 2016: 233.
[35] Ahmed 2016: 176ff.
[36] Dabashi 2013: 120.
[37] Dabashi 2013: 121.
[38] Dabashi 2013: 122.
[39] Dabashi 2013: 124–6.

that is emerging' and that 'the forced binary between a tyrannical theocracy and a militant secularism is a false choice'. Therefore, it is imperative – also for Muslims – 'to cultivate a new sense and intuition of the sacred'.[40] With this rejection of the binaries *dīn/dawla*, religious/secular, sacred/profane, the critic Dabashi implicitly confesses to being a caretaker too.

I conclude that there is far less separating Dabashi and Ahmed than Ahmed's criticism would lead us to believe; something that would escape readers who have no firsthand knowledge of Dabashi's other writings. *What is Islam?* does not stand in contradistinction to Dabashi – and indeed some of Ahmed's other interlocutors – at least not to the degree Ahmed presents in his book. This makes his case for restoring Islam/Islamic as analytical categories in studying Islam and Muslims less persuasive.

Aside from its relevance for rethinking methods and approaches to the study of Islam and the Muslim world, Dabashi's 'Hermeneutics of Alterity' is also related to several other and wider bodies of literature, which – as is the case with Dabashi's own writings – are often not confined to discrete fields of academic specialisation, but are situated on the interstices of scholarship, critique and political engagement. An important aspect of Dabashi's hermeneutics is what Hent de Vries has called 'the turn to religion' in contemporary philosophy, a phenomenon that involves thinkers as diverse as Giorgio Agamben, Alain Badiou, John Caputo, Gilles Deleuze, Jacques Derrida, René Girard, Jean-Luc Nancy, Richard Rorty and Gianni Vattimo.[41]

DECONSTRUCTING THE RELIGION/SECULARITY NEXUS

There are also affinities between Hamid Dabashi's 'Hermeneutics of Alterity' and the investigations of Dabashi's colleague, the literary comparativist Gil Anidjar, in *Semites: Race, Religion, Literature* and *The Jew, The Arab: A History of the Enemy*.[42] Considering the modern history of the Middle East, one might be tempted to assume that the latter is a book about Jewish–Arab animosity. But it is not. Instead, it concerns the projection of Jews and Arabs (a name subsuming other designations like Mohammedan, Muslim, Saracen, Turk) as the respective interior, or theological, and exterior, or political, enemies of Christendom. More recent exponents of this persistent enemy-thinking include al-Qaeda's characterisations of its adversaries as 'near' and 'far enemies'. The implied mutual hostility shows them as different sides of the same coin; the very binaries Dabashi wants to move away from.

---

[40] Dabashi 2013: 136.
[41] De Vries 1999.
[42] Anidjar 2003, 2008.

Gil Anidjar's *The Jew, The Arab* grew out of the author's astonishment about the lack of any serious engagement with the ontology of 'the enemy'.[43] This absence is all the more surprising given the centrality of thinking about love and war in the western (Christian, European) philosophical tradition – because these are the two core commandments that have shaped Christianity: love your neighbour, love your enemies.[44] Tracing its history from Paul through Augustine, Aquinas, Hobbes, Hegel and Freud, Anidjar observes that the enemy is named, but never defined; he remains an 'attribute' and 'accident'" a 'contingency'; 'indeterminate'.[45] It is only with Carl Schmitt's reflections on the Latin terms *inimicus* and *hostis* that philosophy approaches the more penetrating question as to what exactly an enemy *is*. But then Derrida illustrates its very slipperiness by pointing to *hostis*, 'the stranger', as the origin of not only hostility, but also hospitality.[46]

As epitaphs for the chapter 'Religion – Quote, Unquote', Dabashi selected two quotes, one from Anidjar's chapter 'Secularism'[47] and the second from *Kashf al-maḥjūb* by the eleventh-century Sufi Abū al-Ḥasan al-Hujwīrī respectively:

When there was Sufism there was no name for it, when there was a name for it there was no Sufism.

Christianity turned against itself . . . coming to name that to which it ultimately claimed to oppose itself: religion. Munchausen-like, it attempted to liberate itself, to extricate itself from its own conditions; it judged itself no longer Christian, no longer religious. Christianity . . . judged and named itself, it reincarnated itself as secular.[48]

When arguing for a 'renewed conception of "religion"', Dabashi combines Anidjar's critique with Gadamer's insight that the world as lived experience both shapes and is shaped by language.[49] The paraphrasing and reformulation of both quotes into 'when there was Religion there was no name for it, when there was a name for it, there was no Religion' mirrors another of Anidjar's observations, which Dabashi does not cite:

[T]hat one particular 'religion' is the one whose self-identification with, whose understanding and enforced institutionalization of, that most Latin of words shaped the current hegemonic use and dissemination of that very same

---

[43] Anidjar 2003: xxiii.
[44] Anidjar 2003: 14–21.
[45] Anidjar 2003: 75.
[46] Anidjar 2003: 61–2, 72.
[47] Before being included in *Semites*, this text appeared as an article: Anidjar 2006.
[48] Dabashi 2013: 140.
[49] Dabashi 2013: 139.

word and its ensuing division of the real, what Jacques Derrida has called *mondialatinisation* and Peter van der Veer 'the globalization of Christianity'.[50]

In the section on the 'christening of religion', Dabashi specifies that the culprit of the invention of religion is 'the *colonial condition of Christianity*' or 'Western Christianity' not Christianity as such. If Christianity itself had been the culprit, then Gianni Vattimo would have made a very awkward interlocutor for Dabashi.[51] As a further aside, it is worth noting that although it is clear that Dabashi and Anidjar's concern is with semantics, there is a certain irony to the latter's deconstruction of 'religion' in a book entitled *Semites*, when, a century earlier, Ernest Renan remarked that the Christian world does not owe the Semites anything with regard to politics, philosophy, science, the arts or poetry (!), and that their contribution to civilisation consists solely of 'religion'.[52]

Although Dabashi's vocabulary is less accurate when discussing secularity (he uses secularism and secularity interchangeably), it is noted that 'secularism is not just the doppelganger of religion', but *is* religion, and because of the global influence of Christianity, secularity has fetishised other traditions as well, including Islam. He then continues: 'Secularity is religion's greatest invention, and the other way around', while '[s]ecularism is the somber graveyard and the august pantheon of its own manufactured alterities, code-named religions'.[53]

This realisation makes Dabashi very critical of the academic study of religion, because 'professors of religion ... are implicit in acts of religion' and '[d]epartments and disciplines of religious studies are paradigmatic of a false (commodified) consciousness'.[54] Anidjar shows himself to be a bit more generous, referencing the late Jonathan Z. Smith's observation that religion is 'a term created by scholars for their intellectual purposes' and therefore a 'second-order, generic concept'.[55] However Anidjar too is acutely aware that keeping a 'reverential distance ... and leav[ing] religion to scholars of religion, as well as to the interpretive and mobilizing energies of religious communities' is missing the true extent of what Gadamer would refer to as *Wirkungsgeschichte* or the effective-historical workings of the religion-secularity nexus.[56]

If religion is 'the name for de-worlding the world', then – as Dabashi has it – the response should be the 'un-naming of religion' and the 're-worlding

---

[50] Anidjar 2008: 45.
[51] Dabashi 2013: 141.
[52] Ernest Renan, 'The Share of the Semitic People in the History of Civilization', inaugural address on assuming the Chair in Semitic Languages in 'Studies of Religious History and Criticism' at the College de France in 1862. Included in Warner *et al.* (eds) 1917.
[53] Dabashi 2013: 145.
[54] Dabashi 2013: 148.
[55] Anidjar 2008: 42.
[56] Anidjar 2008: 40.

of the world' by 'forgetting about religion' and 'retrieving the polyvocal heter-
onormativity' found in literature, cinema and politics, 'where the face of the
other has become the site and citation of not just an alterity, but an alterity
coming home to be at ease with its self'.[57] This proposition also echoes what
Anidjar observed in the chapter 'Secularism', and what informs his interest in
the relation between religion and literature, which he expands on in the rest of
his book, *Semites*:

> [t]o uphold *secularism* (or, for that matter, religion) as the key word for critical
> endeavors and projects today is, I am afraid, not to be that worldly . . . It is
> to oppose that world and those who inhabit it rather than those who make it
> unlivable . . . Religion cannot be willed out of worldly existence by secularists
> who deny its 'fictional' or oppressive escape while affirming the cultural and
> political importance of that other fictive production based on infinite credit
> and credulousness: literature.[58]

It is precisely because of the Christian baggage that comes along with secularity and its cognates that Dabashi opts for the term 'worldly'. This termino-
logical substitution is unpacked in the chapter that actually precedes 'Religion
– Quote, Unquote', the earlier mentioned '*Din, Dowlat* and *Donya*: Rethinking
Worldliness'. The three Persianised Arabic words (*dīn*, *dawla* and *dunya*) are
introduced to 'raise the linguistic horizon' and demonstrate that there is an
alternative vocabulary that enables us to talk about religion, politics and the
world. The addition of *dunya* (world) serves to drive home an important point:
contrary to claims by Muslims and non-Muslims alike that, because Islam – as
dīn wa-dawla (a religion and a state) – cannot be separated, Islam *is* in fact
entirely able to make that distinction. *Donya/dunya* is not just a referent for
Muslim worldliness, it also offers an opportunity to 'come ashore to a new
globality of our consciousness'.[59]

Dabashi's chapter on the category 'religion' opens with a note on a con-
ference, entitled the 'Future of Secularism and the Public Role of Religion in
Post-Islamist Iran'. The conference formed part of the debates about Samuel
Huntington's *Clash of Civilizations* and gave a new lease on life to Francis
Fukuyama's *End of History*.[60] Recognising his former student's 'folly of forget-
ting that indispensable Enemy', Huntington 'instantly posited Islam and thus
Muslims as its most recent incarnation'.[61] As constituent elements of both

---

[57] Dabashi 2013: 146, 148–9.
[58] Anidjar 2008: 51.
[59] Dabashi 2013: 136.
[60] Fukuyama 1992; Huntington 1996.
[61] Dabashi 2013: 114.

theses, Dabashi mentions the Hegelian spirit and the concept of enemy underlying the philosophy of Carl Schmitt; two philosophers who feature prominently in Anidjar's *The Jew, The Arab*.

Both Anidjar and Dabashi also invoke Giorgio Agamben. In a chapter from *The Jew, The Arab*, entitled 'Muslims', Anidjar notes that Agamben considers the word Muslims the 'perfect cypher' for what is at stake in his books *Homo Sacer* and *Remnants of Auschwitz*: 'Muslim', or more precisely the *Muselmann*, was a concentration camp idiom for the 'resigned extinguished souls who had suffered so much evil as to drift to a waking death' (Elie Wiesel); 'the non-men . . . the divine spark dead in them' (Primo Levi); those prisoners who, 'seeing them from afar, one had the impression of looking at Arabs praying' (Wladislaw Fejkiel).[62] While mentioned extensively in the Holocaust literature, Anidjar notes that this particular use of the term *Muselmann/Muslim* is largely missing from historical, philosophical and literary scholarship on Islam and Muslims. Dabashi notes another omission affecting not only Agamben, but also other relevant philosophers in this regard, such as Hannah Arendt and Emmanuel Levinas. That is, today's successors of the persecuted Jews of the Second World War are often Muslims. Here Dabashi is thinking of Palestinian refugees and Iranian opponents of the Islamic Republic.[63] Wedged between two rounds of university purges in 1979 and 2009 respectively, Iran's academics and students were not only victims of an ideological cleansing, but also of a 'stripping of citizenship to *bare life*', reduced 'from *bios* down to *zoë*'.[64]

Symposium: *Religion as Critique*

Gil Anidjar also participated in a symposium on Irfan Ahmad's *Religion as Critique*, organised online by Yunus Doğan Telliel for the journal *Critical Research on Religion* (CRR). Other contributors included Mayanthi Fernando, Bruce Lawrence and Nada Moumtaz, with Irfan Ahmad acting as respondent. Based on a narrower case study than Shahab Ahmed's 'Balkans-to-Bengal Complex', in *Religion as Critique*, Irfan Ahmad uses the figure of Abu'l Ala Mawdudi as a modern-day illustration of a critical tradition that is endogenous to traditional Islamic learning.[65] While working with the same cultural and historical coordinates of South Asian Islam, in contrast to Ahmed's six questions about what is 'Islamic' about scholarly and artistic fields, through nine penetrating and detailed questions, Ahmad tries to determine what is 'critical' about a tradition.

To this end, Ahmad wrote a 'comparative study of critique' in which he

---

[62] Anidjar 2003: 140.
[63] Dabashi 2013: 115–16.
[64] Dabashi 2013: 120.
[65] Ahmed 2016: 32ff.; Ahmad 2017, chaps. 4 and 6.

builds an argument for an Islamic critical tradition by juxtaposing the legacy of the Prophet Muhammad with that of the founders of other religions and philosophical movements. He engages the literature on what Karl Jaspers called the axial age. What makes Ahmad's project different from Jaspers' is the absence of a concern with the notion of transcendence:

> He instead sees in the axial age an emergence of a close relationship between reflexivity and social reform, which made possible one's being both an insider and an outsider to the community. For him, this is the modality of *effective* critique.[66]

By taking ancient prophetic legacies as the starting point, Ahmad not only makes a case for an Islamic conceptualisation of critique, but also challenges emphatic European post-Enlightenment claims to being the universal model. Considering it one tradition of critical thinking among many, Ahmad qualifies Enlightenment critique as an 'immanent' critique.[67] Aside from using this expansion of scale, Ahmad also consulted the theorising of immanent critique by the anthropologist Talal Asad and the philosopher Alasdair MacIntyre to undergird an interrogation that resonates with the argument put forward by Dabashi and Anidjar, about the Enlightenment and the progenitor of its secular presuppositions, Christendom, in terms of their exercises in 'boundary-making and category-creating: civilized versus uncivilized, rational versus irrational, European/Western versus non-European, pure race versus mixed, traditional versus modern, reason versus fanaticism, and so on'.[68] Irfan Ahmad executes this comparative study of traditions of critique not just for the sake of historical contextualisation, but also 'to reconsider the kind of questions a researcher can ask about critique and its social and political ramifications, as well as the objects, mediums, genres, and registers of critical inquiry that may change from one context to another'.[69]

When restricting his comparison to the European and Islamic traditions, Ahmad zeroes in on an examination of the different grammars of critique underlying the (seemingly) twin notions of reason (*'aql*) and critique (*naqd*). Ahmad attributes the holistic rather than binary aspects of critique in Islam to the linking of *'aql* to the notion of *qalb* (heart).[70] This establishes a more intimate link between intellectual activity and the day-to-day concerns of common believers than is made possible by the dualism that has characterised Enlightenment

---

[66] Telliel 2019: 2.
[67] Ahmad 2011.
[68] Ahmad 2017: 48.
[69] Telliel 2019: 3.
[70] In the symposium, Ahmad (2017: 60) also highlighted the contributions of both Lawrence and Telliel.

thinking since Descartes and Hobbes, and that has carried over into the modern discipline of sociology. To examine this further, Irfan Ahmad engages with Max Weber and the contemporary Germanist William Rasch, who – like Anidjar and Dabashi – has made much of the Enlightenment's Christian roots.

Since Irfan Ahmad draws on theories of immanent critique, the Islamic variant must be regarded as 'an engagement that speaks from within a tradition rather than claiming truth simply based on reason. It addresses the other as a practitioner of that tradition.'[71] For Nada Moumtaz this is an incentive 'to wonder then whether we could think of Ahmad's Axial Age critique as equivalent to Asad's notion of orthodoxy'.[72] Like her fellow interlocutor Mayanthi Fernando, Moumtaz has also reflected on terminology and translation, noting that an immanent critique like Ahmad's 'forces us to historicize the meaning of the terms "tanqīd" and "naqd", which Ahmad renders as critique'.[73] In this regard, I want to briefly note another line of enquiry set out by Alexander Key in *Language Between God and the Poets*. While I do not pursue it any further here, and Key's concerns and interests are first and foremost philological, his translation of *ma ʿnā* as 'mental content' and *ḥaqīqa* as 'accuracy' and its cognates seems to offer exciting interpretative possibilities that may be fruitfully and profitably employed in the study of Islam.[74]

Finally, while Anidjar's contribution to the symposium may contain relatively little immediate engagement and reflection on Irfan Ahmad's book, he makes a very interesting point concerning the French philosopher Pierre Hadot, who proposed to 'narrate the entire history of Western philosophy (though notably, *sans* Kant) as a history of conversion'.[75] This was subsequently picked up by Michel Foucault, who also adopted Hadot's distinction between Platonic *epistrophè*, translated as awakening, recollection and return, and Christian *metanoia* as 'a drastic change of the mind, a radical renewal; it involves a sort of rebirth of the subject by himself, with death and resurrection at the heart of this experience'.[76] Located historically between these two models, Foucault situates a Hellenistic-Roman alternative of self-subjectivation, which he uses as the only proper qualification of Enlightenment as neither a return nor rebirth, but a 'historical ontology of ourselves'.[77]

Anidjar uses this excursion to illustrate Ahmad's claim 'that Kant

---

[71] Moumtaz 2019: 2.

[72] Moumtaz 2019: 4.

[73] Fernando 2019; Moumtaz 2019: 5.

[74] Key 2018: 1–2. There is also an enticing observation regarding a 'conceptual vocabulary in which epistemology and ontology bleed into each other', for which there are no equivalent words in eleventh-century Arabic (Key 2018: 6).

[75] This is Anidjar 2019: 4, referring to Hadot 1953: 31–6.

[76] Anidjar 2019: 4, quoting Foucault 2005: 216.

[77] Anidjar 2019: 5, quoting Foucault 2005: 46.

misunderstood the Enlightenment [and] misunderstood critique'.[78] First, Kant was too focused on knowledge. Second, 'much of critique has been stymied insofar as it has been largely imitative rather than sufficiently reflective, reproductive rather than transformative'.[79] Ahmad's repeated assertions of critique as 'a way of life',[80] 'critique of everyday lives',[81] 'an anthropology of critique'[82] ring with the echoes of the Annales school, but in offering a holistic perspective on critique, 'which *both* illuminates the limits of the Kantian critique *and* offers a different model for critique',[83] he positions himself as a critic who is a caretaker too.

CONCLUSION

Earlier scholars of Islam from Muslim backgrounds, such as Mohammed Arkoun and Muhammad Abid al-Jabri, fit McCutcheon's category of 'critics not caretakers', and would even self-identify as such – sometimes to the irritation of fellow Muslims, frustrated by their unwillingness to profess their belonging (or no longer belonging) to the *umma*.[84] The more recent exponents of the critical study of religion (Islam in particular) presented in this chapter engage differently with the religion from which they come. The ways in which they interrogate their own tradition, reformulate critiques and hermeneutics, indicate that they retain a stake in its future, providing an affirmative answer to Atalia Omer's question whether critics can be caretakers too; while setting new research agendas they may also plot conservative, reactionary, or progressive trajectories.

BIBLIOGRAPHY

Ahmad, Irfan (2011), 'Immanent Critique and Islam: Anthropological Reflections', *Anthropological Theory* 11, no. 1: 107–32.

Ahmad, Irfan (2017), *Religion as Critique: From Mecca to the Market Place*, Chapel Hill: University of North Carolina Press.

Ahmed, Shahab (2016), *What is Islam? The Importance of Being Islamic*, Princeton, NJ: Princeton University Press.

Anidjar, Gil (2003), *The Jew, The Arab: a History of the Enemy*, Stanford: Stanford University Press.

Anidjar, Gil (2006), 'Secularism', *Critical Inquiry* 33, no. 1: 55–77.

---

[78] Anidjar 2019: 5.

[79] Anidjar 2019: 5.

[80] Ahmad 2017: 132.

[81] Ahmad 2017: 195.

[82] Ahmad 2017: 39.

[83] Anidjar 2019: 6.

[84] For example, Mohamed Talbi's attack on Mohammed Arkoun in an interview with the magazine *Jeune Afrique* 2122, 7 September 2001, Kersten 2011: xiv, 225.

Anidjar, Gil (2008), *Semites: Race, Religion, Literature*, Stanford: Stanford University Press.

Anidjar, Gil (2019), 'What *was* Enlightenment?', *Critical Research on Religion* 7, no. 2: 173–81.

Arkoun, Mohammed (1973), 'Arab Humanism': *L'humanisme arabe au 4e/10e siècle*, Paris: Vrin.

Arkoun, Mohammed (1984), *Pour Une Critique de la Raison Islamique*, Paris: Éditions Maisonneuve et Larose.

Dabashi, Hamid (2007), *Iran: A People Interrupted*, London and New York: New Press.

Dabashi, Hamid (2008), *Islamic Liberation Theology: Resisting the Empire*. London: Routledge.

Dabashi, Hamid (2009), *Post-Orientalism: Knowledge and Power in a Time of Terror*. New Brunswick: Transaction Publishers.

Dabashi, Hamid (2010), *Iran, the Green Movement and the USA: The Fox and the Paradox*, London: Zed Books.

Dabashi, Hamid (2011), *Brown Skin, White Masks (The Islamic Mediterranean)*, London: Pluto Press.

Dabashi, Hamid (2012a), *The Arab Spring: The End of Postcolonialism*, London: Zed Books.

Dabashi, Hamid (2012b), *The World of Persian Literary Humanism*, Cambridge, MA: Harvard University Press.

Dabashi, Hamid (2013), *Being a Muslim in the World: Rethinking Islam for a Post-Western World*, New York: Palgrave Macmillan.

Dabashi, Hamid (2015a), *Can Non-Europeans Think?*, London: Zed Books.

Dabashi, Hamid (2015b), *Persophilia: Persian Culture on the Global Scene*, Cambridge MA: Harvard University Press.

de Vries, Hent (1999), *Philosophy and the Turn to Religion*, Baltimore: Johns Hopkins University Press.

Fernando, Mayanthi (2019), 'Critique in Translation', *Critical Research on Religion* 7, no. 2: 182–8.

Foucault, Michel (2005), *The Hermeneutics of the Subject: Lectures at the Collège de France, 1981–1982*, trans. Graham Burchel, New York: Palgrave.

Fukuyama, Francis (1992), *The End of History and the Last Man*, New York: Simon & Schuster.

Hadot, Pierre (1953), 'Epistrophè et metanoia dans l'histoire de la philosophie', *Actes du XIe congrès international de Philosophie* 12: 31–6.

Hughes, Aaron (2014), *Theorizing Islam: Disciplinary Deconstruction and Reconstruction*, Durham: Acumen Publishing.

Huntington, Samuel P. (1996), *The Clash of Civilizations and the Remaking of World Order*, New York: Simon & Schuster.

Kersten, Carool (2011), *Cosmopolitans and Heretics: New Muslim Intellectuals and the Study of Islam*. London: Hurst.

Kersten, Carool (2015), *Islam in Indonesia: The Contest for Society, Ideas and Values*, London: Hurst.

Kersten, Carool (2016), 'Post Everything', *Critical Muslim* 20: 122–31.

Kersten, Carool (2017), 'Islam vs the West? Muslim Challenges of a False Binary', in

Klaus-Gerd Giesen, Carool Kersten and Lenart Škof (eds), *Poesis of Peace: Narratives, Cultures and Philosophies*, New York: Routledge, pp. 81–96.

Kersten, Carool (2019), *Contemporary Thought in the Muslim World: Trends, Themes, and Issues*, London: Routledge.

Key, Alexander (2018), *Language between God and Poets: Maʿnā in the Eleventh Century*, Oakland: University of California Press.

Knecht, Michi, and Jorg Feuchter (2008), 'Introduction: Reconfiguring Religion and its Other', in Heike Bock, Jorg Feuchter and Michi Knecht (eds), *Religion and its Other: Secular and Sacral Concepts and Practices in Integration*, Frankfurt: Campus Verlag, pp. 9–22.

Lawrence, Bruce (2019), 'Trolling for Exemplars of Islamicate Critique', *Critical Research on Religion* 7, no. 2: 189–93.

McCutcheon, Russell (2001), *Critics Not Caretakers: Redescribing the Public Study of Religion*, Albany: State University of New York Press.

McCutcheon, Russell (2003), *The Discipline of Religion: Structure, Meaning, Rhetoric*, London: Routledge.

Moumtaz, Nada (2019), 'Critique, *Naqd*, Orthodoxy', *Critical Research on Religion* 7, no. 2: 194–8.

Omer, Atalia (2011), 'Can a Critic be a Caretaker Too? Religion, Conflict, and Conflict Transformation', *Journal of the American Academy of Religion* 79, no. 2: 459–96.

Robbins, Bruce (1993), *Secular Vocations: Intellectuals, Professionalism, Culture*, New York: Verso.

Telliel, Yunus Doğan (2019), 'Introduction: Islamic Critical Thinking from Mecca to the Marketplace', *Critical Research on Religion* 7, no. 2: 168–72.

Vattimo, Gianni, and Pier Aldo Rovatti (2012), *Weak Thought*, Albany: State University of New York Press.

Warner, Charles Dudley, *et al.* (eds) (1917), *The Library of the World's Best Literature. An Anthology in Thirty Volumes*, New York: Warner Library, https://www.bartleby.com/library/prose/4265.html.

CHAPTER 3

Talal Asad and the Question of Islamic Secularities

HADI ENAYAT

In this chapter I explore Talal Asad's genealogy of the 'secular' and its complex relationship with Christianity and western colonialism. In particular, I critique the notion of secularism as an alien political form imposed by western colonialism on Islamicate societies. Instead, I argue that formations of the secular are better understood in terms of 'uneven and combined development' and 'connected histories'. I then turn to Talal Asad's geneaology of the secularisation thesis which, from his perspective, is seen not as a neutral social theory, but rather as the scientific justification for a technique of statecraft developed and deployed in the nineteenth century as an instrument of nationalism and colonialism. I explore some of these arguments with reference to Asad's critique of José Casanova's restatement of the secularisation thesis in the course of which a qualified defence of 'secularisation' understood as 'functional differentiation' is proffered. The chapter concludes by exploring the potential for synthesising genealogy and sociology to understand secularisation. It is hoped that this discussion will help bring Asad's genealogical approach to the secular into a dialogue with sociological approaches from the Marxist and Weberian traditions.

SECULARISM, CHRISTIANITY AND COLONIALISM

Talal Asad's rich and influential scholarship has been part of a growing international current of thought that seeks to problematise the 'secular' and demonstrate its imbrication with religion, particularly Christianity.[1] The idea that secularity has its roots in Christianity has been argued by Marcel Gauchet (Christianity

---

[1] Chrulew 2015: 144.

as the 'religion of the end of religion') and more recently by Charles Taylor, who maps the emergence of the secular as it develops within and out of Latin Christendom.[2] Other thinkers, such as Carl Schmitt and more recently John Gray, have argued that the political theory of the modern liberal state (especially the concepts of sovereignty and human rights) are secularised religious myths drawn from the Christian narrative.[3] The idea of secularism as disguised Christianity, as a sort of 'Christianity in sheep's clothing', as Aziz al-Azmeh puts it, is a variation 'of an older trope of denigration directed at the Enlightenment, at the French revolution and later at Marxism, and now at secularism'.[4] But as we see further below, this notion of a Christian essence inherent in secularism is problematic, as it posits a structural continuity between historical formations that does not adequately account for the 'historical breaks, structural transformations, innovations and functional differentiations that came with modernity'.[5] It also does not account for the complexity of church–state relations in Europe historically, which were by no means uniform, and do not correspond with this assumption of internal emergence and continuity.[6]

While Talal Asad sees secularism as a western norm and a unique product of post-Reformation western history, he does not see the secular as simply a mask for Christianity, rather he makes a more subtle argument about their co-constitution, tracing the shifting boundaries of 'religion' and the 'secular' to multiple sources and episodes in western history.[7] For Asad the idea that there is some trans-historical and transcultural essence called 'religion' is only about 300 years old. Indeed, the concept of religion as requiring assent to a set of propositions is a legacy of post-Reformation western history. This is counter-posed with religion in the 'non-West' where it is allegedly a communal, embodied and ritualistic set of practices that shapes social and public institutions in a way that is not adequately captured by the concept of 'religion' drawn from the historical experience of Christianity. The Renaissance, the emergence of humanism, the European wars of religion, the Protestant Reformation, the Enlightenment and European colonialism are all relevant to understanding the emergence of the categories of the 'religious' and the 'secular'.[8]

In Asad's schema, it is due to these processes that secularism emerged as a political ideology premised on the assumption that it is possible and desirable to isolate 'religion' from the 'secular' sphere. Specifically, the understanding of 'religion' that secularism presupposes is a product of a reconfiguration of power

---

[2] Taylor 2007; Gauchet 1998.
[3] Gray 2011; Schmitt 1985.
[4] Al-Azmeh 2019: xxxvii.
[5] Al-Azmeh 2019: xxxix.
[6] Al-Azmeh 2019: xxxix.
[7] Asad 2003: 26.
[8] Asad 1993: 27–55, 2003: 22–66, 190–4.

in which ecclesiastical authorities were gradually subordinated to the power of the emerging modern state, which arbitrarily reorganised 'substantive features of religious life, stipulating what religion is or ought to be, assigning its proper content, and disseminating concomitant subjectivities, ethical frameworks and quotidian practices'.[9] Hence, Asad understands secularism as primarily the power to control and ultimately define 'religion'. Moreover, the religious–secular distinction accompanies a number of other distinctions in western modernity; namely, distinctions between the public and the private, religion and politics, and church and state.[10] According to Asad, these distinctions operate discursively to legitimise certain kinds of practices and delegitimise others. They make religion essentially interior, private, and distinct from the secular, public sphere.[11] Thus, a religion like Protestantism can coexist with secularism because it is voluntarist and because a citizen's private loyalty to God is separated from her public loyalty to the state, whereas more publicly and politically oriented religions such as Islam cannot and must conform to this model to be accepted.[12]

Asad's analysis of secularism is drawn almost exclusively from western European history. This is not problematic because, he argues, 'Euro-America' is the privileged site for the exploration of non-European encounters with secularism and thus the correct starting point from which to understand secular formations in non-western contexts.[13] The legacy of colonialism and the overlapping histories of the European and non-European world have had profound consequences for the ways in which 'the doctrine of secularism has been conceived and implemented in the rest of the modernizing world'.[14] As Asad argues, this is not only due to the West's political, military or industrial dominance, but also its 'power to construct a "universal progressive history" which the other [non-European] tradition does not possess'.[15] This means that non-westerners who 'seek to understand their local histories must also inquire into Europe's past'. Here Asad seems to be referring to a tradition in western philosophy, from Vico to Hegel, based on the assumption that western reason and progress – the West's ability to transcend its past – was a result of it having written 'universal and progressive' histories that other civilisations did not have (at least to the same degree).[16] This gave the West a critical self-consciousness lacking

---

[9] Mahmood 2016: 3.
[10] Asad 2003: 183.
[11] Asad 2003: 245–8.
[12] Asad 2003: 186. Asad greatly simplifies Protestantism here. The godly republics of the seventeenth century did not presuppose a division of church and state. Likewise, commentators on Weber often forget that he only described certain forms of Protestantism. Ironically, states like Calvin's Geneva have much in common with contemporary Islamist states. I thank Philip Wood for this point.
[13] Asad 2003: 25. See also Bangstad 2009: 192.
[14] Asad 2003: 25.
[15] Asad 1993: 231.
[16] One could argue that this kind of history is not unique to the West: there is a progressive narrative

in non-western cultures.[17] Thus, western political, economic and ideological power 'unleashed in Enlightenment Europe' 'continues to restructure the lives of non-European peoples, often through the agency of non-Europeans themselves'.[18] In his introduction to an earlier volume, *Anthropology and the Colonial Encounter* (1973), Asad anticipated Edward Said's thesis in *Orientalism* (1979) by emphasising the discursive power of the West which gave it

> access to cultural and historical information about the societies it has progressively dominated, and thus [it] not only generates a certain kind of universal understanding, but also reinforces the inequalities in capacity between the European and non-European worlds (and derivatively, between the Europeanized elites and the 'traditional' masses in the Third World).[19]

From this perspective secularism and 'formations of the secular' are seen as part of the 'regime of truth' instituted by western colonial power.

Though not so boldly stated, Talal Asad's understanding of secularism is similar to some Indian post-colonial theorists, such as Ashish Nandy, who have viewed political secularism as a 'colossus standing on feet of clay'.[20] According to this view, beneath a thin stratum of westernised state elites who inherited an anti-religious orientation from the colonial regime, most people in post-colonial states reject secularism as an inauthentic norm that is increasingly shunned in favour of more public and politicised expressions of religion. Indeed, in some post-colonial analyses we get the impression that the 'natural' religiosity of the population is ranged against the ideological secularism of political and academic elites.[21] These perspectives on secularism are the antithesis of the earlier Marxist and nationalist discourse: whereas secularism used to be regarded as a means of liberation from the constraints of traditional and religious authority, religion now appears as a space of freedom, and secularism as an instrument of regimentation and of exclusion.[22] This perspective has now found expression in radical theory and scholarship in which, as Aamir Mufti puts it, there is a 'mood' in which religion as 'belief, ritual, institution, worldview, or identity' is seen as a means of healing the 'shattered totality of life in [colonial] modernity'.[23]

As a genealogy of certain forms of 'assertive secularism', such as the current

---

embedded in Islamic history (and a narrative in Chinese history of self-sufficiency and a return to the status quo). Moreover, multiple Eurasian cultures have different complexes of stereotypes that are used to classify the barbarian other and compete with one another. I thank Philip Wood for this point.

[17] Bhambra 2007: 22.
[18] Asad 1993: 229.
[19] Asad 1973: 16.
[20] Weir 2015: 3.
[21] Chibber 2013: 18.
[22] Wohlrab-Sahr and Burchardt 2012: 5.
[23] Mufti 2000: 87–8.

manifestation of French *laïcité*, Asad's intervention is convincing. But at the same time, Asad's understanding of secularism rests on a Eurocentric and *internalist* social ontology that overlooks the multiple and interactive character of social development. Consequently, it sets up an epistemological distinction between the 'West' and the 'Rest' as theoretically incommensurable, and turns the study of the origins of secularism into an exclusionary process in which the agency of non-western societies is overlooked or erased, particularly in understanding amalgamated sociopolitical and cultural-ideological forms such as secularism.[24] One way out of this theoretical impasse may be by adapting Leon Trotsky's idea of 'uneven and combined development' as the intellectual basis of an ontologically pluralist social theory. This has been done recently by Kamran Matin who calls for a social theory that assigns 'a co-constitutive and generative theoretical status to "the international"'. Such a theory can help us understand the 'heterogeneity of modernity and multilinearity of history as the organic products of an intrinsically international process of social change'.[25] As Matin relates:

> Uneven and combined development can therefore engender a radical 'provincializing of Europe' through theoretical foregrounding of the international dimension of the (trans)formation of capitalist modernity and geopolitical and geo-economic fractures that were, and arguably remain, constitutive of its variegated forms. By the same token, uneven and combined development also dispels the reificatory effects of the conceptualizations of the non-West' as a geo-culturally unified zone.[26]

From this perspective, social development can rarely be understood as purely internal to a particular society or culture, but is conceived as 'ineluctably *multilinear, causally* polycentric and *co-constitutive* by virtue of its very interconnectedness'.[27] Adopting this approach potentially opens up a space for critical dialogue between postcolonial scholars such as Asad and 'uneven and combined development approaches' mainly advanced by neo-Marxist scholars. Moreover, it can help us integrate power asymmetries ('unevenness') as well as multiplicity and contradiction ('combination') to understand the development of political and economic formations. This suggests that it is not sufficient to see secularism as a purely western imposition or in terms of its multiple incarnations in distinct national contexts as if they were independent from one another. The formations of the secular are better seen in terms of 'connected histories': while

---

[24] Nişancıoğlu and Anievas 2015: 5.
[25] Matin 2012: 370.
[26] Matin 2012: 370.
[27] Nişancıoğlu and Anievas 2015: 46.

they follow distinct historical trajectories and have different religious genealogies, they are also closely intertwined, sometimes with each other, but more
importantly with the hegemonic power of western modernity and colonialism.[28]
Thus, although we cannot ignore the legacy of colonialism and modernism in
shaping the formations of the secular, we cannot reduce secularism to a mere
copy of the western model.[29] As Nilüfer Göle argues, instead of seeing secularism
as the mirror of an ideal western model and measuring its deficiencies, we need
to understand the ways secularism is 'semantically adopted, politically rein-
vented, collectively imagined and legally institutionalized'.[30] Indeed, empirical
studies of secularism in Muslim-majority societies show that they exhibit a range
of religion–state arrangements and multiple secularities that defy essentialist
notions of typically 'Islamic' religion–state relations, often inspired by the ques-
tionable view that Islam knew no separation between religion and state.[31]

Some have investigated secularism in practices and discourses produced at sites
throughout global modernity.[32] For example, scholars have examined the ways
in which specific societal and political contexts impinged on the formulations
of secularism in the colonial encounter. In cases such as Kemalist Turkey and
Pahlavi Iran, for example, elites and state actors faced challenges posed by religious establishments in instituting secularising reforms as part of a state-building
project designed to resist imperial power – 'the whip of external necessity' – a
paradigm of reform that has been described as 'defensive modernization'.[33] In
these contexts, secular ideology was closely intertwined with anti-imperialism
and nationalism and was a powerful mobilising force in these societies – even if
some of the specific secular reforms, such as forced unveiling, were unpopular.
Others have employed Shmuel Eisenstadt's concept of 'multiple-modernties' in
order to understand the emergence of 'multiple secularities' around the world.
This perspective assumes a minimal, unifying concept of modernity from which
a diversity of developmental paths is then mapped.[34]

Adopting a similar approach, which focuses on 'imperial-modernities', Peter
Van der Veer examines how supposedly western ideas of rationality and progress
were produced and universalised in the expansion of European power. Focusing
on state and elite groups, Van der Veer identifies continuities in Chinese state
secularism from the Imperial period to Maoism and compares them to the
secularism of similarly elite groups in India. 'This entails close attention to the
pathways of imperial universalization. Examining secularism in India and China

---

[28] On 'connected histories', see Bhambra 2007.
[29] Göle 2015: 54, 57.
[30] Göle 2015: 58.
[31] Künkler et al. 2018.
[32] Weir 2015: 3.
[33] Curtin 2000.
[34] Eisenstadt (ed.) 2017; Wohlrab-Sahr and Burchardt 2012.

uncovers some of the peculiarities of this universalization by showing how it is inserted in different historical trajectories in these societies.'[35]

In a similar vein, Amartya Sen has characterised the rule of the Indian emperors Ashoka and Akbar as an indigenous form of Indian secularism based on pluralism and tolerance that has been an inspiration and justification for contemporary Indian secularism.[36] Whether the term 'secularism' is appropriate here is debatable, but as Charles Taylor points out, when a term such as 'secularism' is transplanted from one civilisational and historical context to another 'the useful question may not be "Is this move right?" but rather "What in our understanding of the term has to change if we are to make sense of the transfer?"'[37] Souleymane Bachir Diagne, for example, has studied how *laïcité* has been understood in Senegal in ways very different from its contemporary French version.[38] Although internally contested, the currently dominant understanding of *laïcité* in France generally advocates accommodation between different religious and philosophical views, something that can only come about if we create a special, neutral space between all religions.[39] This means that the public square or 'les espaces de la République' must be free from religious symbols, and public discussion should be conducted in a discourse without religious references.[40] Bachir Diagne's account of Islam in Senegal reveals a somewhat different understanding of *laïcité* in a country in which Sufi brotherhoods are the main vehicles of religious life and in which a number of them coexist in the same political space, along with non-Muslim minorities. Here the animating ideal of *laïcité* is not so much one of religious neutrality as one inspired by a powerful spiritual ethos which embraces pluralism and tolerance. This means that it can accommodate recognition of different religious communities, and even celebrate them, without undermining state neutrality or religious equality. Bachir Diagne tries to show that pluralism and equality may be generated from within a religious matrix and a deeply felt piety.[41] He also argues that a key

---

[35] Van der Veer 2014: 144–6.

[36] Sen 2006: 16–18.

[37] Taylor 2016: 252.

[38] Bachir Diagne 2016.

[39] For an interpretation of *laïcité* that attempts to give more space for religion in the public sphere, see Baubérot 2012.

[40] Taylor 2016: 255.

[41] Bachir Diagne 2016: 42; Taylor 2016: 256. One might comment here that while these ideas may be effective to justify and foster accommodation and pluralism among different religious communities, an adequate secular regime should also provide guarantees to protect the rights of individuals in the various communities. What are the costs of conversion for example? Is the regime of family law set up in ways that protect the rights of 'minorities within minorities' – for example women and children? There is no space to discuss these questions adequately here, but it is worth noting that Senegal moved to unify its family law after independence and implemented a secular family code applicable to all, irrespective of religion. However, strong opposition from the Sufi brotherhoods forced the government to make an exception for the Muslim community in the area of succession law in the Code de la Famille of 1972. This illustrates that while Sufism can be an important and effective resource for

component of this spiritual ethos requires one to maintain a distance from political power, and is thus inimicable to the idea of an 'Islamic state'.[42]

Bachir Diagne's position is similar to that of other reformist thinkers, such as the Iranian Abdolkarim Soroush and the Indonesian Nurcholis Madjid, who have argued that the most important reason for a separation of political and religious authority is to protect the integrity of Islamic ideals from corrupt governments and state monopolies.[43] The Turkish reformer Mustafa Akyol has argued that an Islamic precedent for opposing theocracy can be traced back to the Murji'a of the seventh century who embraced the doctrine that religious disputes had to be postponed until the afterlife because only God could judge them.[44] Thus, the state had no right to impose religious orthodoxy, and the Murji'a developed an almost Pauline theology that saw faith as internal and spiritual (a model of religion which, as we have seen, Asad has characterised as distinctly Protestant and liberal) rather than as displayed by works and exterior actions.[45] The Sudanese scholar and human rights activist Abdullahi an-Na'im has attempted to define an alternative foundation for a diverse and democratic society, one founded on his fundamental commitment as a practising Muslim. Such a society requires a kind of secularism, but not one that attempts to privatise religion or prevent the presentation of religiously based reasons in public debate. Rather, it requires that the state remain neutral with regard to religious and philosophical worldviews. Thus, he calls for a separation of religion and state but not a separation between religion and politics.[46] An-Na'im roots these arguments in a historical and comparative analysis of religion and state in Islamicate history. Drawing on the work of historians such as Marshall Hodgson and Ira Lapidus, he shows that much of the time there was a de facto separation between religion and state. Therefore, a secular state is not a wholly alien import that is necessarily harmful to Muslims.[47]

SECULARISATION THEORY AND ITS DISCONTENTS

We now turn to discuss the relationship between two perspectives on secularisation in connection with the Islamicate: first, the genealogical approach of Talal Asad, and second, the variety of differentialist sociological theory advocated by José Casanova. Foucault conceived of genealogies as critical 'histories of the

---

accommodating pluralism, it is still a generally conservative force based on communal authority, especially in the area of women and the family (Sezgin 2013: 41).
[42] Bachir Diagne 2016: 29.
[43] Hefner 2004.
[44] Aykol 2011.
[45] Aykol 2011: 83–5.
[46] An-Na'im 2008: 5.
[47] An-Na'im 2008: 45–84.

present' which, unlike conventional history, start with the present rather than the past, and uncover the conditions of possibility of our present practices and institutions. This method of historical and philosophical enquiry is oriented to uncovering the concealed meanings and functions of concepts and institutions, highlighting their contingency, their complicity with power; and tracing their roots to multiple, seemingly unrelated sources.[48] Theorisations of structural and functional differentiation have a long history in sociological theory, including in Max Weber's concept of the autonomisation of value spheres and his sociology of religion, Émile Durkheim's conceptualisation of the division of labour and his sociology of religion, and more recently Niklas Luhmann's theory of social systems.[49] Differentialist theory seeks to understand the lateral shrinkage in the social space occupied or influenced by religion, and the subsequent reallocation of religious functions in society, polity and culture.[50] Differentialist theory generally understands the process of lateral shrinkage as driven by the emergence of modern state-formation, generalised market relations, transnational flows and the concomitant division of labour that enabled a decisive separation between the political and economic spheres of existence, and thus an emerging civil society. As a result of this process of differentiation, 'the private world of "meaning" and the public arena of "legitimacy" were substantially separated'.[51]

There is a tension between these two approaches that derives largely from the genealogical assertion of the Eurocentric secular bias embedded in differentialist theories. Likewise, proponents of differentialist theories have sometimes critiqued genealogy for its excessively nominalist approach and its inability to grapple with the materialist dimensions of the universalising processes of colonialism and capitalism. Using Asad's genealogy of secularisation theory as a starting point, the following section will critically assess these two approaches to understanding secularisation in Islamicate societies, then discuss the prospects for a synthesis of the two ostensibly opposed theoretical paradigms.

Asad's genealogy of secularisation theory

The study of religion and modernisation lay at the roots of the sociological imagination being a prominent component in the work of Marx, Weber, Durkheim and Simmel.[52] Indeed, what became known as the 'secularisation thesis' – that modernisation inevitably fosters secularisation – became intrinsically interwoven with all theories of the modern world and with the self-understanding

---

[48] Foucault 1977; Koopman 2013.
[49] Dressler et al. 2019: 21.
[50] Vanaik 2017.
[51] Vanaik 2017.
[52] Turner 2011: 134.

of modernity.[53] This thesis has come under attack since the 1980s with the apparent 'return of the sacred' and the alleged onset of a 'post secular' society. Secularisation theory has long faced the charge that it is prescriptive rather than descriptive, ideological rather than sociological. For example, Peter Berger, one of the most influential theorists of religion, warned against 'assassination by definition', by which he meant those negative definitions of religion which 'serve to provide quasi-scientific legitimations of a secularized world-view' and easily lend themselves to ideological ends: religion as 'false consciousness' (Marxism), as 'the disease of language' (Müller), as 'imperfect philosophy' (Tyler) or as 'the childhood of man' (Freud).[54] Other critical histories have identified 'secularisation' not as a neutral social theory, but rather as 'the scientific auxiliary of a technique of statecraft developed and deployed in the nineteenth century to unify nations and divide colonial populations'.[55] The discourse of 'secularisation' has thus helped to legitimise the constitutional arrangements and policies deployed by modern states and elites who have sought to regulate religion and, in the process, reinforced the 'immanent frame' in which religion is now located.[56]

Talal Asad has also questioned the grand narrative of 'secularisation' theory that has been central to liberalism, Western colonial domination, and anthropology. He traces the ways in which terms such as 'secular' and 'secularism' became ideologised in earlier micro-political episodes. Asad's analysis of the invention of the term 'secularism' by George Holyoake in 1851 is a case in point.[57] Holyoake's neologism was designed to distinguish 'secularism' from 'atheism' and he was at pains to point out that it was an ethical worldview and not a doctrine designed to undermine ecclesiastical power or religion in general (note that this sematic slip has occurred in much of the Muslim world where the Arabic word for secularism, 'almaniyya, is largely understood as 'atheism' though the Arabic word for the latter is ilhād).[58] Nevertheless, Asad argues, it was this more anti-theistic concept of 'secularism' that was gradually co-opted by liberal elites and used to legitimise the project of political and cultural secularisation.[59] In this way, 'long-standing habits of indifference, disbelief, or hostility among individuals towards Christian rituals and authorities' became 'entangled with

---

[53] Casanova 2006: 20.

[54] Berger 1974: 128; Vanaik 1997: 71.

[55] Weir 2015: 1.

[56] Taylor 2007; Weir 2015: 1.

[57] Asad 2003: 23–4; Weir 2015: 10.

[58] The Arabic word for secularism is sometimes rendered as 'almaniyya (worldliness) and sometimes as 'ilmaniyya (positivism/scientism), both of which have negative connotations as they are associated with the desire to undermine the influence of religion in society. They are both distinct however from the Arabic for 'atheist' and 'atheism' which is, respectively, mulhid and ilhād.

[59] Asad 2003: 24; Weir 2015: 10.

projects of total social reconstruction by means of legislation'[60] and this marks the moment in which the anticlericalism of marginal groups of free-thinkers such as Holyoake, Owenite socialists, and subaltern radicals was transformed and passed on to the more powerful social forces of British liberalism.[61] For Asad, as we have seen, the larger context of this shift was the emergence of the modern bureaucratic nation state and its regime of 'governmentality' which sought to manage populations and render them as secular, rational individuals and consumers.[62] As José Casanova points out, from this perspective the secularisation of western European societies can be understood more in terms of the victory of the 'regime of truth' of secularism than of the impersonal processes of 'secularisation' such as urbanisation, education and rationalisation.[63] Thus 'secularisation' became a self-fulfilling prophecy in Britain, and eventually in Europe as a whole, once a critical mass of the population accepted the basic premise of the secularisation thesis: namely, that secularisation is a teleological process of social change and that modernisation inevitably fosters secularisation. 'Secularity' became a sign of modernity which was symptomatic of a society on the path of progress.

Most modernisation theories of the 1950s and 1960s, whether Weberian or Marxist, subscribed to this thesis and foresaw a process of secularisation in the newly independent and industrialising post-colonial states.[64] Instead, the late 1970s onwards witnessed the dramatic rise of politicised religion across the Middle East and South Asia as well as the growing popularity of the New Christian Right in the United States. It seemed that the secularisation thesis was not being borne out and some pronounced it dead in the water.[65] But others tried to modify it in ways shorn of its normative and predictive teleology. A prominent example is Casanova's influential restatement of the Weberian theory of secularisation.[66] Weber argued that modernity entails (1) an increasing structural differentiation resulting in the separation of religion from politics, economy, science, and so on; (2) the privatisation of religion; and (3) the declining social significance of religious belief and institutions. In brief, Casanova argues that all three elements are not necessary for modernity and that only (1) is viable. Thus, while functional differentiation is clearly occurring, modernity does not entail the privatisation of religion and it is possible for religion to exist in the public political space without necessarily threatening the essential

---

[60] Asad 2003: 24.
[61] Weir 2015: 10.
[62] Asad 2003: 24.
[63] Casanova 2006: 17.
[64] Chatterjee 2006: 58.
[65] For example, see Stark 1999.
[66] Casanova 1994.

components of liberal modernity.[67] Divested of their roles as grand narratives, 'responsible for integrating society as a whole, religions can become movements and pressure groups that vie with rivals in the public sphere'.[68]

Asad claims that Casanova's theory is incoherent because 'when religion becomes an integral part of modern politics, it is not indifferent to debates about how the economy should be run, or which scientific projects should be funded or what the broader aims of national education should be'.[69] Thus, public religions (and Islam in particular) cannot accept functional differentiation. Indeed, Asad goes further and argues that Casanova's theory smuggles in normative and secularist assumptions because it presupposes a certain kind of religion compatible with liberal modernity. The public roles of a religion are acceptable only when they unequivocally recognise the functional differentiation of social spheres – that is, when they agree to operate in the framework of secularisation.[70] Casanova has responded to Asad's arguments,[71] but we do not need to decide here whether his liberal approach to public religions is more convincing than Asad's distinctly negative view of liberalism. The issue partly turns on whether it is possible to have a value-free social science – a subject that has been a bone of contention in the philosophy of the social sciences since Weber and that is not discussed here. But in terms of understanding the relationship between modernity and religion, Casanova's arguments about functional differentiation (however we evaluate this process normatively) are difficult to contest, as we shall see further below.

Proto-secularities in premodern Islamicate societies: siyāsa justice

While Asad is correct to show that the domains of the religious and the secular were discursively shaped in the context of western modernity, there were analogous – though not identical – distinctions and differentiations between religious and non-religious spheres in non-western, early and premodern contexts.[72] Indeed, this differentiation and its tensions are by no means a uniquely modern phenomenon; both were visible in the post-prophetic Muslim community in which much of the time there was a de facto separation of religion and state and a separation between religious and secular law.[73] Examples of these conceptual distinctions in Islamic discourses can be found between *shar'* and *'urf* (custom), sharia and *siyāsa* (administrative law), and between *dunyā*

---

[67] Casanova 1994.
[68] Gorski and Altınordu 2008: 58.
[69] Asad 2003: 181–2.
[70] Asad 2003: 183.
[71] Casanova 2006: 12–29.
[72] Dressler et al. 2019: 10.
[73] An Na'im 2008; Hefner 2004.

('this world') and *ākhira* (the 'other world').[74] The semantic ties between these binaries may have played a role in Muslim appropriations of modern secularity and deserve further attention – for example the Persian word for 'secularisation' is *urfishodan* ('becoming *urfi*'). Moreover, Sherman Jackson (2017) has argued that there is an 'Islamic secular' from 'within Islam'. Jackson discerns this in the juridical debate on the domain of sharia and conceives of the 'Islamic secular' as that which lies beyond this sphere but which is nevertheless still within the Islamic tradition. In his historically informed inquiry, Jackson's 'Islamic secular' is not contrasted with Islam, but is seen as integral to it – though it is a part which is not governed in any specific way by the sharia. In this sense Islamic secularity is not only the realm of that which is differentiated from religion, but also is a realm that is relatively untouched by divine injunctions and, consequently, distinct from the realm of sharia.[75] As we shall see below, these spheres – such as sharia and *siyāsa* – are functionally differentiated but at the same time 'share valences of interdependence'.[76] These differentiations have sometimes been understood under the rubric of 'secularity' or – in connection with the Islamicate – 'Islamicate secularity' rather than the more normative concepts of 'secularism' or 'secularization'.[77]

An example of the 'Islamic secular' or of 'Islamicate secularity' (however it is conceived) can be discerned in the relationship between *siyāsa* and sharia, which is one of the main subjects of Khaled Fahmy's *In Quest of Justice* – a study of law and medicine in khedival Egypt. Fahmy discusses Asad's critique of secularism's separation of morality from law and his assumption that 'secularism did not exist in Egypt prior to modernity' and that prior to modernity, 'the moral subject [was] not concerned with state law as an external authority'. In Muslim tradition, Asad argues,

> the capability for virtuous conduct, and the sensibilities on which that capability draws, are acquired by the individual through tradition-guided practices . . . *Fiqh* is critical to this process not as a set of rules to be obeyed but as the condition that enables the development of the virtues.[78]

Through a careful archival study of the *siyāsa* councils in khedival Egypt, Fahmy shows how *fiqhī* morality was not the only ethical framework in premodern Egypt and how a *siyāsī* morality, one that derives from the rich *siyāsa* literature and the reciprocal rights and duties that this literature stipulates for rulers

---

[74] Dressler *et al.* 2019: 25.
[75] Jackson 2017: 11; Dressler *et al.* 2019: 15–16.
[76] Yavari 2019.
[77] Yavari 2019.
[78] Asad quoted in Fahmy 2018: 25.

and the ruled alike, was also imagined. *Siyāsa* and *fiqh* worked together and were complementary, but were also differentiated, as they were administered in different courts and informed by different legal logics. In the *fiqhī* world, the principle that binds relationships together is 'equivalence' not 'equality'.[79] This situation was similar to the Aristotelian view that defined justice as giving each their due or treating people according to their rank or nature. Thus, the qadi does not see individuated, isolated people when passing his judgements, but is bound to consider the social and communal relationships in which they are embedded and the relations of reciprocity which bind individuals together. This meant that before passing a ruling he had to consider such factors as the gender, religion, sanity, and age of the litigants and witnesses appearing in his court, as well as whether they were free or slaves. Therefore, the amount of *diyya* (blood money), the amount of inheritance, the number of witnesses to be heard – all these and other questions cannot be addressed until 'the *qadi* has paid close attention to whether his litigant is a man or a woman, a Muslim or a non-Muslim, a slave or a free person'.[80]

By contrast, the *siyāsa* council had at its disposal a number of impersonal bureaucratic procedures, and as a result could deal with individuals largely irrespective of their freedom, gender or religion (though these factors were not completely absent from legal proceedings). As Fahmy shows, this was evident at every stage of a criminal investigation. For example, instead of *'udūl* witnesses[81] who were effectively the linchpin between the qadi and the community, and who could establish not only the identity of the litigants and witnesses but also their reputation, the *siyāsa* councils relied on the textual devices of the modern state: the census record, the *daman* (a voucher establishing someone's good standing in the community), the *tadkhara* (passport), legal domicile, and simple patronymic names. They also relied on legal procedures which were inadmissible in qadi courts, such as the admission of circumstantial evidence and the acceptance of doubt (*shubha*), in order to secure a prosecution.[82] Moreover, in nineteenth-century Egypt these procedures were not simply copied from European models, but were developed from the earlier legal tradition of *siyāsa* justice that dated to the Abbasids.[83] On these bases, Fahmy argues that, *contra* Asad:

the idea of equality before the law in Egyptian legal thinking, which is so central in most accounts of secularization, was not born out of any deep

---

[79] Rosen 2000: 153–76.
[80] Fahmy 2018: 131.
[81] *'Udūl*, from the root ('-d-l) meaning 'just' or 'equitable' has been translated by Tyan as 'reliable witness' (Tyan 1960: 239; Rosen 2000: 8).
[82] Fahmy 2018: 92–117.
[83] Fahmy 2018: 126.

belief in the Enlightenment ideals of the value of each and every individual. Nor was it the result of pressure applied by European diplomats on leading intellectuals in Istanbul or Cairo to treat their Muslim and non-Muslim subjects equally. Furthermore, the concept of equality (as opposed to equivalence) that was established between members of the same polity in Egypt was made thinkable not because, as Asad argued, morality was divorced from the law, for this had happened when *fiqh* was combined with *siyāsa* – that is in the very early days of sharia. Rather, legal equality was born as a result of *siyāsa*'s successful attempt to uphold and maintain *fiqhi* principles and to do so by embracing modern medical and bureaucratic devices. In other words, sharia became secularized in khedival Egypt not because it was limited to the realm of personal status but because its partner in crime, the *siyāsa* councils, were successful in embracing the bureaucratic and medical techniques of the modernizing centralizing state.[84]

In light of this, Fahmy argues that *siyāsa* constituted an indigenous premodern and precolonial bureaucratic tradition – one which separated morality and law – and thus made a secular rule of law possible in the Egyptian legal sphere.

Functional differentiation in colonial modernity

Though they were transformed in complex ways, these distinctions formed the basis for the process of structural differentiation that accompanied colonial modernity in the Islamicate world. An integral part of these transformations was what Sami Zubaida calls the 'dis-embedding' of religion from social institutions and practices.[85] From the eighteenth century onwards – in a distinctly uneven and varied set of processes across the 'Muslim world' – the spheres of law, education, productive property, and *awqāf* (charitable endowments) were disengaged from religious control and brought under the control of the state (sometimes administered by state employed *'ulamā*).[86] While this differentiation was something that took place over the *longue durée* and was often an organic and untheorised process, in the modern era it was sometimes imposed by autocratic modernising regimes such as Kemalist Turkey, Pahlavi Iran and Bourguiba's Tunisia.[87] This created a backlash with the rise of political Islam and its calls for Islamicising the state and pushing back against the depredations of a corrosive

---

[84] Fahmy 2018: 132.
[85] Zubaida 2011: 3.
[86] Note that in many countries the *'ulamā* continued to oversee and administer civil law and *waqf* but as employees of the state in state ministries and courts.
[87] On secularisation in Turkey, see Berkes 1999. On legal secularisation in Iran during the early twentieth century, see Enayat 2013. On secularisation in Tunisia, see Dalacoura 2007.

and alien secularisation. But even within these contexts the logic of functional differentiation seems to reassert itself. Indeed, functional differentiation has been integral to capitalist modernisation even in states that have experienced enforced projects of desecularisation, such as the Islamic Republic of Iran, where the dis-embedding of religion from areas such as law, education and popular culture continues despite the project to Islamicise these spheres after the 1979 revolution.[88]

Religious authorities and their followers in many regions, including much of the 'Muslim world', have been largely reconciled to this specialisation. Even though many of the 'ulamā would dispute the theoretical legitimacy of the kind of differentiation of social spheres that Casanova identifies, they have long accepted some such differentiation in practice. A prominent example of this acceptance, even in theory, is India's premier Deobandi organisation, the Jamiat Ulama-i-Hind which, shortly after India's independence in 1948, formally accepted this specialisation and announced that it would restrict its activities to 'religious, cultural and educational rights and obligations'.[89] Nevertheless, this differentiation has clearly caused tensions, and some movements (such as the Muslim Brotherhood and some of its affiliates, as well as some Deobandi and Salafi organisations), fearful at their loss of control over certain social spheres, have responded with political and moralistic campaigns aimed at re-establishing control, especially in the area of gender, sexual morality, education and artistic expression. However, this has tended to happen *within* functionally differentiated spaces, sometimes with the longer-term strategy of countering secularisation by Islamicising these spheres in ways which, it is hoped, will eventually filter 'upwards' into state and political institutions. Thus, as Zubaida points out, in the Middle East as in much of the 'Muslim world', we have the paradox of largely secularised societies and polities combined with the advocacy of Islamist and fundamentalist ideologies by regimes and social movements.[90] The societies are secularised in that many of their institutions and practices have little or no relation to religion and it is precisely this functional differentiation that 'fundamentalism' is reacting against.

These structural transformations are not unilinear, nor are the differentiated spheres of the religious and the secular mutually exclusive. Moreover, they do not map neatly onto the public and private spheres. Furthermore, these assertions do not mean that the 'secular' always has primal causality over the 'religious', or that religion is purely epiphenomenal. Indeed, they are deeply intertwined and the unpredictable complexity of causes in human affairs means that the lines of

---

[88] On secularisation in the Islamic Republic of Iran, see Roy 2004; Schirazi 1998; Khosrowkhavar 2013.
[89] Zaman 2012: 138.
[90] Zubaida 2011: 4.

causality between them frequently switch places. Nevertheless, I would suggest that in the political, economic and cultural spheres, over time, the *tendency* of modernisation is toward secular functional differentiation. Indeed, it is this differentiation – experienced as moral disintegration by 'reactionary radicals' like Khomeini – that sparks movements for societal reintegration under the sacred canopy of religion.

Asad's genealogies of the secular provide a way of deconstructing the teleo-logical assumptions of the social sciences and encouraging a more reflexive and critical sociological imagination. But his tendency to conflate the sociological concept of functional differentiation with a normative secularism is not con-vincing and the theory of functional differentiation remains a useful analytical framework for a comparative research agenda. Indeed, it is a useful paradigm for understanding the dialectic of secularisation and desecularisation in terms of the advance and retreat of the state (or in terms of functional differentiation and de-differentiation). In the 1990s, for example, neoliberal reforms led to the shrinking of state sectors in many countries, including Egypt and India; as a result, religious movements such as the Muslim Brotherhood and the Bharatiya Janata Party (BJP) filled this space by providing social services to the poor, and this led to their increased popularity. Thus, the process of secularisation is not unilinear and, by virtue of operating in a wider political economy of capitalist development, frequently and in various contexts, is characterised by interrup-tions, halts and reverses.[91]

Towards a synthesis of genealogy and sociology

As we have seen, the critiques of secularisation theory by postcolonial gene-alogists such as Asad stem from a number of issues discussed above, including the biased definitions of the 'religious' and the 'secular' and their imbrication in regimes of truth that underpin colonialism, liberalism and capitalism. But more broadly, they also derive from a strong nominalist and anti-foundation-alist thrust which 'puts at its centre the aporias of all kinds of universalistic arguments'.[92] Thus, the supposed incompatibility of Foucauldian genealogy and more conventional Marxist and Weberian historical sociology rests largely on the assumption that the former's commitment to the contingency of our beliefs and practices is incompatible with the latter's assertion of the neces-sity of universal processes such as secularisation. But as Colin Koopman has shown in a recent study of the genealogical method, the two approaches are not necessarily incompatible, and Foucault allowed room for a conception of

---

[91] Vanaik 2017.
[92] Chernilo 2013: 5.

universalisability in parameters established by his concern with contingency and complexity.[93] While the concept of universalism embedded in conventional sociology was too entangled with simplification and necessity for his purposes, Koopman argues that Foucault left open the possibility of an idea of universalisability consistent with contingency. It is worth quoting Koopman here at length:

> It was one of Foucault's best insights to develop analytic and diagnostic orientations that simultaneously faced both of these directions. According to such an account, universality in the sense of processes of universalizability turns out to be nothing more surprising, but also nothing less remarkable, than the way in which some objects and concepts proliferate across just about any context and get packaged into portable forms that can be transported just about anywhere. . . . If something as quotidian as standards of measurement and communication can be regarded as universalizable without requiring an overarching transcendental story to explain their gradual proliferation across the planet, then something as complex as modern sexuality or modern punishment may be universalizable in just the same way, with requisite accounting for complexity. How did we get, in less than a century, from the spectacle of torture to the ubiquity of imprisonment? How, in so short a time, did the prison, which was once unheard of, become the only viable option for punishment in our society? The story of these standardizations is very much at the heart of Foucault's genealogy of discipline. Genealogical problematization can thus be understood as a critical inquiry into the conditions of the possibility of the proliferation of practices and problematizations.[94]

Here Koopman makes a seemingly simple but nevertheless important point that 'contingency picks out a modality, and universality picks out a scope', hence, there is 'no obvious (no necessary) contradiction in their being deployed together'.[95] He goes on to develop this argument into a convincing defence of what he terms 'contingent universals' that are themselves the outcome of complex and ongoing processes of universalisation whose outcomes are uncertain.[96] As Foucault noted:

> Instead of deducing concrete phenomena from universals, or instead of starting with universals as an obligatory grid of intelligibility for certain concrete

---

[93] Koopman 2013: 222.
[94] Koopman 2013: 119–20.
[95] Koopman 2013: 224.
[96] Koopman 2013: 239–40.

practices, I would like to start with these concrete practices and, as it were, pass these universals through the grid of these practices.[97]

In short, ostensibly objective and universal definitions of 'secularisation' and the 'secular' are divorced from the social world they describe because as Erlenbusch-Anderson puts it they ignore processes of historical change, conceptual transformation, contestations over political categories, resistance to hegemonic concepts, and the practices these concepts make possible'.[98] Moreover, a definitional approach to objects of social reality (which sometimes characterises differentialist theory and its deployment of 'ideal types') runs the risk of importing static concepts leading to a 'rarefied, impoverished, decontextualised, and ahistorical account' of secularisation.[99] These arguments about genealogy can be usefully applied to understanding (and problematising) the conditions of possibility for the proliferation of normative/political concepts such as 'religion', 'secularism' or 'human rights', as well as impersonal processes and theories such as 'functional differentiation'. Thus, genealogy can help advance the process of conceptual amelioration based on and informed by a critical analysis of the historical formation of the concepts to be reconstructed.[100] Despite the strong epistemological and ideological disagreements between the two methodological traditions, genealogy and sociology can be synthesised. Empirical sociology and ethnography can be informed by an anti-essentialist and genealogical awareness of diversity, plurality and context.[101] This can help us understand complex and sometimes contradictory trajectories of differentiation and de-differentiation as well as the multiple secularities in the Islamicate world while not losing sight of the discursive hegemonic construction of these concepts. Finally, integrating genealogy and secularisation theory may help forge a more reflexive and critical secularisation theory more attuned to the persistence of religion in modernity.

BIBLIOGRAPHY

Abdel Razek, Ali (2012), *Islam and the Foundations of Political Power*, ed. Abdou Filali-Ansary, trans. Maryam Loutfi, Edinburgh: Edinburgh University Press.

---

[97] Foucault 2010: 3.
[98] Erlenbusch-Anderson 2018: 112
[99] Erlenbusch-Anderson 2018: 112. Note that Erlenbusch-Anderson is making these arguments in connection with the concept of 'terrorism' but I would argue that they apply to concepts such as 'secularization' or 'secularism' as well.
[100] Erlenbusch-Anderson 2018: 113.
[101] Angela McRobbie for example, has argued that part of the reason cultural studies has not been able to engage in policy debates is due to the dearth of concrete, empirically grounded research. She suggests that the 'three Es' – empiricism, ethnography and experience – 'be reconceptualized in the light of the "anti-Es": anti-essentialism, post-structuralism and psychoanalysis'. See McRobbie 1999: 25.

Ali, Souad T. (2009), *A Religion Not a State: Ali 'Abd al-Raziq's Islamic Justification of Political Secularism*, Salt Lake City: University of Utah Press.

an-Na'im, Abdullahi Ali (2008), *Islam and the Secular State: Negotiating the Future of Shari'a*, Cambridge, MA: Harvard University Press.

Asad, Talal (1973), *Anthropology and the Colonial Encounter*, London: Ithaca Press.

Asad, Talal (1993), *Genealogies of Religion: Disciplines of Power*, Baltimore: Johns Hopkins University Press.

Asad, Talal (2003), *Formations of the Secular: Christianity, Islam, Modernity*, Stanford: Stanford University Press.

Asad, Talal (2015), '"Do Muslims Belong in the West?" An Interview with Talal Asad', *Jadalliya*, 3 February, http://www.jadaliyya.com/pages/index/20768/do-muslims-belong-in-the-west-an-interview-with-ta.

Aykol, Mustafa (2011), *Islam Without Extremes: A Muslim Case for Liberty*, New York: W. W. Norton & Company.

al-Azmeh, Aziz (2019), *Secularism in the Arab World: Contexts, Ideas and Consequences*, Edinburgh: Edinburgh University Press.

Bachir Diagne, S. (2016), 'The Sufi and the State', in Akeel Bilgrami (ed.), *Beyond the Secular West*, New York: Columbia University Press, pp. 28–41.

Bangstad, Sindre (2009), 'Contesting Secularism/s: Secularism and Islam in the Work of Talal Asad', *Anthropological Theory* 9, no. 2: 188–208.

Baubérot, J. (2012), *La Laïcité Falsifiée*, Paris: Éditions la Découverte.

Berger, Peter (1974), 'Some Second Thoughts on Substantive versus Functional Definitions of Religion', *Journal for the Scientific Study of Religion* 13, no. 2: 125–33.

Berkes, N. (1999), *The Development of Secularism in Turkey*, Montreal: McGill University Press.

Bhambra, G. (2007), *Rethinking Modernity: Postcolonialism and the Sociological Imagination*, New York: Palgrave Macmillan.

Bowen, I. (2014), *Medina in Birmingham, Najaf in Brent: Inside British Islam*, London: Hurst Publishers.

Casanova, José (1994), *Public Religions in the Modern World*, Chicago: University of Chicago Press.

Casanova, José (2006), 'Secularization Revisited: A Reply to Talal Asad', in D. Scott and C. Hirschkind (eds), *The Powers of the Secular Modern: Talal Asad and his Interlocutors*, Stanford: Stanford University Press, pp. 12–30.

Chatterjee, P. (2006), 'Fasting for Bin Laden: The Politics of Secularization in Contemporary India', in D. Scott and C. Hirschkind (eds), *The Powers of the Secular Modern: Talal Asad and his Interlocutors*, Stanford: Stanford University Press, pp. 57–74.

Chernilo, D. (2013), *The Natural Law Foundations of Modern Social Theory*, Cambridge: Cambridge University Press.

Chibber, V. (2013), *Postcolonial Theory and the Specter of Capital*, London: Verso.

Chrulew, M. (2015), 'Genealogies of the Secular', in T. Stanley (ed.), *Religion After Secularization in Australia*, New York: Palgrave Macmillan, pp. 139–58.

Cohen, J. (2018), 'On the Genealogy and Legitimacy of the Secular State: Bockenforde and the Asadians', *Constellations* 25, no. 2: 207–24.

Curtin, P. (2000), *The World and the West: The European Challenge and the Overseas Response in the Age of Empire*, New York: Cambridge University Press.

Dalacoura, Katerina (2007), *Islam, Liberalism and Human Rights*, London: I. B. Tauris.

Dressler, Markus, Armando Salvatore and Monika Wohlrab Sahr (2019), 'Islamicate Secularities: New Perspectives on a Contested Concept', *Historical Social Research* 44, no. 3: 7–34.

Eisenstadt, Shmuel (ed.) (2017), *Multiple Modernities*, Oxford: Routledge Publishers.

Enayat, Hadi (2013), *Law, State and Society in Modern Iran: Constitutionalism, Autocracy and Legal Reform 1906–1941*, New York: Palgrave Macmillan.

Erlenbusch-Anderson, V. (2018), *Genealogies of Terrorism: Revolution, State Violence, Empire*, New York: Columbia University Press.

Fahmy, Khaled (2018), *In Quest of Justice: Islamic Law and Forensic Medicine in Khedival Egypt*, Berkeley: University of California Press.

Foucault, Michel (1977), *Discipline and Punish: The Birth of the Prison*, New York: Vintage.

Foucault, Michel (2010), *The Birth of Biopolitics: Lectures at the Collège de France, 1978–1979*, eds M. Senellart, F. Ewald, A. Fontana and A. I. Davidson, trans. G. Burchell, New York: Palgrave Macmillan.

Gauchet, Marcel (1998), *La Religion dans la Démocratie: Parcours de la Laïcité*, Paris: Gallimard.

Göle, N. (2015), *Islam and Secularity: The Future of Europe's Public Sphere*, Durham, NC: Duke University Press.

Gorski, P. S., and A. Altınordu (2008), 'After Secularization', *Annual Review of Sociology* 34: 55–85.

Gray, J. (2011), *Black Mass: Apocalyptic Religion and the Death of Utopia*, London: Penguin.

Hefner, R. (2004), 'Book Review of Talal Asad's *Formations of the Secular*', *H-Gender-Mid-East*, https://networks.h-net.org/node/6386/reviews/6632/hefner-asad-formations-secular-christianity-islam-modernity.

Jackson, Sherman (2017), 'The Islamic Secular', *American Journal of Islam and Society* 34, no. 2: 1–38.

Khosrowkhavar, F. (2013), 'Two Types of Secularization: The Iranian Case', in S. Arjomand and E. P. Reis (eds), *Worlds of Difference*, London: Sage, pp. 121–55.

Koopman, C. (2013), *Genealogy as Critique: Foucault and the Problem of Modernity*, Bloomington: Indiana University Press.

Künkler, M., J. Madley and S. Shankar (2018), *A Secular Age Beyond the West: Religion, Law and the State in Asia, the Middle East and North Africa*, New York: Cambridge University Press.

Mahmood, S. (2016), *Religious Difference in a Secular Age: A Minority Report*. Princeton NJ: Princeton University Press.

Matin, K. (2012), 'Redeeming the Universal: Postcolonialism and the Inner Life of Eurocentrism', *European Journal of International Relations* 19, no. 2: 353–77.

Matin, K. (2016), 'The Iranian Revolution in the Mirror of Uneven and Combined Development', Lecture at London Middle East Institute at SOAS, https://www.soas.ac.uk/lmei/events/cme/08mar2016–the-iranian-revolution-in-the-mirror-of-uneven-and-combined-development.html.

McRobbie, A. (1999), *In the Culture Society: Art, Fashion and Popular Music*, London:

Routledge.

Mufti, A. (2000), 'The Aura of Authenticity', *Social Text* 18, no. 3: 87–103.

Nişancıoğlu, K., and A. Anievas (2015), *How the West Came to Rule: The Geopolitical Origins of Capitalism*, London: Pluto Press.

Rosen, Laurence (2000), *The Justice of Islam*, Oxford: Oxford University Press.

Roy, Olivier (2004), *Globalized Islam: The Search for a New Ummah*, New York: Columbia University Press.

Schirazi, A. (1998), *The Constitution of Iran: Politics and the State in the Islamic Republic*, London: I. B. Tauris.

Schmitt, C. (1985), *Political Theology: Four Chapters on the Concept of Sovereignty*, Chicago: University of Chicago Press.

Sen, A. (2006), *The Argumentative Indian: Writings on Indian History, Culture and Identity*, London: Penguin.

Sezgin, Y. (2013), *Human Rights under State-Enforced Religious Family Laws in Israel, Egypt and India*, Cambridge: Cambridge University Press.

Stark, R. (1999), 'Secularization RIP', *Sociology of Religion* 60, no. 3: 249–73.

Taylor, Charles (2007), *A Secular Age*, Cambridge, MA: Harvard University Press.

Taylor, Charles (2016), 'A Secular Age Outside Latin-Christendom', in A. Bilgrami (ed.), *Beyond the Secular West*, New York: Columbia University Press, pp. 246–61.

Turner, Bryan S. (2011), *Religion in Modern Society: Citizenship, Secularization and the State*, Cambridge: Cambridge University Press.

Tyan, E. (1960), *Histoire de l'organisation judicaire en pays d'Islam*, Leiden: Brill.

Vanaik, A. (1997), *The Furies of Indian Communalism: Religion, Modernity and Secularization*, London: Verso.

Vanaik, A. (2017), *The Rise of Hindu Authoritarianism: Secular Claims, Communal Realities*, London: Verso Books.

Van der Veer, P. (2014), *The Modern Spirit of Asia: The Spiritual and the Secular in China and India*, Princeton, NJ: Princeton University Press.

Weir, T. (2015), 'Secularism and Secularization: Postcolonial Genealogy and Historical Critique', Reprints and Working Papers of the Centre for Religion and Modernity, Munster University, https://www.uni-muenster.de/imperia/md/content/religion_ und_moderne/preprints/crm_working_paper_7_weir.pdf.

Wohlrab-Sahr, Monika, and Marian Burchardt (2012), 'Multiple Secularities: Towards a Cultural Sociology of Secular Modernities', *Comparative Sociology* 11: 875–909.

Wohlrab-Sahr, Monika, and Marian Burchhardt (2017), *Revisiting the Secular: Multiple Secularities and Pathways to Modernity*, Working Paper Series of the HCAS 'Multiple Secularities: Beyond the West, Beyond Modernities' (Leipzig University), https:// www.multiple-secularities.de/media/wps_wohlrabsahr_burchardt_revisitingthesecu lar.pdf.

Yavari, Neguin (2019), *Secularity in the Premodern Islamic World*, Working Paper Series of the HCAS, https://www.multiple-secularities.de/publications/companion/seculari ty-in-the-premodern-islamic-world/.

Zaman, M. Qasim (2012), *Modern Islamic Thought in a Radical Age*, Cambridge: Cambridge University Press.

Zubaida, Sami (2011), *Beyond Islam: A New Understanding of the Middle East*, London: I. B. Tauris.

CHAPTER 4

Territory at Stake!
In Defence of 'Religion' and 'Islam'

Susanne Olsson and Leif Stenberg

Religion is a multifaceted phenomenon studied from a variety of scholarly perspectives. The Danish historian of religions, Jeppe Sinding Jensen, describes religion as a human social construct, no more mysterious or inaccessible than language, sports or politics. In the preface of his book *What is Religion?* (2014), Sinding Jensen observes that 'religion is not ontologically mysterious nor is it epistemically intractable: religion consists of beliefs and behaviours held and performed by humans. That is all that there is to it.'[1] This portrayal of religion is not unique either. Questions concerning the scholarly conceptualisation of the term 'religion' and the issue of how the study of religions should be conducted as an academic discipline have been present since the birth of the field.[2]

Discussions about how to study religions ranges from the idea of continuing to study texts and practices defined as religious to positions that challenge scholars of religion by questioning the need for a study devoted to religion. For example, religious studies scholar Timothy Fitzgerald rejects the validity of using the category 'religion' at all, including the existence of a specific discipline for the study of religions.[3] Fitzgerald problematised the use of 'religion' as a cross-cultural analytical concept, because of its close connection to 'the secular'. The historian Brent Nongbri similarly stated that 'religion' should not be

---

[1] See Sinding Jensen 2014: ix.
[2] In the nineteenth century, scholars like Max Müller (d. 1900) and William James (d. 1910) presented ideas on the origin of religion and discussed how to study what they perceived as religion and the religious experience; see, for example, their respective Gifford Lectures. For a contemporary example of a discussion of the question 'What is Religion?', see Bergunder 2014.
[3] Fitzgerald 1999.

used cross-culturally.[4] Taking these discussions as a starting point, we examine questions about understanding religion in an academic context. Furthermore, in this chapter we also take a position concerning how scholars researching and teaching in the broader study of religions understand and use categories such as 'religion', 'Islam' and 'Muslim'. In this contribution, the study of religions should be a critical, comparative and non-confessional field. If used carefully, categories such as 'religion' can function as scholarly tools.

In the following, we discuss 'religion', 'Islam', 'Muslim', and problematise their use as academic categories. After arguing that 'religion' ought to be considered a map, not a territory, we elaborate on the categories 'Islam' and 'Muslim'. Our aim is to stress that they necessarily must be critical categories in order to avoid confessional or apologetic stances, while also acknowledging the heterogeneous character of all categories. As the heading of this article indicates, territory is at stake. Consequently, the aim of our article is to defend the territory, that is, the study of religions. The purpose is to maintain it as a critical discipline, in which analytical categories are our main tools to perform our critical task as scholars in the study of religions. Hence, in the conclusion, we emphasise the importance of a critical academic study of religions.

On 'Religion'

Scholars usually agree with historian of religion Jonathan Z. Smith (d. 2017) that a map is not a territory (1993).[5] Smith uses this geographical metaphor to argue that representations of religions are not the same thing as 'religion'. Like many other scholars of his time, Smith actively attempted to distance himself from the Romanticism and essentialism represented by historian of religion Mircea Eliade (d. 1986), as do many in the broader field of the study of religions today. One principal way of separating analysis from empirical material involves a careful usage of categories and typologies, and discussions of what we have except for maps.[6]

Cultural anthropologist Talal Asad's discussion on 'religion' as a non-universal category has significantly influenced conceptualisations of the term 'religion'. He has stressed that all definitions are historically situated. For example, the contemporary usage of the category 'religion' is coloured by a Protestant Christian focus on 'religion' as something related to an interior world of humans. An earlier example of a similar approach is Islamicist Wilfred Cantwell Smith's (d. 2000) view, which can be seen, for example, in *The Meaning and End of Religion: A New Approach to the Religious Traditions of Mankind* (1962), in which

---

[4] Nongbri 2013.
[5] An idea presumably inspired by Max Weber's thinking about ideal types.
[6] This question echoes the title of Paul Matthews Wright's article from 2010.

he writes about personal, genuine and religious feelings opposed to an external understanding of religion. In Smith's view, people have always been religious, and 'religion' was defined as a way to systematise religiousness. In his study, he includes behaviours, as well as everyday religion and people who are not religious. Since Smith presented his ideas, these discussions have progressed, and the definition of the category 'religion' affects the comprehensiveness of the empirical material and the scholarly questions that can be asked:

> Anyone familiar with what is called the sociology of religion will know of the difficulties involved in producing a conception of religion that is adequate for cross-cultural purposes. This is an important point because one's conception of religion determines the kinds of questions one thinks are askable and worth asking.[7]

Today many scholars of religion have acknowledged and accepted Asad's approach to the study of religions. Scholars usually avoid definitions of 'religion' that are narrowed down to what is usually called faith or interior moods, experiences, and the like. However, aside from the difficulty of using 'religion' across cultures, scholars studying, for example, Islam, Hinduism or Shinto, still tend to go ahead and use the word religion as a wide empirical and theoretical category anyway.

In recent years, a question has arisen concerning whether a cross-cultural use of the term 'religion' is valid. Brent Nongbri is critical of the cross-cultural use of 'religion' since not all languages and cultures have an equivalent term. He argues that applying contemporary terminology to historical material may not be a fruitful way forward. As Nongbri states, 'What is modern about the ideas of "religions" and "being religious" is the isolation and naming of some things as "religious" and others as not "religious"'.[8] Nongbri criticises how conceptualisations of the term 'religion' and related terms have been used. Many, like Nongbri, ask whether we should use the concept of 'religion' for premodern phenomena, and whether we can translate concepts from premodern sources as 'religion'. Nongbri holds that this would be an anachronistic application of the category 'religion', one used for explanatory purposes, and that, therefore, the product of such an approach will result in a form of descriptive account of a premodern 'religion'; this stated since 'religion' as a word was not used or carried

---

[7] Asad 2009: 16.

[8] Nongbri 2013: 4. Scholars in other disciplines have not focused on 'religion', but more on the 'modern'. Eickelman and Piscatori state that the contemporary times involve intellectual challenges and questions about Islam. The answers to these questions have produced a view on religion as an abstract and self-contained system that can be compared and distinguished from other belief systems. The construction of the self-contained system emanates from a supposedly authentic version of the 'religion'. They described this as an objectification of Islam; see Eickelman and Piscatori 1996: 38ff.

the same meaning in the sources available to historians. Nongbri's criticism concerns the concept of 'religion' being associated with so many contemporary features, in particular the idea of secularisation.[9] Therefore, using this charged category may lead us to misinterpret the sources and ascribe things to them that are not there.[10]

In his work *The Ideology of Religious Studies* (1999), Timothy Fitzgerald states: 'Though all categories may to some extent be culturally and ideologically charged, some are more useful than others. There are other less ideologically loaded categories that can be used instead.'[11] Therefore, he suggests that the study of 'religions' should not have its own departments, but rather be part of cultural studies or anthropology. Nonetheless, it is not at all apparent that 'culture' would serve as a less loaded term or category. This broader reflection on the category 'religion' was reflected in the call for the initial workshop leading to this publication that asked, 'What do we gain by describing a phenomenon as religious? (when a more precise term might be found)'. Hence, we should ask whether we can find more accurate terms. It is difficult to find a universal conceptualisation of the term 'religion'. In our view, substituting 'religion' with 'culture' is not the way forward, especially if we understand religions as humanly constructed expressions and parts of cultures. In current discussions about identity politics, it is also difficult to support the idea that the use of the term 'culture' is less ideological than the term 'religion'.[12] Another possible way to make categories more precise is to use confessionally grounded terminology. For example, we could use the term *dīn* when related to Muslims. Yet, abandoning categories such as 'religion' or 'Islam', or replacing them with others, does not address the question of whether 'religion' as a scholarly category has a universal value or how the word can be operationalised in a scholarly way to study the past and the present. Instead, it replaces one set of problems with another.[13]

Anthropologist Benson Saler states: 'The testimony of various ethnographies affirms that people do not need a category or term for religion to "have" a religion or to be religious in ways that accord with notions of religiosity entertained by anthropologists.'[14] Nongbri holds that 'this is a very tricky statement'.[15] He claims that Saler uses the term 'religion' redescriptively[16] and clarifies his usage

---

[9] For a discussion on the terms 'secular' and 'secularisation', see Hadi Enayat's contribution in this volume.
[10] See also Broucek 2015.
[11] Fitzgerald 1999: 4.
[12] For a discussion on contemporary identity politics, see Fukuyama 2018.
[13] Saler 1999: 403.
[14] Saler 1993: 70.
[15] Nongbri 2013: 22.
[16] Nongbri 2013: 22.

and the meaning of the word redescriptively: 'religion is "notions of religiosity entertained *by anthropologists*"' and people '"have" religion only insofar as anthropologists are free to impose their own framework for the purpose of study'.[17] Nongbri states that *redescriptive* accounts 'freely employ classification systems foreign to those of the people being observed'.[18] In a critical review of Nongbri's book *Before Religion*, James Broucek, a scholar in the study of religions, discusses the role of scholars in the following way:

> Our responsibility as scholars, as I see it, is to endeavor to use words in ways that help us solve pressing problems of research. We need not worry about defending their traditional meanings, unless we take these meanings as important for our purposes of inquiry.[19]

The quotation from Broucek parallels the idea that a map is not a territory, a point that is also apparent in other academic disciplines, such as, for example, translation studies: 'Translating takes up someone else's thinking and effects a revival (*Wiederholung*) of it, although it does not produce a replica of it.'[20] It is worth noting that mapping is a scholarly project and ideally should not support or oppose a particular religion or religious idea. The religious studies scholar Russell T. McCutcheon, whom Nongbri referred to, also discussed scholarly depictions of things 'religious': 'All scholarship, whether it is simply a well-intentioned and even sympathetic descriptive restatement or a rigorous, explanatory analysis of indigenous systems of classification and collective representations, is by definition a reduction or a translation.'[21] McCutcheon's statement underlines that it is not possible to translate something, or describe a phenomenon, and create a replica. An act of translation or description involves an act of interpretation.

In scholarly terminology in the study of religions, the terms 'insider' and 'outsider' have become a prevalent method to distinguish between confessional and non-confessional approaches. They mirror the usage of two other terms, 'emic' and 'etic'. It is common to use the terms 'emic' and 'etic' to distinguish between levels of understanding and terminology, and to differentiate between various accounts and viewpoints. 'Etic' refers to an outsider's perspective, while 'emic' is an insider's perspective. The use of emic terms and accounts to explain a particular culture or phenomenon is problematic because an emic account analysis is conducted from outside the etic position, and as such, it includes an act of

---

[17] Nongbri 2013: 22.
[18] Nongbri 2013: 21.
[19] Broucek 2015: 107.
[20] Groth 2017: 140.
[21] McCutcheon 2001: 11.

interpretation. If one were to use the Arabic word *dīn* instead of 'religion' when referring to Islam or Muslims, it would not solve the problems outlined above. *Dīn* is part of an Islamic terminology that has been conceptualised and understood in a wide variety of ways throughout history and is burdened by changing ideological presuppositions. Different intellectuals use the Islamic terminology in different ways to pursue their own agendas. It is not a stable or universal terminology, even if it is often claimed to contain an Islamic authenticity.[22]

Whether or not 'religion' is an emic (insider) term is not the critical issue here. In scholarly examinations, clarity concerning the perspective of the researcher is important to distinguish between an etic approach, founded on a language linked to a methodology and theory in an academic discipline, and an emic approach embedded in the religious tradition under study. Ideally, the etic approach enables a scholar to evaluate empirical material critically, and clearly define the analytical terminology applied. To use Nongbri's wording again, scholars make *redescriptive* accounts in which they freely employ classification systems grounded in a language separated from the empirical material. In this way, we support and develop our academic territory and strive to uphold a critical and analytical perspective. In such a perspective the term 'religion' becomes part of the analytical language. Jonathan Z. Smith supported the use of 'religion' as a scholarly and critical term:

> 'Religion' is not a native term; it is a term created by scholars for their intellectual purposes and therefore is theirs to define. It is a second-order, generic concept that plays the same role in establishing a disciplinary horizon that a concept such as 'language' plays in linguistics or 'culture' plays in anthropology. There can be no disciplined study of religion without such a horizon.[23]

The function of 'religion' as such a second-order category is heuristic and necessary in making limitations concerning the empirical material. It is also important to maintain a polythetic and inclusive definition of the category. As social and cognitive scientist Dan Sperber expresses it:

> I don't see religion as a unitary phenomenon. I don't believe that all or even most human societies have had a religion in any useful sense of the term. What we find rather across societies is a variety of ideas, practices, and institutions that can be said to have 'religious' features in some vague sense of this polythetic term. Wittgenstein could well have used 'religion' instead

---

[22] See, for example, Gardet 2012.
[23] Smith 1998: 269.

of 'game' (another apparent cultural universal) to illustrate his idea of mere family resemblance.[24]

The notion of family resemblance emphasises the ambiguity of categories that are usually broad and general in meaning. Family resemblance can be defined as follows:

> Family resemblance categories are fuzzy categories where the members are generally similar to each other, but where there is no set of defining properties that any and all examples have. Family resemblance traditionally has been defined in terms of matching and mismatching properties or attributes, where the individual properties are treated as independent of and unrelated to each other.[25]

Note that in the above quotation from the scholars of psychology Medin, Wattenmaker and Hampson, family resemblance shows similarities in shape, language, beliefs, morality, and stories of how the world and humans originated, but it does not necessarily speak about contextual interpretations and the creation of meaning. For example, descriptions of football are often interchangeable with those used in the domain of 'religion': faith, devotion, worship, ritual, dedication, sacrifice, commitment, spirit, prayer, suffering, festival, and celebration. While it is obvious that football and religion share a number of common features, such features tend to be reduced to just one of these or bypassed altogether. Jeppe Sinding Jensen suggests that one definition of 'religion' bears in mind the idea of family resemblance:

> Typically religions include such elements or components as: explanations of the origin (cosmogony) and classifications of what makes up the world (cosmology); ideas about matters, objects and agents that are sacred, ultimate and inviolable; beliefs in spiritual beings such as superhuman agents; special powers and knowledge that such beings and agents have and which humans may gain access to; beliefs concerning human fate and life after death; ritual actions of various kinds (from silent prayer to bloody sacrifice) that ensure the communication with the sacred or 'other world'; institutions setting the limits and conditions for such communication and containing rules for human conduct in systems of purity, hierarchy and group relations; ethics and morality.[26]

---

[24] Sperber 2018: 447.
[25] Medin et al. 1987: 243.
[26] Sinding Jensen 2014.

Sinding Jensen's definition does not evaluate or justify what is 'real', 'true' or 'imagined' religion. It does not matter if people actually believe or practice in accordance with religious traditions or if rituals are invented, and if practices share some 'religion-like' traits. With the help of definitions like the one above, scholars can explore correlations and differences between football fans and religious belonging.[27] In line with the notion of family resemblance and emphasising the need for historical contextualisation, Sinding Jensen's category of religion includes explanations of the stereotypical and outdated image of religion presented in the universe of the TV series *Star Trek*.[28]

From a position like the one outlined above, the consideration of normative questions about what Islam *is*, or the identification of the most authentic and genuine form of Islam is irrelevant. Answering questions about the 'true practice of Islam' requires a bounded category of 'religion'. From the perspective of the study of religions, we can note that a majority of those calling themselves Muslims believe that Muhammad is the last prophet, but that some who call themselves Muslims believe prophecy has continued; for example, this is the official theology of Ahmadiyya.[29] The majority of those calling themselves Muslims do not think that humans can be divine. However, if we consider the theology of the Nation of Islam, devotions of Sufi saints, and the role of imams for the Shia, we can see that some do believe humans can have characteristics of divinity.[30] Scholars in religious studies may also categorise the Nation of Islam as a new religious movement, or even a UFO religion.[31] These are samples of an unbounded and borderless category called 'religion' and 'Islam' as a set of discursive traditions. Talal Asad states:

> A tradition consists essentially of discourses that seek to instruct practitioners regarding the correct form and purpose of a given practice that, precisely because it is established, has a history. These discourses relate conceptually to a *past* . . . and a *future* . . ., through a *present* . . . An Islamic discursive tradition is simply a tradition of Muslim discourse that addresses itself to the conception of the Islamic past and future, with reference to a particular Islamic practice in the present.[32]

---

[27] Ludwig 2015.

[28] Porter and McLaren 1999: 1–3.

[29] For an introduction to the Ahmadiyya, see Valentine 2014.

[30] On the Nation of Islam, see Fishman and Soage 2013.

[31] Urban 2015; Finley 2012. 'UFO religion' is an umbrella term conceptualising ideas among individuals and groups who believe in extra-terrestrial life. Contact with aliens is often framed in eschatological and soteriological ideas about salvation or the improvement of humanity (see Östling 2016).

[32] Asad 2009: 20. For an example of how this type of thinking can materialise in a study of a discourse on the relationship between Islam and modern science, see Stenberg 1996.

The thinking about Islam as a discursive tradition is reminiscent of the detached approach to 'religion' that is often expressed in the discipline of sociology of religion. One example is a Durkhemian focus on 'religion', which maintains that its social functions, beliefs and practices bind people together to dominate and strengthen social organisation. Another example is the Weberian view that 'religion' aims to answer existential questions and dilemmas, and makes the world meaningful. Sociologist of religion Bryan S. Turner has pointed out several problems with the definitions of religion founded on Durkheim and Weber. For example, presuming a social uniformity and shared culture in societies, without taking pluralism or the more mundane needs of people into consideration, risks definitions that end in cognitive reductionism.[33] However, in this context, it is sufficient to note that this form of definition is separate from the empirical material. The definition is crafted in a scholarly domain and is applicable to a variety of examples of 'religion'. In addition, definitions may not be bound in time since they are concerned with terms like 'meaning', 'control' and 'organisation'. Below we return to the issue of discursive traditions, family resemblance and definitions, but now we turn to discuss the category of 'Islam' in more depth.

ON 'ISLAM'

Historian Andrew Rippin, the editor of *Defining Islam: A Reader*, comments on the definition of 'Islam' in the book's introduction:

> The issue that lingers, of course, and that cries out for definition, is what do we mean by 'Islam'? The goal of this book [*Defining Islam: A Reader*] is, after all is said and done, to bring into focus the nature of the 'critical category' – in this case, 'Islam' – that functions as a definition of the entire discipline of Islamic studies.[34]

Based on this goal, in *Defining Islam: A Reader*, the chapters are divided thematically into theology, the social sciences, religion, civilisation, and the media, in order to illustrate a wide range of themes and perspectives that have developed in Islamic studies over time. To speak not only about Islam, the reader also contains texts from the past and present that represent various positions on Islam written by Muslim authors from Abū Ḥanifa (d. 767) to Islamicist Mohammed Arkoun (d. 2010) and historian of religion Abdelkader I. Tayob. He concludes the introduction by stating:

---

[33] Turner 1991, 2013.
[34] Rippin 2007: 1.

For academics, the study of Islam is a microcosm of the discussions that are protracted within the disciplines that make up religious studies. Just what is it we are studying? What assumed categories of thought are being used to approach the topic? How do we reconcile what we are told about the religion by insiders with what we might observe as historians or sociologists?[35]

Thus, *Defining Islam: A Reader* does not present us with a single definition of 'Islam', but rather stresses that 'Islam' is a critical category, with a wide range of meanings for people who express ideas about Islam (independent of whether they are Muslims or not), while connoting a wide range of empirical diversity throughout history. Understanding Islam as being in a state of ongoing fluid development is a statement that can also be applied to analyse the academic discussion about Islamic studies and to public debates about Islam and its meanings. Academics, local imams, politicians and opinion makers (both Muslim and non-Muslim) are all examples of personal or impersonal stakeholders who influence how Islam is understood in academia and in public spaces.[36]

Although as academics we acknowledge the empirical diversity of Islam, we still use expressions such as 'classical Islam' and problematise the statement by saying that it comes close to resurrecting 'orthodoxy' as an etic analytical term.[37] Perhaps this is the case, and is a result of taking a position related to, or against, orientalism, and out of concern about possible accusations of essentialising or forming stereotypes of Islam. A related concern is the way scholars make vague, uncritical and apologetic comments on 'Islam' and 'Muslims'. The risk is that scholars, voluntarily or involuntarily, may participate in a constructive theological debate about what 'Islam' is (or should be), or what is good 'Islam' or a good 'Muslim'. We argue that this is only a risk if we do not carefully consider how we use categories such as 'religion', 'Islam' and 'orthodoxy'. To avoid this peril, we are obliged to apply a meticulous use of categories and their definitions.

One example that may illustrate apologetic tendencies is the following citation from Omid Safi, professor of Asian and Middle Eastern Studies at Duke University and the director of the Islamic Studies Center. In his edited book, *Progressive Muslims*, he holds that:

> this book represents the collective aspirations of a group of Muslim thinkers and activists . . . and [we] seek to implement the Divine injunction to enact the justice (*'adl*) and goodness-and-beauty (*ihsān*) that lie at the heart of the Islamic tradition . . . It may not be an exaggeration to state that unless

---

[35] Rippin 2007: 13.
[36] Olsson and Stenberg 2015: 207 n.5.
[37] Social anthropologist Samuli Schielke also noted this risk in his discussion on 'Islam' (Schielke 2010: 1ff.).

we succeed in doing so, the humanity of Muslims will be fully reduced to correspond to the caricature of violent zealots painted by fanatics from both inside and outside the Muslim community.[38]

Comprehending the quotation as an expression of Islamic hermeneutics we can recognise Safi's definition of Islam as normative and prescriptive. His call to justice and goodness-and-beauty as the heart of *the* Islamic tradition enables him, and those who share his position, to interpret and evaluate Islam according to these overarching values, and to judge the opinions and behaviours of others.[39]

To return to the term 'Islam', social anthropologist Samuli Schielke seems to say that those who stress seeing Islam as a set of discursive traditions are comparable to those who hold an essentialist position.[40] We would propose the contrary, namely, that recognising something as a discursive tradition opens up a critical and analytical approach and the study of the umbrella term 'Islam', without requiring that we discuss in a normative manner what 'Islam' is. From our perspective, making general and universal claims about authentic Islamic practice is not a question for scholars in Islamic studies. Among those calling themselves Muslims, and those who do not, 'Islam' has many different histories, interpretations, notions, practices and truth claims. At the same time, 'Islam', as 'religion', is part of our academic classification system. The key question is not what 'Islam' is. That kind of question is not necessarily part of an academic repertoire of questions, in our view. We utilise Brent Nongbri to illustrate this point: 'We would no longer ask the question "Is phenomenon X a religion?" Rather, we would ask something like "Can we see anything new and interesting about phenomenon X by considering it, for the purpose of study, as a religion?"'[41]

Nongbri also stresses the importance of keeping a watching eye on definitions of 'religion' – and suggests that we could exchange 'religion' with 'Islam' here:

What sorts of interests are involved in such decisions of defining religion? *Who* is doing the defining and *why*? In other words, a good focus for those who would study 'religion' in the modern day is keeping a close eye on the *activity* of defining religion and the *act* of saying that some things are 'religious' and others are not.[42]

---

[38] Safi 2003: 1f.
[39] Our discussion on Safi's position reflects the debate on Islamic studies primarily between Omid Safi and Aaron Hughes. For one account of their debate, see Sheedy (ed.) 2018.
[40] For Shielke's justification for the statement, see Shielke 2010.
[41] Nongbri 2013: 155.
[42] Nongbri 2013: 155.

It is significant that we approach 'Islam' as a set of discourses that are con-stantly being reproduced in each generation and context according to a chang-ing paradigm. It is our impression that most academics already share such an approach, and assert that the idea of a continuity of Islam or Muslim identity across time and space is a confessional and ideological position. The discursive-ness of 'Islam' is a historical and empirical reality. In line with the view of 'Islam' as a set of regulated and evolving traditions, 'Islam' has a history. Throughout history 'Islam' has been situated and referenced by many people, Muslims and non-Muslims, and has been given a wide variety of meanings. A confessional approach that advocates 'true' Islam as a constant is one thing, but the multi-tude of interpretations, practices and ideas have their empirical presence in any given study and cannot be ignored. The many meanings of 'Islam' need to be dealt with also by confessional Muslims, and of course they have been.

The book by the late Harvard Islamic studies scholar Shahab Ahmed enti-tled *What is Islam? The Importance of Being Islamic* (2016) asks how we con-ceptualise the term 'Islam' as a historical and human phenomenon. To answer his question Ahmed suggests an understanding of Islam as a hermeneutical engagement with revelation. Ahmed explained revelation as the premises for the revelation, the history, the texts, and the contexts – all these are parts of a process of making meaning of Islam itself. 'Islam' becomes a creation of meaning in theology and everyday life produced by Muslims. In his view the process of Islam-making is key because, in such a process, what are identified as similarities in the past and present are what constitutes Islam. Also, to make something Islamic, Muslims speak and act in their capacity as Muslims and share a notion of Islam. As stated in reviews, Ahmed does not clearly outline when something is Islamic or not.[43] Therefore, the definition of Islam is ambiguous, although Ahmed gives Islam a certain agency. In many ways, this is an interesting and challenging book in which he discusses a sizable body of scholarship on Islam; however, the majority of what he reviews is North American. Beyond the Quran, the empirical examples he cites to illustrate many points are primarily from pre-nineteenth-century texts. Consequently, this ambitious book that aims to tell readers what Islam is, and that gives 'Islam' agency, almost entirely ignores gender, female Muslim authors, questions of power, Muslims as communities in Europe and North America, popular culture in its many forms, issues of literacy and non-literacy, state formation, and many other questions that have formed the general notion of 'Islam', crafted by Muslims and non-Muslims, over the last century. Perhaps Ahmed's circum-vention of all these questions, and his focus on a select number of scholars in order to establish his image of the study of Islam, was a way to sidestep research

---

[43] Doostdar 2017.

and researchers in sociology, anthropology, religious studies, Islamic studies, ethnology, literature, philosophy, history, and other disciplines for whom his ideas are neither novel nor compelling. Or, by avoiding certain questions the work carries an apologetic element that renders it difficult for Ahmed to make his claim that Muslims share a 'massive *notion* called "Islam"'.[44]

The Moroccan Muslim 'feminist' Fatima Mernissi (d. 2015) represents a concrete example of a confessional response to change in history. Note that Shahab Ahmed's book does not cite Mernissi, who differentiated between 'islam' and *islam risāla*, that is, she delineated between Islam as practised by Muslims, and what she defined as the true message of Islam.[45] Other examples of a similar kind are the contemporary Muslim orientations that are sometimes labelled 'Salafi Islam'. Salafis desire to live in accordance with the examples of the first generations of Muslims. They acknowledge that Muslims have practised Islam very differently throughout history, but that the Islam practised by the first generations of Muslims is the ideal to be emulated. Muslim interpretations and practices that emphasise a return to an idealised past, like the more pragmatic forms of European Muslims, and modelling a Muslim individual life according to an understanding of how the Prophet Muhammad lived his life, are examples of contemporary interpretations and practices that strive to reject what they regard to be cultural practices they see as innovations, *bid 'a*. In all cases the aim is to establish what they consider to be true Islamic interpretation and practice. Thus, it is commonplace to differentiate between individual and collective Muslim understandings of 'Islam', that is, between authentic *religious* practices and *cultural* practices.[46]

Ultimately, from a scholarly point of view there is no reason to create a universal definition of Islam. The attempts to construct a universal definition founded on texts such as the Quran and the hadith, literary and interpretative traditions, ideas about absolute monotheism, and ideas about specific rituals becomes an elitist and narrow definition of 'religion'. Shaping such a definition usually leaves more questions asked than answered. The Islam that is produced by Muslims and non-Muslims in the past and present overlaps with regard to theology, perceptions, practice and terminology. The process of producing a definition necessarily relates to local and transnational circumstances to such an extent that the process of creating an 'Islam' becomes more interesting than the product itself.

---

[44] Ahmed 2016: 259.
[45] Mernissi 1993: 5, 1991: 65. For a scholarly discussion on Mernissi's perspective, see Varisco 2005: 92ff.
[46] For more examples, see Olsson 2009.

ON 'MUSLIM'

When the category 'Muslim(s)' is used it is not always evident what, or whom, the term refers to. It is used as both an emic and etic category. It is

> both a category of analysis and a category of social, political and religious practice; and the heavy traffic between the two, in both directions, means that we risk using pre-constructed categories of journalistic, political, or religious common sense as our categories of analysis.[47]

The sociologist Rogers Brubaker analyses a set of articles dealing with Muslims in European countries, and focuses on etic categories of analysis and emic categories of practice. Brubaker notes that:

> As a category of practice, 'Muslim' is used to identify oneself and to identify others. (In the important case of collective self-identifications, it is used to identify oneself and others at the same time: to speak not just of but for others, to subsume others, along with oneself, into a collective 'we').[48]

The idea of identifying and labelling oneself in a certain manner, and including others to establish a collective is a process that involves an exercise of power. The process also intentionally or unintentionally generates notions about that collective – in this case 'Muslims'. Brubaker holds that all identity categories (self- and other-identifications) are interdependent. He states:

> self-identifications and other-identifications are interdependent: self-identifications are profoundly shaped by the prevailing ways in which people are identified by others; and other-identifications may be shaped – though usually less profoundly, especially where major asymmetries of power are involved – by prevailing idioms of self-identification, especially by publicly proclaimed collective self-identifications.[49]

In Europe, the sense of what constructs the other and how others are defined has changed in recent decades following developments related to migration in most western European countries. A variety of interests are involved in the interdependency that shapes the 'Muslim' identity and one should not underestimate the extent to which non-Muslim agency plays a role in forming general

---

[47] Brubaker 2013: 2.
[48] Brubaker 2013: 2.
[49] Brubaker 2013: 2.

and public ideas about the category 'Muslim'. For Brubaker, the overarching category 'Muslim' has become a common categorisation of othering: 'Other-identifications of immigrants have shifted in Europe. Previously, identification followed lines of national/regional origin, socio-economic, demographic, legal or racial categories. For example, Algerians, immigrants, blacks. Such terms have also been connected to religion, notably "Muslim" . . .'[50]

Brubaker also stresses that there has been a shift in public representations that has altered the scene in Europe and that people self-identify as Muslims. He holds that such self-identification is often a reaction to hegemonic other-identifications, especially when these are perceived as stigmatising. In a sense, this is a strategy of 'reclaiming' the category 'Muslim' and conceptualising the term differently. Such self-identification may also be intensified in situations when Muslims, seen as a single collective, are expected to account for what other Muslims say or do. Brubaker continues: 'This experience has led some who are not themselves religiously observant to identify – or to identify more strongly – as Muslims, sometimes specifically as "secular" or "cultural" Muslims . . .'[51] Hence, discussions that take place from the level of the individual to the level of national and international politics may increase the stereotypical questions asked about 'Muslims', questions that assume Muslims constitute a universal and like-minded community.

However, public discussions about the term 'Muslim' should not cause us to refrain from using the category 'Muslim(s)'. We cannot avoid using terms like 'Islam' and 'Muslims' in scholarly studies. However, we need to be on the alert to avoid misrepresentations and unwarranted generalisations concerning the terms 'Islam' and 'Muslims'. This too has been noted by Brubaker who stresses that when we define someone as Muslim, we create a distance. He says: 'Identifying one's object of analysis as "Muslims", for example, highlights religious affiliation and, at least implicitly, religiosity; it also marks the population of interest as different from the surrounding population in both religion and religiosity.'[52] Moreover, like Schielke's claim that 'there is too much Islam in the anthropology of Islam',[53] Brubaker notes that an academic focus on radical Islamists may bring about a misrepresentative image, given the intense focus on their identity as Muslims. He labels this focus a 'methodological Islamism'. He argues that scholars focus on 'conspicuously visible, vocal and devout practitioners'. Likewise, Garbi Schmidt argues that this risks reinforcing 'public understandings

---

[50] Brubaker 2013: 2.
[51] Brubaker 2013: 3.
[52] Brubaker 2013: 5.
[53] Schielke's statement is perhaps not primarily directed toward the study of religions, but to anthropology as an academic discipline (Schielke 2010: 1).

of Muslims as particularly (and dangerously) religious'[54] as well as reproducing ideological ambitions among Islamic movements, with their 'privileging of Islam as the supreme guideline of all fields of life'.[55] According to Brubaker, the focus on radical Islamists may lead to a 'methodological Islamism', due to the exclusive focus on 'Muslimness' and treating 'Muslim' as a master status and a continuously salient self-identification.[56]

We can probably assume that most scholars in the broad field of religious studies, the history of religions, and Islamic studies are aware of the risk of 'methodological Islamism' and reflect this in their studies. We can also postulate that scholars in the broad field of religious studies are interested in activists, even though there is an increasing interest in unorganised 'Muslims', popular culture, and everyday 'Islam'. The interest in phenomena, such as activists or extremists at the margins of a society, is also visible in other fields of study, for example, in the disciplines of sociology, anthropology, and political science. On the usage of analytical categories, Brubaker states:

My argument is not about what categories we should use; it is about how we should use them. We may have no good alternative to using analytical categories that are heavily loaded and deeply contested categories of practice; but as scholars we can and should adopt a critical and self-reflexive stance towards our categories. This means, most obviously, emphasizing that 'Muslims' designates not a homogeneous and solidary group but a heterogeneous category.[57]

Brubaker and other researchers referenced in this article stress the need for critical awareness and the use of categories. In addition to the statement quoted above, that the key is how we use categories rather than which category we use, Brubaker also notes that we must focus on

the changing ways in which the category 'Muslim' works, both as a category of analysis and as a category of self- and other-identification in practice. In this way we can make the category 'Muslim' the object of analysis, rather than simply using it as a tool of analysis.[58]

Consequently, this implies that how the term 'Muslim' is conceptualised in societies is one aim of scholarly studies. The process of conceptualisation becomes part of the empirical material from a scholarly and etic point of view. In

---

[54] Schmidt 2011: 1217.
[55] Schielke 2010: 2.
[56] Brubaker 2013: 6; see also Meer and Modood 2013.
[57] Brubaker 2013: 5.
[58] Brubaker 2013: 5f.

Brubaker's words, the term 'Muslim' is also an emic category of self-identification that scholars can analyse to understand self-designations and strategies of othering. This implies that the language of scholarly analysis is separated from the language of empirical material, and if 'Muslims' functions as a critical and analytical concept, it must be utilised carefully so that the reader is kept aware of the concept's internal heterogeneity.

In sum, in order to apply the term 'Muslim(s)' and avoid ambiguity, scholars must carefully distinguish between analytical language and the way the term is utilised in specific empirical material. It is also necessary to recognise the heterogenous character of the category in scholarly work.

ON TERRITORIAL DEFENCE

From the discussion on 'religion', 'Islam' and 'Muslims' above, we can conclude that a map is not a territory. This statement is founded on several theoretical and methodological concerns discussed in the text. Reverting to the introductory discussion of Jonathan Z. Smith, we can also conclude that maps are all we have from a scholarly perspective. Simultaneously, the discussion above shows that territory is at stake. The territory we want to support is the study of religions, as a non-confessional discipline, founded on critical, reasonably and cautiously defined categories. To do this, as a prerequisite, we must acknowledge that all categories and theories we use are maps, or models. Based on these, scholars approach history and the present. This certainly does not imply that a term like 'religion' can easily be conceptualised (synchronically or diachronically) in a universal category. Rather, the recognition of categories and theories as maps signifies that we need to approach the world we study from scholarly and conceptual frames that have been consciously discursively constructed. Being constantly aware of these unavoidable limitations brings a critical edge to the study of religions. Mark C. Taylor, a scholar of religions, expressed this in the following way:

> If terms are to be useful for the contemporary study of religion, they must not only be strategically selected but must also be critically assessed. 'Critical' means, *inter alia*, crucial, decisive, important, momentous, pivotal. . . . the notion of criticism has been inseparable from the self-reflexivity of self-consciousness.[59]

Critical terms, according to Taylor, are also the foundation for comparisons. Here comparison should not be confused with phenomenology in its philosoph-

---

[59] Taylor 1998: 16.

ical or essentialist mode. Discussing the role of comparisons, Michael Stausberg, historian of religions, states: 'Comparing is a common sense routine cognitive activity; there is no way of getting around comparison.'[60] In his view, comparing others to ourselves, searching for similarities and differences, is a common human practice. Stausberg also stresses the importance and role of categories in comparisons:

> Even if one sometimes cannot help finding some phenomena to be strikingly similar, academic comparisons are not discoveries of relations given by nature; they are the products of academic work, starting with the scholarly categories that serve as their points of departure.[61]

In Stausberg's view this process is not *a* method of comparison but rather *comparative research designs*. He continues, 'Far beyond being a distinct method among others, comparison is an often unacknowledged yet undeniable part of the scholarly project of the study of religion/s in each of its various approaches.'[62] He underlines the importance of comparison when we form scholarly categories, and, as the citation above indicates, comparisons are part of most kinds of research. Categories are used to describe and analyse our material, and function as platforms for cross-cultural and systematic studies. Moreover, typologies and classifications are, according to Stausberg, constructed using comparisons.[63]

Following the view of 'Islam' as a set of diverse, evolving, and socially embedded discursive traditions opens the category to a wide empirical field, including the study of conceptualisations of the terms 'religion' and 'Muslim'.[64] Moreover, if scholars are careful and aware of the various theoretical and methodological problems involved, we may still critically use categories such as 'religion', 'Islam' and 'Muslim'. In such a way scholars refrain from painting stereotypical or essentialist images of territory. In our opinion most scholars of 'religion' already do this and take for granted that 'Islam' is not a heterogeneous phenomenon and cannot be given agency, and that 'Muslims' do not act and think alike in accordance with one singular and normative version of 'Islam'.

One may acknowledge that all categories are critically and comparatively founded and are historically situated. Among academics there is a criticism of using such categories because of their origin in a European and North American cultural and academic context. According to this criticism these categories may

---

[60] Stausberg 2011: 21.
[61] Stausberg 2011: 33.
[62] Stausberg 2011: 21.
[63] Stausberg 2011: 33f.
[64] This statement also reveals how the broad field of religious studies has been influenced by discussions on theory and method in the humanities and social sciences.

carry ideological assumptions. It would appear that this form of criticism does not take into consideration the effects of globalisation in academia or the problems inherent in categorising something as 'the West'. This type of thinking usually has a political edge and is part of an identity politics that divides the world into stereotypes such as 'Islam' and 'the West'. In our opinion it is important to use analytical categories to sustain and encourage a critical perspective and language use. In this way scholars studying 'religion' can produce research results that are falsifiable. Constructing categories based on family resemblance acknowledges such a comparative aspect of definitions and boundary construction, and it stresses polythetic and unbounded boundaries of a category such as 'religion'. In the words of Saler:

> Terms such as 'religion', 'sacrifice', 'value' and so forth are conveniences. They allow us to talk about things that interest us in more or less intelligible fashion. And we can do so even though the terms themselves are polysemous and the categories to which they pertain are organized by family resemblances. We need to be cognizant of their complexities and subtleties, however, if we are to avoid using them in rigid and otherwise nonproductive ways. And we need also to have some sense of their connotations.[65]

Even if the idea of family resemblances is a tempting tool in research it is also criticised. Fitzgerald assesses family resemblance-based theories of 'religion', stating that it is an 'overextended family usage, where religion is used in a haphazard way to include just about everything'.[66] He holds that the 'all-inclusive usage renders religion meaningless as an analytical concept. It picks out nothing distinctive – Christmas cakes, nature, the value of hierarchy, vegetarianism, witchcraft ... There is not much within culture that cannot be included as "religion".'[67] We agree with his opinion in this matter, but rather consider it a positive consequence that supports a distanced non-normative, etic, outsider and academic approach to the study of 'religions'. With an unbounded and borderless approach to 'religion', we can include both 'Islam' and 'Pastafarianism' as empirical data in which it is possible to encompass both the flying spaghetti monster and Allah in a constructed category like 'supernatural beings'. From a scholarly perspective, we do not have to define Star Trek fans as a 'quasi-religion', or as a 'religious-type movement', as a part of our comparative approach, or to state that 'Star Trek (ST) fandom is a phenomenon unlike any other.'[68] Why should we (re)describe ST fans as a quasi-religion or something extraordinary?

---

[65] Saler 1999: 403.
[66] Fitzgerald 1999: 25.
[67] Fitzgerald 1999: 26.
[68] Jindra 1994: 27.

If scholars do, they are supporting the view that there *are* religious phenomena that are not quasi-religion, but representations of a real, authentic and objective religion. In our view, such assertions about phenomena as quasi-religions can easily become normative claims, and not examples of academic accounts of empirical material. In scholarly accounts, we do not have to consider 'religion' to be something extraordinary or even connected to something divine or otherwise supernatural – but we often do this without reflecting on it.

In our capacity as scholars, some phenomena appear or are evaluated as more 'religious' than others. This is stated even if scholars personally do not believe in an ontology of religion. Mentioning Pastafarianism and Star Trek is not intended to mock someone or something. It is to underline a significant aspect of how many view 'religion', even when they are well-read in theories and epistemological issues related to the study of 'religion'. An example is the discussion by Robert H. Sharf, a professor in Buddhist studies, on 'experience' in which he discusses claims of mystical experience and meetings with supernatural beings, and how scholars approach different claims in very different manners. Studies related to mystical religious experiences are often confined to the characteristics of claims and their philosophical implications.[69] In addition, we note a certain respectful approach among academics writing about certain mystical experiences. However, Sharf eloquently shows that the same is not the case when the study concerns an individual who claims to have been abducted by aliens or supernatural beings, whose stories are met with scepticism. Claims of alien abductions are not taken as expressions of true and sincere experiences and reductionist explanations are the rule. Those claiming to have been abducted cannot produce any observable evidence; several of the narratives of abductions have furthermore been processed through hypnosis; and the 'abductees' have been accused of talking nonsense. As cognitive psychologist Susan Clancy notes, dismissing these stories and laughing at them does not help us much.[70] She states that 'Abductees do not believe what they believe because of scientific evidence'.[71] As Sharf puts it: 'The question is unavoidable: Is there any reason to assume that the reports of experiences by mystics, shamans, or meditation masters are any more credible as "phenomenological descriptions" than those of the abductees?'[72] We argue that Sharf's question can be answered in the negative: it is very difficult to evaluate mystical experiences in this manner.

To conclude, above we describe the reasons we need to critically and carefully assess our use of categories, and recognise that they are part of a historically and discursively bound terminology. This assessment should be carried out in the

---

[69] Sharf 1998: 103.
[70] Clancy 2005: 6.
[71] Clancy 2005: 7.
[72] Sharf 1998: 110.

same manner scholars in the study of 'religions' analyse their empirical material. Any analytic category that scholars employ requires a justification in terms of usefulness as a comparative category, and all analytical categories serve redescriptive purposes. All descriptions become mirrors or replicas. They become maps – a reduction of territory. This awareness and reflection, as well as the use of unbounded and borderless categories, contributes to a critical and contextualised study of 'religions', in which 'religion' is considered something quite ordinary, everyday and human. According to this perspective, 'religion' *is* a human phenomenon. Paraphrasing the statement from Schielke about the presence of 'too much Islam in the anthropology of Islam', there is too much theology in the study of religions in general, such that understandings of 'religions' founded on confessional or apologetic perspectives are part of the scholarly analysis.

Ultimately, the only scholarly answer to the initial question of this article, namely what 'religion' *is*, is thinking about 'religions' from an academic perspective as ordinary, human, dynamic, socially embedded, and without any inherent values. However, according to our scholarly perspective, it is also clear that the definition of 'religion' is not the first question we should ask, nor is it a particularly interesting one. As scholars of 'religions', for the answer to most other questions we look to empirical material that should be redescriptive and analytical accounts based on categorisation, classification systems, and a language foreign to the material studied.

Bibliography

Ahmed, Shahab (2016), *What is Islam? The Importance of Being Islamic*, Princeton, NJ: Princeton University Press.

Allievi, Stefano (2005), 'How the Immigrant Has Become Muslim', *Revue Européenne des Migrations Internationales* 21, no. 2: 2–21.

Asad, Talal (2009), 'The Idea of an Anthropology of Islam', *Qui Parle* 17, no. 2: 1–30.

Bergunder, Michael (2014), 'What is Religion? The Unexplained Subject Matter of Religious Studies', *Method and Theory in the Study of Religion* 26: 246–86.

Broucek, James (2015), 'Thinking about Religion before "Religion": A Review of Brent Nongbri's *Before Religion: A History of a Modern Concept (Review)*', *Soundings: an Interdisciplinary Journal* 98, no. 1: 98–125.

Brubaker, Rogers (2013), 'Categories of Analysis and Categories of Practice: A Note on the Study of Muslims in European Countries of Immigration', *Ethnic and Racial Studies* 36, no. 1: 1–8.

Clancy, Susan A. (2005), *Abducted: How People Come to Believe They Were Kidnapped by Aliens*, Cambridge, MA: Harvard University Press.

Doostdar, Alireza (2017), 'Review of Shahab Ahmed, *What is Islam? The Importance of Being Islamic*', *Shi'i Studies Review* 1–2: 277–82.

Eickelman, Dale F., and James Piscatori (1996), *Muslim Politics*, Princeton, NJ: Princeton University Press.

Finley, Stephen C. (2012), 'The Meaning of "Mother" in Louis Farrakhan's "Mother Wheel": Race, Gender, and Sexuality in the Cosmology of the Nation of Islam's UFO', *Journal of the American Academy of Religion* 80, no. 2: 434–46.

Fishman, Jason, and Ana Soage (2013), 'The Nation of Islam and the Muslim World: Theologically Divorces and Politically United', *Religion Compass* 7, no. 2: 59–68.

Fitzgerald, Timothy (1999), *The Ideology of Religious Studies*, Oxford: Oxford University Press.

Fukuyama, Francis (2018), *Identity: Contemporary Identity Politics and the Struggle for Recognition*, London: Profile Books.

Gardet, Louis (2012), 'Dīn', in P. Bearman, T. Bianquis, C. E. Bosworth, E. van Donzel and W. P. Heinrichs (eds), *Encyclopaedia of Islam*, 2nd edn, online, http://dx.doi.org. ezp.sub.su.se/10.1163/1573-3912_islam_COM_0168 (last accessed 6 March 2019).

Groth, Miles (2017), *Translating Heidegger*, Toronto: University of Toronto Press.

Hughes, Aaron (2012), 'The Study of Islam Before and After September 11: A Provocation', *Method and Theory in the Study of Religion* 24, nos. 4–5: 314–36.

Jenkins, Richard (1997), *Rethinking Ethnicity: Arguments and Explorations*, London: Sage.

Jindra, Michael (1994), 'Star Trek Fandom as a Religious Phenomenon', *Sociology of Religion* 55, no. 1: 27–51.

Ludwig, Frieder (2015), 'Football, Culture and Religion: Varieties of Interaction', *Studies in World Christianity* 21, no. 3: 201–22.

McCutcheon, Russell T. (2001), *Critics Not Caretakers: Redescribing the Public Study of Religion*, New York: State University of New York Press.

Medin, Douglas L., William D. Wattenmaker and Sarah E. Hampson (1987), 'Family Resemblance, Conceptual Cohesiveness, and Category Construction', *Cognitive Psychology* 19, no. 2: 242–79, www.doi.org//10.1016/0010-0285(87)90012-0.

Meer, Nasar, and Tariq Modood (2013), 'Beyond "Methodological Islamism"? A Thematic Discussion of Muslim Minorities in Europe', *Advances in Applied Sociology* 3, no. 7: 307–13, www.doi.org//10.4236/aasoci.2013.37039.

Mernissi, Fatima (1991), *The Veil and the Male Elite: a Feminist Interpretation of Women's Rights in Islam*, Reading, MA: Addison-Wesley.

Mernissi, Fatima (1993), *The Forgotten Queens of Islam*, Cambridge: Polity Press.

Nongbri, Brent (2013), *Before Religion: A History of a Modern Concept*, New Haven: Yale University Press.

Olsson, Susanne (2009), 'Religion in Public Space: "Blue-and-Yellow Islam" in Sweden', *Religion, State and Society* 37, no. 3: 277–90.

Olsson, Susanne, and Leif Stenberg (2015), 'Engaging the History of Religions – from an Islamic Studies Perspective', *Temenos* 51, no. 2: 7–23.

Östling, Erik (2016), 'What Does God Need with a Starship? UFOs and Extraterrestrials in the Contemporary Religious Landscape', in James R. Lewis and Inga B. Tollefsen (eds), *The Oxford Handbook of New Religious Movements: Volume II*, New York: Oxford University Press.

Porter, Jennifer E., and Darcee L. McLaren (1999), *Star Trek and Sacred Ground: Explorations of Star Trek, Religion, and American Culture*, Albany: State University of New York Press.

Rippin, Andrew (2007), 'Introduction', in Andrew Rippin (ed.), *Defining Islam: A Reader*, London: Equinox.

Safi, Omid (2003), *Progressive Muslims: On Justice, Gender and Pluralism*, Oxford: Oneworld.

Saler, Benson (1993), *Conceptualizing Religion: Immanent Anthropologists, Transcendent Natives, and Unbounded Categories*, Leiden: Brill.

Saler, Benson (1999), 'Family Resemblance and the Definition of Religion', *Historical Reflections/Réflexions Historiques* 25, no. 3: 391–404.Schielke, Samuli (2010), 'Second Thoughts about the Anthropology of Islam, or How to Make Sense of Grand Schemes in Everyday Life', *Zentrum Moderner Orient Working Papers* 2: 1–16, https://d-nb.info/1019243724/34.

Schmidt, Garbi (2011), 'Understanding and Approaching Muslim Visibilities: Lessons Learned from a Fieldwork-Based Study of Muslims in Copenhagen', *Ethnic and Racial Studies* 34, no. 7: 1216–29.

Sharf, Robert H. (1998), 'Experience', in Charles Taylor (ed.), *Critical Terms for Religious Studies*, Chicago: University of Chicago, pp. 94–116.

Sheedy, Matt (ed.) (2018), *Identity, Politics and the Study of Islam: Current Dilemmas in the Study of Religions*, Sheffield: Equinox Publishing.

Sinding Jensen, Jeppe (2014), *What is Religion?*, Hoboken: Taylor and Francis.

Smith, Jonathan Z. (1993), *Map is Not Territory: Studies in the History of Religions*, Chicago: University of Chicago Press.

Smith, Jonathan Z. (1998), 'Religion, Religions, Religious', in Mark C. Taylor (ed.), *Critical Terms for Religious Studies*, Chicago: University of Chicago Press, pp. 269–84.

Smith, Wilfred Cantwell (1962), *The Meaning and End of Religion: A New Approach to the Religious Traditions of Mankind*, New York: Macmillan.

Sperber, Dan (2018), 'Cutting Culture at the Joints?', *Religion, Brain and Behavior* 8, no. 4: 447–9, doi.org//10.1080/2153599X.2017.1323783.

Spielhaus, Riem (2010), 'Media Making Muslims: The Construction of a Muslim Community in Germany through Media Debate', *Contemporary Islam* 4, no. 1: 11–27.

Stausberg, Michael (2011), 'Comparison', in Michael Stausberg and Steven Engler (eds), *The Routledge Handbook of Research Methods in the Study of Religions*, London: Routledge, pp. 21–39.

Stenberg, Leif (1996), *The Islamization of Science: Four Muslim Positions Developing an Islamic Modernity*, Stockholm: Almqvist and Wiksell International.

Taylor, Mark C. (1998), 'Introduction', in Mark C. Taylor (ed.), *Critical Terms for Religious Studies*, Chicago: University of Chicago Press, pp. 1–20.

Turner, Bryan S. (1991), *Religion and Social Theory*, London: Sage.

Turner, Bryan S. (2013), *The Religious and the Political: A Comparative Sociology of Religion*, Cambridge: Cambridge University Press.

Urban, Hugh B. (2015), *New Age, Neopagan, and New Religious Movements: Alternative Spirituality in Contemporary America*, Oakland: University of California Press.

Valentine, Simon Ross (2014), 'Prophecy after the Prophet, Albeit Lesser Prophets? The Ahmadiyya Jama'at in Pakistan', *Contemporary Islam* 8, no. 2: 99–113.

Varisco, Daniel Martin (2005), *Islam Obscured: The Rhetoric of Anthropological Representation*, London: Palgrave Macmillan.

Wright, Peter Matthews (2010), 'After Smith: Romancing the Text when "Maps Are All We Possess"', *Religion and Literature* 42, no. 3: 93–122.

Yildiz, Yasemin (2009), 'Turkish Girls, Allah's Daughters, and the Contemporary German Subject: Itinerary of a Figure', *German Life and Letters* 62, no. 4: 465–81.

CHAPTER 5

Power Practices and Pop:
The Islam of Zain Bhikha

JONAS OTTERBECK

In this chapter I demonstrate how a critical understanding of power practices can help us analyse the diverse ways of addressing and living Islam. The aim is to offer a strategy for studying the actual enunciations of individuals that, taken together in their contradictory, complementary and overlapping multitude, make up the abstraction 'Islam'. The chapter suggests a critical, but constructive, rereading of Talal Asad's influential concept of 'discursive tradition' with the help of Foucauldian theories about power and ethics, and further stressing the importance of semiotics.

After developing the theoretical perspective, and with the help of it, I explore the enunciated Islam of one person, South African singer-songwriter Zain Bhikha, who has composed, recorded and performed pop nashid since 1994. The aim is to convince the reader of the importance of taking the issues raised by the theory into consideration when researching Islam.

Pop nashid is a genre of music inspired by Islamic piety and ethics. *Nashīd* (pl. *anāshīd*) simply means song in Arabic. Historically, *nashīd* has been used to refer to a variety of musical forms. The music I am referring to in this chapter shares the typical traits of popular music, that is, with regard to the length of songs (3–5 minutes), the structure (with intros, verses and repeated centrally placed choruses), production and marketing. As there are other forms of *nashīd*, I use pop nashid as an analytical concept. In English, fans at times spell the genre 'nasheed'.[1]

Over the years, Zain Bhikha has gained popularity – his official YouTube channel features twelve music videos that have been played at least one million

---

[1] Otterbeck 2021.

times, the most popular has been viewed seventeen million times – and he has collaborated with almost every major pop nashid artist and act. Despite this success, Zain Bhikha remains an amateur; he still works full-time at his father's company. Any surplus from sales or concerts goes to charity.

How does Zain Bhikha express Islam in songs, texts, interviews, promotional material, music videos and on stage? Most artists take advice on clothing, stage performances, music video directing and lyrics from trusted friends and collaborators; Zain Bhikha acknowledges this, so evidently, his expressions are not entirely his own. I analyse the Islam expressed by the artist persona of Zain Bhikha, rather than Zain Bhikha as a private person, though he himself often stresses that there is no difference between his private self and his artist persona. Finally, I discuss my results and theoretical perspective.

. . . AND ACTION!

Musicologist Christopher Small provocatively proclaims 'there is no such thing as music. Music is not a thing at all but an activity, something that people do. The apparent thing "music" is a figment, an abstraction of the action.'[2] Proceeding, he coins the term 'musicking', a present participle of the seldom-used verb 'to music',[3] to describe this practice- and performance-directed approach. Islamic studies needs something similar, though 'Islamicising' or 'Islaming' do not work.

A reified Islam – that is, Islam seen as a thing – implies that performances are not important for what Islam is. Islam becomes a one-way communication; the believer is merely receiving the message according to his or her ability – the richer and fuller, the better. This has often been the preferred understanding of religious specialists[4] working within different Islamic traditions. But if instead we stress that religions are the results of the actions – oral, written, and bodily – of believers, and others, from different social positions, a power practice-oriented understanding is central. Sociologist of religion Peter Beyer argues: 'The central religious paradox lies in the fact that the transcendent can only be

---

[2] Small 1998: 2.
[3] Small 1998: 9.
[4] Bryan S. Turner (1991: chap. 4, 1996: chap. 4) stresses the material preconditions of the 'virtuosi' (a Weberian term) that enables them to pursue knowledge and provide blessings, religious expertise, and ritual leadership. At times, Turner uses the term 'religious specialists' (Turner 1991: 87) to emphasise that religious virtuosi designate an economic category. I follow Turner in this, as I consider 'virtuosi' to have many connotations to excellence, charisma, talent, which is a part of Weber's discussion. Further, 'religious specialist' is more neutral in general discussions than are emic words like priest, monk or *'ulamā*. Finally, religious specialist is a broader category that can include both women and men who make their livelihood by providing religious services outside the intellectual, often institutionalised, spheres; for example, by wandering shaykhs engaged in dream interpretation and the selling of cures and amulets.

communicated in immanent terms, and this by definition: communication on the basis of meaning is always immanent, even when the subject of communication is the transcendent.'[5] Communication about Islam is always immanent and discursive, and involves unruly and contradictory power practices as well as senders and receivers that frequently switch places, as senders devise their communication based on being receivers themselves – of language, ideas and genres. The power practices of enunciations contain the potential for difference or repetition, or the (re-)invention of the wheel, and are not under the full control of individuals' intensions (as communication never is). Statements might aspire to communicate an assumed transcendence, but transcendence is not accessible for analysis, only the statements are, as they crystalise in languages in time and space. Thus, scholars of Islamic studies must accept the above as the very condition for research on Islam and must focus their attention on the verbal, bodily, or emotional deeds and claims – or the material results thereof.

REREADING ASAD'S DISCURSIVE TRADITION

In 1986, the anthropology professor Talal Asad launched the concept of 'discursive tradition' in a working paper. He attempted to formulate an alternative to ahistorical, essentialist representations of Islam and particularistic analyses that disconnect and fragment local contexts from each other and ultimately dissolve Islam into an abstraction worthy of study. His concern was to rethink what an anthropology of Islam implied theoretically. Later, he turned his interest to the concepts 'religion' and 'secular' by pursuing an anthropology of concepts.[6] Asad was inspired by an understanding of discourse and power informed by the historian of ideas Michel Foucault. Although Asad's 1986 paper does not refer to Foucault, later texts by Asad frequently do. Asad suggests an anthropology of multiple, interrelated power practices – all with a historicity – specifically pointing out that 'indigenous discourses' and 'political-economic conditions' cannot be omitted.[7] At the heart of Asad's argument are ideas expressed in the following two quotations:

Islam as the object of anthropological understanding should be approached as a discursive tradition that connects variously with the formation of moral selves, the manipulation of populations (or resistance to it), and the production of appropriate knowledges.[8]

---

[5] Beyer 1994: 5.
[6] Asad 2003. See also Enayat, this volume.
[7] Asad 1986: 9.
[8] Asad 1986: 7.

An Islamic discursive tradition is simply a tradition of Muslim discourse that addresses itself to conceptions of the Islamic past and future with reference to a particular Islamic practice in the present.[9]

In unpacking the above-quoted lines, two initial things need to be addressed: Asad's use of tradition and discourse. Asad sees traditions as consisting of intertwined discourses with a rich history that very likely share a future. This is mainly borrowed from the philosopher Alasdair MacIntyre. Asad acknowledges the many varying discourses in existence – in history and in the present – but claims that they are interrelated, in spite of their differences. He further insists on the need to study and analyse the discourses in relation to sociopolitical conditions in real societies. The discourses are upheld and changed by actors who through their power practices both define and learn the rules and orders of the discursive orthodoxy. Asad prefers a Foucauldian understanding of orthodoxy, seeing it as a 'relationship of power', especially the disciplinary power of what is deemed correct and incorrect, a power practice he allocates to everyone from the learned specialists to 'an untutored parent'.[10] As such, the discursive power practices of orthodoxy become a disciplinary reminder of the past in the present with the ability to marginalise, stigmatise, and possibly exclude or include, regulate, form and institutionalise behaviours and ideas, affecting, for example, gendered subjectifications. In the first quote, Asad mentions 'moral selves'. In later writings, Asad expands on his reading of Foucault's ideas about ethical selves. I return to this concept below to clarify the gender dimension of this situation.

Despite its prominence, Asad does not often include the concept of 'discursive tradition' in his writing. For example, it only features twice in *Genealogies of Religion* (1993), his first major book after the 1986 working paper.[11] Asad does not abandon the concept. It is used occasionally, but is not developed or defended. However, the concept of 'tradition' features fairly frequently, enabling Asad to argue that the vast varieties of expressions in history relating to 'Islam' can be understood in relation to each other as they produce something larger by existing: the Islamic discursive tradition.

CRITICISM

Anthropologist Sindre Bangstad has been persistent in his critique of Asad.[12] In particular, he accuses Asad of prioritising a text-based understanding of

---

[9] Asad 1986: 14.
[10] Asad 1986: 15.
[11] In fact, the book is a compilation of earlier arguments and articles, yet excludes the working paper.
[12] Bangstad 2008, 2009.

Islam.[13] Rereading Asad, after scrutinising Bangstad's critique, I end up with two possible readings. In my first reading, I agree with Bangstad, who is suspicious about the theologising tendencies expressed in quotations like 'If one wants to write an anthropology of Islam one should begin, as Muslims do, from the concepts of a discursive tradition that includes and relates itself to the founding texts of the Qur'an and the Hadith' and 'Clearly, not everything Muslims say and do belongs to an Islamic discursive tradition'.[14] Does this imply that the founding texts set limits for possible inclusion? Asad's essay and later writings do not explicitly address the issue of change; rather, he assumes that change does and will happen, though the question is not addressed properly.[15]

My other reading challenges Bangstad's criticism and is more generous to Asad. When Bangstad points out that Islam is not always the reference point of actions or thoughts for 'Muslims' (in this case, it would be preferable to write 'people with a Muslim family history' to stress that everyone living in such a relationship with Islam is not always in their role as Muslims),[16] he is, in fact, complying with Asad's ideas and the second of the two Asad quotes given in the last paragraph. Bangstad seems to want Asad to do something else and asks for an anthropology of Muslims rather than an anthropology of Islam.[17] Regarding the accusation of a text-based focus, Asad mentions, for example, Sufis, unlettered parents, and many local contexts as producing Islamic discourse. Still, the odd formulation about the Quran and hadith chafes and clearly gives priority to the founding texts. In fact, the formulation that Bangstad criticises is so careless, so Sunni-centrist, and so unrepresentative of the working paper at large that I find it difficult to consider it part of the theory. In my mind, I rewrite it to mean that the discursive tradition has a historical origin and some of its symbolic centres are the founding texts that supply vocabulary, narratives and symbols that are related in discourse. When Asad writes 'includes and relates' it does not imply that expressions must exclusively originate in the founding texts.

Due to the many signals in the working paper of the opposite, and the way Foucauldian logic steers away from a preference for a text-centred interpretation, my reading differs from Bangstad's as it is informed by Islamic studies, albeit Islamic studies inspired by anthropology, culture studies and sociology. An anthropology of Islam trying to understand how the abstract concept 'Islam' is embodied, conjured up and creatively moulded particularly appeals to me, though it may not appeal to Bangstad.

---

[13] Bangstad 2008: 246, 2009: 197.
[14] Asad 1986: 14.
[15] Bangstad 2008.
[16] Otterbeck 2010, 2015.
[17] Bangstad 2008: 252.

DEVELOPING THE FOUCAULDIAN ELEMENT

If we accept my reading of the working paper, which differs from Bangstad's, Asad's contribution becomes an inspiring attempt, but not nearly developed enough to help operationalise an anthropology of Islam. The theory must be clearer on power and practice, and on the relation between the specific and the general. It also requires an understanding of change and the genealogy of ideas.

Power practices and authority are intertwined, but authority is not only found at traditional centres. The formulations of Islam by religious specialists should not automatically be given priority by social scientists and humanists. Even theological writings are enunciated power practices subject to development, feuds, claims, dominant trends, individual struggles, and are affected by context. No doubt skilful religious specialists formulate concise understandings of respective faith better than most, but why should such interpretations be given precedence over other honest attempts to live or conceptualise a faith? When recognising all enunciations as power practices, contextualisation becomes essential so that they can be understood properly and realistically. In societies marked by mediatisation and a globalising tendency this becomes increasingly difficult but still essential to recognise. By perceiving the discursive tradition to be in flux and, at any given point in history, diverse, even in rather central dogma, the field of Islamic studies can include almost anything.[18]

In order to assess enunciations, we must acknowledge that all can be described as both unique and as general. When uttering a *duʿā* (supplication), the words may have been said before, but the immediate situation, the intonation, the emotions they awaken (or not) and its purpose at a specific time are all unique. Finding the unique in the general and vice versa is at the heart of a practice-oriented discourse study, particularly a genealogical one.[19]

A genealogy attempts to explain how ideas and enunciations are tied to earlier expressions. Religious discourses are by definition disciplined, but to a certain extent are also open to impulses from the outside, meaning that religious discourse can change over time and still keep its imagined coherence. Studies in the history of religions often challenge religious discourse precisely because of discourses' tendency to change, while claiming continuity.

Genealogical studies utilise a key strategy, namely, asking not what utterances or gestures mean, but why they exist, 'what it means for them to have appeared when and where they did – they and no others'.[20] Foucault aimed to historicise enunciations, not by evaluating the claims they make, but by viewing

---

[18] Asad 1986; Curtis 2014.
[19] Foucault 1998.
[20] Dreyfus and Rabinow 1983: 51.

their appearance as power practices in relation to discourses and thus as clues to the composition of the discourse.

From the perspective of area studies, I treasure unique expressions and would like to nurture both sides in my research. Borrowing from literary scholar Jonathan Culler, I consider it of great value to 'understand' enunciations, not only to 'overstand' them.[21] Understanding implies a benign reading following the intended logic of a text or a series of bodily expressions and the faithful communication of this to a reader, and overstanding entails asking critical questions and seeking answers that might or might not please the studied individual or groups or those invested in earlier interpretations of a text.

According to the literary scholar Roland Barthes, when a word, gesture, symbol – a sign – is interpreted in the context of other signs, these additional signs help anchor meaning.[22] Signs are the building blocks of discourses mobilised through practices. Signs get coded by prior use, which enables a normal, or common, use but also satire, irony or provocation. The signs historically associated with an Islamic discursive tradition can be mobilised by Muslims as well as non-Muslims, and new signs may be introduced and accepted or rejected – wholly or partly – by the practices of the many.

Researchers in Islamic studies should respectfully 'understand' the expressions studied, give these expressions space to stress their uniqueness. Further, they must acknowledge that everyone – researchers, believers, hecklers – approaches Islamic enunciations from specific knowledge positions. Research is a power practice in itself and must be performed ethically and reflexively, but merely to acknowledge this and 'understand' is not enough, research must also 'overstand' expressions, which requires theoretically informed critical analysis.

ZAIN BHIKHA

In this part of the chapter, I focus on the religious enunciations of Zain Bhikha, who is not part of an Islamic organisation, or a spokesperson for a social movement. He is not a religious specialist and has no formal higher education in Islam. He is, and for the last twenty-five years has been, a singer-songwriter and civil society activist engaging with audiences, youth, charities and fellow artists. He aspires to be perceived as presenting an Islamic message to the world. To do this, he acts in relation to the Islamic discursive tradition and its resources. He not only adheres to a script, but also models Islam through his enunciations and according to his own mould.

---

[21] Culler 1992.
[22] Barthes 1997.

Early career

Zain Bhikha was born in 1974 in South Africa into a family with Indian roots. His father owns a business where Zain Bhikha works full-time.[23] He grew up in a family with a very positive attitude to music, though he lived in a Muslim neighbourhood where most other families were critical to music. He grew up with contemporary pop music, not least Anglo-American and South African.

As a young man, Zain Bhikha was not politically engaged despite growing up during Apartheid.[24] When his friend Mubeen Yusuf Rasool died in the political havoc around the first South African general election of 1994, Zain Bhikha was shaken awake from his rather carefree youth. He started to ask himself pivotal questions about the meaning of life, justice and fairness. Given that he came from a devout Muslim family, supported by his parents, he turned to his inherited faith.

To channel his grief and his new interest in Islam, Zain Bhikha penned a number of songs in praise of Allah, Muhammad and an Islamic lifestyle. Because his family had means, he was able to record his songs (in vocals-only) in a studio. He was raised speaking English and found it natural to record songs in English. A demo cassette tape was produced and a few hundred copies were circulated, as was normal at that time. These songs from 1994 are probably the first studio recordings of someone singing Islamic *nashīd* in English. Islamic *anāshīd*, traditional devotional songs celebrating Allah, Muhammad and other key Muslim figures, or an Islamic lifestyle, were growing in popularity at the time, in part because of a wave of new compositions reflecting the sociopolitical context of Muslim activists worldwide.[25] Pirated copies of Yusuf Islam (formerly Cat Stevens) singing a few children's songs in English had circulated among Muslim activists earlier, but these were live recordings that were not authorised by Yusuf Islam.

While this cassette did not propel Zain Bhikha to world fame, he was given the opportunity to perform his songs on a few occasions and, with some experience of recording and performing, he wrote new songs. Soon he had recorded a number of independently distributed albums and his reputation grew.

Zain Bhikha remembers the confusion that his music caused in the early days. He was compelled to engage in discussions about whether it was acceptable to praise Allah in songs in English, not because of a well-established taboo but

---

[23] Unless specified, the information about Zain Bhikha is either taken from the three DVD set *Zain Bhikha: Songs of a Soul* (2014) (this includes a documentary and a concert); his website: zainbhikha. com; or an online interview (sound + image) I did with him in October 2017.

[24] This story is often repeated by Zain Bhikha and, although it has likely been rationalised through repetition, while interviewing him I got the distinct impression that the description was as fair as possible.

[25] Otterbeck 2021.

because such an enunciation was unfamiliar. In his context, the very idea of singing praise was tied to the established musical forms and poetic lyrics in archaic Urdu and Arabic. Instead, Zain Bhikha used North American pop music styles and his lyrics were very straightforward and not as elaborate as might be expected. By performing songs praising Allah in English, he created something new and exciting for some, but alien and problematic for others.

At live performances, the way he embodied his role also caused debates. Zain Bhikha mentions an occasion when he was asked to sing his songs in a mosque; after engaging in discussions about English and the form of the songs, he was offered a cloak – a signal of Islamic authority – which he politely declined.

When new forms, expressions and communication styles are introduced, negotiations take place. At the time, even if the messages of his songs were grounded in Islam, the aesthetics and form were simply not part of the discursive tradition; the new devotional English pop nashids were not yet disciplined and ordered and thus difficult to interpret, especially because language and form generated associations to non-Islamic expressions. Over the years, this type of new Islamic songs has been successfully embraced in many contexts worldwide and is now almost a standard part of any larger Islamic conference or event.[26]

Zain Bhikha's father frequented Islamic conferences and once ran into Yusuf Islam and handed him one of his son's cassettes. Together with Zain Bhikha's growing reputation, that small act of networking proved decisive.

London calling

Zain Bhikha was invited to London in 1999 to contribute to a new album by Yusuf Islam. It was to be a collection of children's songs in English and Yusuf Islam asked two singers who had recorded Islamic children's song to back him up. The other singer was the Canadian Dawud Wharnsby who had been recording Islamic songs in English since 1996. With his connections to pioneering Canadian Islamic media house Sound Vision, Dawud Wharnsby's recordings were fairly well distributed in North American Sunni circles. The record was released in 2000 as *A is for Allah*.

Working with Yusuf Islam and Dawud Wharnsby brought a lot of changes. Apart from gaining two lifelong friends, Zain Bhikha learned from their ways of working. He was signed to Jamal Records, a subdivision of Yusuf Islam's recording company Mountain of Light. In 2005, Zain Bhikha Studios was formed; he ended the contract with Jamal Records on good terms. Most importantly, he found a future collaborative partner in Dawud Wharnsby, who was of his generation. Over the coming years, they recorded, performed and wrote together.

---

[26] Otterbeck 2021.

The established amateur

Twenty-five years into his career, Zain Bhikha is an established artist with sixteen original albums. Ever since the yearly list of most influential Muslims, *The Muslim 500*, was first published in 2009, Zain Bhikha has been featured in the 'Arts & Culture' section, along with Yusuf Islam and Dawud Wharnsby.

Having been a public persona for decades, Zain Bhikha, now in middle-age, is aware of his influence and thus, as he sees it, his responsibility. To me, he stressed:

> You are mixing your faith with your creativity, two very, very powerful things. If you just did music without faith, without spirituality, without anything else and you're just an artist being creative, it would have been easy, but you're combining these two things, so who you are as a human being and who you portray yourself to be and who you think you are have to be all connected.

This ethical responsibility and awareness that Zain Bhikha refers to is reflected in his songs, music videos and performances, but also in his life on and off stage. For the last fifteen years this has inspired him to hold regular workshops. In particular, he engages in youth empowerment through creativity and holds regular workshops on this, especially in sub-Saharan Africa.

My study does not include how audiences receive Zain Bhikha's music, or what use they make out of it, but there is a great need for such studies regarding this type of music. Judging from meetings with fans of pop nashid music, observations at concerts and from discussions online, I suspect that artists and songs within the pop nashid genre inspire people to love Islam and live ethical lives inspired by Islam. The genre offers music and artists that many Muslims take pride in; the phenomenon is seen as contemporary and fresh. At the very least, Zain Bhikha provides an Islamic soundtrack to some lives. We now turn to the artistic output of Zain Bhikha.

Lyrics

Zain Bhikha mainly sings about three topics: Islam, the personal experience of faith, and Islamic empowerment versus social problems.[27] At times, he records other people's songs, but here I concentrate on his own. On the cover of *The Beginning* (2009), he cites the famous Muslim intellectual, Abū Ḥāmid al-Ghazālī (d. 1111), who said: 'The purpose of songs is to inspire the

---

[27] This section is based on a study of all the lyrics of Zain Bhikha's released songs.

listener to the love and remembrance of Allah . . .'. This quotation sums up Zain Bhikha's ambition quite well. However, he recontextualises and reinterprets the quote – according to al-Ghazālī, listening to music (*sama*') was a sacred act that could only be controlled and utilised by experienced Sufis. But by anchoring his interpretation in Islamic discursive tradition using the rhetorically powerful figure of al-Ghazālī, Zain Bhikha attempts to promote his music, or at least intends to present it as part of a tradition.

When singing about Islam, he praises Allah and asks Allah to bless the Prophet Muhammad. Typically, he relates the stories of Muhammad, his closest Companions, and Quranic stories. The lyrics to a recent recording, 'The Farewell Sermon' (from *Cotton Candy Sky*, 2018) is a shortened version of Muhammad's well-known farewell sermon given at his last visit to Mecca; the sermon highlights the importance of tolerance and care. Another example, 'Mount Hira' (from *Faith*, 2001), retells the narrative of how Muhammad was called to Islam:

> The same moon, the same star
> Gazed right down at Rasulullah [the messenger of Allah]
> They saw him climb, down from Hira[28]
> Now a Prophet, Prophet of Allah
> And in the sky, was Angel Gibraeel [Gabriel]
> He said O Muhammad, O Rasulullah
> And so he walked, into Makka [Mecca]
> In his heart echoed Iqra, Iqra ['recite'][29]
> And from the world, darkness was gone
> with salvation, rising with dawn
> for here was a blessing, a gift from Allah
> and the light of Muhammad, outshone that star.

The lyrics make use of well-known tropes in classical Muslim history. For example, the final prophet – later in the lyrics Muhammad is referred to as such – has an inner light that is often manifested physically in poetry and quite often also in hagiographic accounts of Muhammad. He sees the angel Gibraeel, all around him on the horizon, after he received the first short passage of the revelation in the cave of Hira, outside Mecca.

When writing about Islamic topics, Zain Bhikha does not challenge Sunni orthodoxy, rather he refers to it through central Islamic concepts, abbreviated narratives (a technique that suggests 'other stories without themselves being

---

[28] That is, the cave where Muhammad allegedly received the first revelation.
[29] According to common Islamic historiography, this was the first word revealed to Muhammad.

stories'),[30] and intertextual references; that is, he makes frequent references to signs generally associated with the Islamic discursive tradition.

As in many English-language nashids, the lyrics use several words originating in Arabic, expressing well-known key terms associated with the Islamic discursive tradition. What is sometimes referred to as Islamic English (the mixing of primarily Arabic Islamic phrases into English) is an aesthetic choice meant to signal authenticity and set the lyrics apart from pop music that might sound similar but is recorded with other purposes. Zain Bhikha also quite consistently uses 'Allah', yet another signal that these songs carry an Islamic message, and are differentiated from songs in English referring to 'God', which would be less precise in Zain Bhikha's context.

When Zain Bhikha writes about the individual's personal faith, he does so by addressing life's hardships and doubts, or happy times and good relations. Often either Zain Bhikha's 'I', a general 'we' or an undefined 'you' dominate the lyrics. For example, 'Allah Knows' (from the 2006 album of the same name) has the following lyrics:

When you lose someone close to your heart
See your whole world fall apart
And you try to go on but it seems so hard
Allah knows, Allah knows
You see we all have a path to choose
Through the valleys and hills we go
With the ups and the downs, never fret, never frown
Allah knows, Allah knows.

In such lyrics, the solution is clear. Trust in Allah and, regardless of hardship, you will find His compassion, mercy and love. This will help you move forward in life.

There are also generally positive songs that have very few references to Islam. For example, 'Mum and Dad' (from *The Beginning*, 2009) only contains a few lines about a 'gift from Allah' and a wish for Allah's blessing. The song is simply a celebration of his parents' role in helping him overcome sorrow following the death of his childhood friend. On the same album, he sings to a child, 'You are very special'. Similarly, this does not mention Islamic issues much; it merely contains a few lines like 'may Allah grant you wisdom' and 'Allah is always there'.

In these songs, Zain Bhikha connects to ethics that are well-grounded in Islam but also relations based on what he himself seems to believe; his songs

---

[30] Straub 2005: 62.

generally promote a respectful non-authoritative vision of parenthood and relationships. At the same time, Zain Bhikha considers this in tune with Islam, as is obvious from, for example, his live introduction to 'My Mum Is Amazing', when he reminds the audience of the respect they owe to their mothers according to Islam (*Songs of a Soul*, filmed concert, 2014). In this way, Zain Bhikha anchors his song in the Islamic discursive tradition even when the lyrics do not do this explicitly.

The final main topic deals with Islamic empowerment versus social problems. It overlaps with the former topic that addresses individual empowerment through Islam. In this case, empowerment is more on a collective level. When interviewing Zain Bhikha in 2017, he stressed that as he has become older, he has felt the urge to address social problems. This is not a step away from faith-based songs, rather, according to him, it is the opposite; considering one's faith in relation to society and religious communities is a way forward. Still, the lyrics are meant to be optimistic and bring hope. Typical examples are 'Orphan Child' (from *Our World*, 2002); 'Can't You See' (from *Allah Knows*, 2006) about drug abuse; 'Freedom Will Come' (from *The Beginning*, 2009) about Palestine; 'Better Day' (single release, 2011) about domestic violence against women and children; and 'Dare To Believe' (from *Cotton Candy Sky*, 2018) about refugees. This development has run in tandem with his increased engagement in workshops with social topics. The lyrics from 'Orphan Child' may serve as a typical example:

> She was just standing there, little girl all alone
> Barely covered head to toe, barely just twelve years old
> Why is she all alone, why's the world just so cold?
> Why don't we play our part?
> What has hardened our hearts?

Here the narrator addresses everyone, pointing to our lack of solidarity as the problem. As the 'we' in the song can be understood as 'we Muslims' it also appeals to the specific commands in the Quran to care for orphans. The lyrics stress that Muhammad himself 'was an orphan'. The solution to social problems can be found through Islamic empowerment and ethics.

The music videos

As the music videos were not directed by the artist, I concentrate on those arts that Zain Bhikha was presumably in control of. I have examined how he presents himself, the settings, and the narratives stressed by the music videos.[31] Like the lyrics, the music videos are unambiguous and rather straightforward.

With few exceptions, Zain Bhikha appears as his artistic persona, leisurely dressed in versions of *shalwar kamees* or in T-shirt, jacket and trousers. He almost always wears head gear, most often a *topi* (a cap, or a white knitted skull cap signalling Islamic masculinity). Sometimes he wears an (army) cap – this is common in the more political songs. He is bearded, at times with a goatee, at times with a full beard but with shaved upper lip, again consciously signalling an Islamic masculinity. He seems to like the *tasbīḥ* (prayer beads) that appear from time to time in his hand, on an album cover, or around his neck to indicate piety. In one music video, 'Mountain of Mekkah' (2005), the colour of the *tasbīḥ* matches his clothing. The colour scheme of his clothing matches his environment and the topic of each song.

The body language and the timbre of Zain Bhikha's voice, which he often strains to reach high notes, emphasise the emotional lyrics. He gesticulates with his hands, most often for general emphasis but at times using Islamic semiotics – like signalling one god with a raised index finger, or raising both his hands as if in *du'ā'* (supplication). Zain Bhikha never dances to the music. Live, he taps his foot to keep the beat, but does nothing more than that. Generally, dancing is not part of the repertoire of pop nashid artists, neither on stage nor in music videos. It is widely held to be inappropriate by the artists, managers, video directors and Islamic scholars I have interviewed or read.[32] Just as Islamic religious specialists in all their diversity have produced discourses attempting to discipline the use of music, they have targeted dance as sexually suggestive and disruptive. However, attitudes consciously change. Rashid Bhikha – Zain Bhikha's now-adult son, who he has recorded and performed with since Rashid Bhikha was a child – does hip-hop moves in a music video 'Heartbeat' (2011) and on stage with his father (*Songs of a Soul*, filmed concert, 2014) but it is not part of Zain Bhikha's way of expressing himself.

Zain Bhikha's music videos generally portray one of four different settings: religious settings including stock photos from Mecca and Medina or footage from mosques; nature settings; happy, loving settings featuring couples, children or parents, often of (symbolically) different ages and ethnicities; settings featuring shabby buildings and streets in poor areas (these appear quite often without clear markers of religious adherence, stressing that help should be given to all the dispossessed, not just Muslims).

When Zain Bhikha's lyrics narrate Muhammad's life or deeds, they are often

---

[31] This section is based on analyses of thirty-nine music videos, twenty-six available on *Zain Bhikha: Songs of a Soul* (2014), three DVD set, and thirteen more recently available songs on Zain Bhikha's official website.

[32] Otterbeck 2021.

illustrated with religious imagery related to Arabo-centric Islamic aesthetics from the historical mosques of Saudi Arabia or similar scenes. Less iconic general mosque interiors feature as inviting, safe spaces for contemplation, prayer and meetings, always sunlit and spacious.

Nature features prominently, as illustrations of the vastness, beauty and ingeniousness of 'Allah's creation'. For example, in the refrain to 'Allah Remains' (2015), when the words of the title are repeated, the footage shows nature's splendour. Zain Bhikha's album covers also feature illustrations of nature. Nature as a proof of the existence of Allah is common in Sunni Islamic apologetics and in pop nashid videos; it is, of course, used widely in Muslim thought more generally.[33]

Apart from the obvious narratives of the lyrics, music videos emphasise the social engagement of Zain Bhikha's songs. The two most prominent themes – gratitude and love he expresses for those who stand up for others and support them, and the call for solidarity with orphans, the poor, refugees, and those taking a wrong turn in life – are two sides of the same coin. Like other successful pop nashid artists, Zain Bhikha is engaged in charity work and charity concerts. Two of the music videos to the *Cotton Candy Sky* album (2018) – the title song and 'Get Up Again' – feature the Islamic Relief logo and its aid workers, the second largest Muslim aid provider, second only to the Aga Khan Development Network.[34] The music videos portray Syrian refugees and poor people in South Africa. References to Islam play a minimal role in these videos. Religious affiliation is not a condition of solidarity. In these and similar songs, Zain Bhikha is dressed in a more neutral, less overtly Muslim fashion.

In most of his music videos, children feature prominently. Zain Bhikha trusts the rhetorical power of images of children – happy or sad, playing or working, relaxed or struggling. Children are at the very heart of Zain Bhikha's creativity, as audiences, as partners in the creative process (his own kids singing, children's choirs, or children acting in music videos), or as sung about with admiration or in deep solidarity. In fact, I think I have never come across any other expression of Islam so deeply ingrained with a children's perspective as that of Zain Bhikha, who is aware of the notion that Muhammad was particularly fond of children.

Zain Bhikha appears to be a caring, loving, engaged and deeply devout man, not obsessed with rules but with compassion. Nothing matters more than the future of our children, and, to Zain Bhikha, all children of all ethnicities and all classes are *our* children, period.

---

[33] Otterbeck 2021.
[34] Juul Petersen 2015: 120.

MUSIC MATTERS

All of Zain Bhikha's recordings are vocals-only or vocals and percussion. When discussing the beginning of his career, Zain Bhikha explains his three main reasons for recording vocals-only: first, he did not know how to play an instrument; second, his South African roots offered him a drums and vocals music heritage that he loves and nurtures; and finally, there is an issue in Islamic discourse of the permissibility of musical instruments. At the time he began his career, in Islamic activist circles recordings were only made with percussion, and it was in these circles that most new forms of Islamic *anāshīd* were developing.[35] These activists and musicians were informed by substantial discussions about the legality of music, instruments, singing and listening that I cannot relate in detail here. Suffice it to note that there is a long tradition that considers string and wind instruments part of the Devil's allure and dismisses so-called western music as foreign and immoral.[36]

From the mid-1990s until around 2004, the dominant discourse maintained that Muslims should avoid instrumentation. Around 2004, several pop nashid musicians started to record with instruments and tour with full bands. Religious specialists reacted to the development in two ways: one side took a lenient, inclusive position, and the other side took a conservative, partly reactionary position. The first reaction has created space for new music styles and production techniques and the aesthetics of a contemporary consumer music culture, though within limits: the lyrics must be 'clean' and some scholars object to sounds that they interpret as sexually suggestive. The conservatives continue to claim that most instruments are forbidden. Even when acknowledging the artists' good intentions, they consider them misguided and on a slippery slope. In many places, for example in Afghanistan, Algeria, Iran, Iraq, Pakistan, Palestine, Saudi Arabia and Somalia, reactionary people have attacked, at times killed, musicians and listeners for engaging in music.[37]

While several of his closest collaborators and friends – Yusuf Islam, Dawud Wharnsby, and his son – all record using instruments, Zain Bhikha has chosen to maintain his form. But extensive use of digital studio techniques, including vocal pads, enable and facilitate the creation of a rich sound texture.

---

[35] Otterbeck 2021.
[36] See Otterbeck 2016; Shiloah 1995.
[37] Otterbeck 2008.

What Islam is produced by Zain Bhikha?

Zain Bhikha is not a religious specialist but his enunciations exert influence nonetheless. He is reaching out in a way that few intellectual theologians have the means, skills, or knowledge to do. According to the unique enunciation of Zain Bhikha, Islam entails a deep love for Allah, Muhammad, early Islamic history, and gratitude for creation. To celebrate this, Zain Bhikha's devout lyrics and music videos use signs and abbreviated narratives that he assumes will awaken associations to Islam with the listeners. Further, to Zain Bhikha, Islam is an ethical code calling people to solidarity with the dispossessed and wretched, with the orphans and widows, to paraphrase the Quran. Through his songs and music videos he aims to mobilise others. To this end, he runs a charity and cooperates with other charities. Furthermore, taking Islam seriously includes expressing the love you feel for those close to you. In his lyrics, voice timber and gestures, Zain Bhikha is unreservedly and intentionally sentimental in expressing his affection for his parents, wife, children and friends.

When overstanding the work of Zain Bhikha and his artist persona, especially in analysing its general aspects, it is clear that he is part of three larger trends: one that is specific to consumer society; one that relates to ethics; and one in relation to the idea of empowerment.

The tonal language, song structures and sound production of Zain Bhikha and other pop nashid artists are generally indistinguishable from other contemporary popular music. Zain Bhikha's songs stand out because they are vocals-only recordings, but apart from that, the musical ideals and ideas can be traced, genealogically, to Anglo-American and, in Zain Bhikha's case, South African popular music. The pop nashid genre is a new phenomenon in the Islamic discursive tradition. It illustrates how a number of artists and companies have managed, through their creativity and marketing, to change the discourse through their power practices. The conscious anchoring of lyrics in Islamic discourse, the ethical profile of the artists, and the appealing contemporaneity of the expressions have succeeded in creating a new, beloved component in the Islamic discursive tradition, even though its marketing forms are largely copied from general popular culture. Of course, the Islamic nature of pop nashid is contested by some, but even more often it is defended.

To come across as credible – when singing about his faith and when addressing social issues – Zain Bhikha signals an ethical Muslim masculinity in interviews, on stage, in promotional material and lyrics. I stress masculinity as the scene that Zain Bhikha acts within is highly gendered. Most successful singers are men. Being handsome and well-dressed is beneficial to the careers of Muslim pop nashid artists who are constantly in the spotlight of modern consumer society celebrity culture. Yet, as artists present their bodies, they must try to avoid transgression – not least overt sexualisation – and enact an Islamically informed gendered ethical self. In a sexist world, this has proven more difficult for women artists. Zain Bhikha carefully models himself on advice to men from Sunni *'ilm al-akhlāq* (the knowledge of the character) manuals, but not to the letter. He is Islamically dressed, yet modern; controlled in movements, yet has a stage presence; is pious and polite in speech and lyrics, yet has contributed with something new and appreciated. In fact, the carefully crafted artist persona of Zain Bhikha enacts a Muslim masculinity that is sought after by Muslim audiences, an ethically based counter-masculinity to the often-mediatised raging, gun-toting Islamists.[38]

The stress on ethics in lyrics and the expected ethical persona, together with the aesthetic expectations of a global consumer culture, frame the enunciations of Zain Bhikha. These factors make him part of a trend that connects an ethical Islam to empowerment. Such an empowerment discourse can be found in Islamic social movement organisations and in Islamic social movements, but it is also a general trend among Muslims;[39] the main idea being that if Islam is taken seriously, civil society and political engagement can improve societies. It is an Islam with an ethical emphasis stressing solidarity, charity, education, and at times equality, vegetarianism and environmental awareness, rather than an Islam that is focused on detailed rules. Such an Islam is increasingly visible in Muslim enunciations, and pop nashid is its soundtrack. Pop music and Zain Bhikha are indicative of the changes and potentials in the Islamic discursive tradition.

This study of one man's – albeit a famous artist – expression of Islam illustrates the usefulness of a developed understanding of Asad's discursive tradition. By focusing on details and processes – the power practices that mobilise signs through enunciations – in this chapter, I have demonstrated how a new expression in relation to the discursive tradition can be included through negotiation, even if it is not accepted by everyone. But plurality and struggles are the expected normality of something as abstract as a discursive tradition called Islam.

BIBLIOGRAPHY

Zain Bhikha's albums

Faith (2001) [CD].
Our World (2002) [CD].
Allah Knows (2006) [CD].
The Beginning (2009) [CD].
Zain Bhikha: Songs of a Soul (2014) [DVD set].
Cotton Candy Sky (2018) [CD].

---

[38] Otterbeck 2021.
[39] Otterbeck 2021.

Zain Bhikha's music videos
'Mountain of Mekkah' (2005).
'Better Day' (2011) [single, music video].
'Heartbeat' (2011).
'Allah Remains' (2015).
'Cotton Candy Sky' (2018).
'Get Up Again' (2018).

Literature and internet
Asad, Talal (1986), *The Idea of an Anthropology of Islam*, Center for Contemporary Arab Studies Occasional Papers Series, Washington, DC: Georgetown University.
Asad, Talal (1993). *Genealogies of Religion: Discipline and Reason of Power in Christianity and Islam*, Baltimore: Johns Hopkins University Press.
Asad, Talal (2003), *Formations of the Secular: Christianity, Islam, Modernity*, Stanford: Stanford University Press.
Bangstad, Sindre (2008), 'Fotnoter til antropologien om islam', *Norsk Antropologisk Tidskrift* 19, no. 4: 243–55.
Bangstad, Sindre (2009), 'Contesting Secularism/s: Secularism and Islam in the Work of Talal Asad', *Anthropological Theory* 9, no. 2: 188–208.
Barthes, Roland (1997), *Image–Music–Text*, London: Fontana Press.
Beyer, Peter (1994), *Religion and Globalization*, London: Sage.
Bunt, Gary (2000), *Virtually Islamic: Computer-Mediated Communication and Cyber Islamic Environments*, Cardiff: University of Cardiff Press.
Culler, Jonathan (1992), 'In Defence of Overinterpretation', in S. Collini (ed.), *Interpretation and Overinterpretation*, Cambridge: Cambridge University Press, pp. 109–24.
Curtis IV, Edward (2014), 'Ode to Islamic Studies: Its Allure, Its Danger, Its Power', *Bulletin for the Study of Religion*, http://www.equinoxpub.com/blog/2014/05/ode-to-islamic-studies-its-allure-its-danger-its-power-reflections-on-islamic-studies/ (last accessed 28 October 2019).
Dreyfus, Hubert L., and Paul Rabinow (1983), *Michel Foucault: Beyond Structuralism and Hermeneutics*, Chicago: University of Chicago Press.
Foucault, Michel (1998), 'Nietzsche, Genealogy, History', in J. D. Faubion (ed.), *Aesthetics, Method, and Epistemology: The Essential Works of Foucault*, vol. 2, New York: New Press, pp. 369–92.
Juul Petersen, Marie (2015), *For Humanity or for the Umma? Aid and Islam in Transnational Muslim NGOs*, London: Hurst & Company.
The Muslim 500, https://www.themuslim500.com/ (last accessed 28 October 2019).
Otterbeck, Jonas (2000), *Islam på svenska. Tidskriften Salaam och islams globalisering*, Stockholm: Almqvist & Wiksell International.
Otterbeck, Jonas (2008), 'Battling over the Public Sphere: Islamic Reactions to the Music of Today', *Contemporary Islam* 3, no. 2: 211–28.
Otterbeck, Jonas (2010), *Samtidsislam – Unga muslimer i Malmö och Köpenhamn*, Stockholm: Carlsson.
Otterbeck, Jonas (2015), '"I Wouldn't Call them Muslims!": Constructing a Respectable Islam', *Numen* 62, nos. 2–3: 243–64.

Otterbeck, Jonas (2016), 'The Sunni Discourse on Music', in K. van Nieuwkerk, M. LeVine and M. Stokes (eds), *Islam and Popular Culture*, Austin: University of Texas Press, pp. 151–68.

Otterbeck, Jonas (2021), *The Awakening of Islamic Pop Music*, Edinburgh: Edinburgh University Press.

Shiloah, Amnon (1995), *Music in the World of Islam: A Socio-Cultural Study*, Aldershot: Scolar Press.

Small, Christopher (1998), *Musicking: The Meanings of Performing and Listening*, Middletown, CO: Wesleyan.

Straub, Jürgen (2005), 'Telling Stories, Making History: Toward a Narrative Psychology of the Historical Construction of Meaning', in J. Straub (ed.), *Narration, Identity, and Historical Consciousness*, New York: Berghahn Books, pp. 44–98.

Turner, Bryan S. (1991), *Religion and Social Theory*, London: Sage.

Turner, Bryan S. (1996), *For Weber – Essays on the Sociology of Fate*. London: Sage.

CHAPTER 6

Islam in the Making:
History, Discourses, the Quran and Modern Science

LEIF STENBERG

The late eighteenth century was a period of rapid and global technological change. It witnessed innovations in transportation, warfare, industry, agriculture and health care. Moreover, the opportunity to influence larger groups of people improved thanks to innovations like the modern printing press and faster communications. The rapid changes in this period correspondingly encompassed the transformation of human perceptions and attitudes. Power relations also shifted as the importance of the Safavid, Mughal and Ottoman empires dwindled, and the British, French and Russian empires grew in strength.[1]

The nineteenth century was a major period of institutional transformation. New educational systems, sometimes even national systems of schooling, were established in many European countries. In the cases of France and the United Kingdom, these developments also affected the educational systems in colonised parts of the world. In higher education, the first modern universities emerged. New disciplines in medicine, the sciences and engineering emphasised inductive reasoning, and the influence of religion over education decreased in school systems and at universities. In addition, the disciplines and the theories and methods of the social sciences and humanities were established in the nineteenth century.[2] The emphasis on empirically founded research, critical thinking and analysis, academic freedom, and organising universities into an

---

[1] For a variety of aspects concerning European empires and their engagement with Islam, see Motadel (ed.) 2016.

[2] Auguste Comte (d. 1857), Karl Marx (d. 1883), Émile Durkheim (d. 1917) and Max Weber (d. 1920) are instrumental for the development of social sciences. In the case of the humanities, it is more difficult to refer to single individuals, but the eighteenth-century division between the disciplines, such as the natural sciences and the human sciences (*Geisteswissenshaften*), is important. See Ritzer 1983; Bod *et al.* (eds) 2014.

increasing number of disciplines reflected and drove change in societies across the world. These transformations posed serious challenges to the understandings and practices of religion, religious authority, and the conventional role of religion in societies of the time.[3]

To followers of most religions, encountering new cross-cultural and liberal ideas about how to form societies, and about the creation of nation states, posed philosophical as well as very practical challenges.[4] Technological innovations and changes to everyday life were also visible parts of these trials, especially for people who understood religion as a social philosophy and a source of practice in daily life.

In the case of Muslims, these social, political and technological changes produced a number of intellectual and practical reactions. Religious scholars and laypeople discussed the Islamic response to new commodities, financial instruments, technologies and material culture.[5] In the everyday practice of religion there also arose issues of how to interpret and practice Islam under new political circumstances. The military victories of the early Muslims had been seen as a proof of the truth of Islam. Therefore, when the British and French began to extend their domination into areas with a Muslim-majority population, this was a significant existential challenge. It became necessary to read and find out more about the intellectual and philosophical foundations of the colonisers. One goal was to find Islamic explanations.[6]

With regard to the Islamic response to this encounter, the many novel questions that appeared among Muslims at this time – questions concerning everyday life as well as power politics – catalysed thinking about the practice and meaning of Islam. Famous individuals produced responses, legal opinions and new thinking about Islam developed in the nineteenth and twentieth centuries. The new challenges to Muslims and Islam were discussed in a number of works by Muslim scholars, including those of Jamāl al-Dīn al-Afghanī (d. 1897), Sir Syed Ahmed Khan (d. 1898), Muhammad ʿAbduh (d. 1905), Rashīd Riḍā (d. 1935) and Said Nursi (d. 1960). As part of this trend, al-Afghanī proposed pan-Islamism

---

[3] In this context, the ambiguous term 'religion' is conceptualised in an overarching way and is given a general meaning usually attached to the word that describes the phenomenon in the past and present. For a discussion on the usage of the term 'religion' in religious studies, see Olsson and Stenberg's contribution in this volume.

[4] Halevi 2019 is an excellent study that displays the dilemmas new and ordinary technologies, commodities, financial instruments and material culture pose for religious scholars who have had to produce legal opinions in response to questions concerning new objects, and determine whether or not they could be used from an Islamic standpoint.

[5] The rejection of the tomato (in Aleppo) as a Frankish invention is perhaps seen today as a humorous example, but at the time it was part of a serious discussion on how to approach what were perceived as new and foreign commodities; see Issawi 1988: 87.

[6] An illustrating portrait of how relations between scholars from Britain, France and Muslim societies generated new thinking in the field of astronomy, and also on reading science into the Quran, is found in Determann 2018: 39–70.

as a means to create an empire able to challenge foreign political influence; Syed Ahmad Khan founded the Muhammadan Anglo-Oriental College, the predecessor of the Aligarh Muslim University, to contest the intellectual and cultural dominance of the British; ʿAbduh emphasised a new educational system that would combine religion, modern science and reason; Riḍā formulated reform-oriented legal opinions in response to questions from Muslims in many countries; and Nursi was instrumental for discussions on Islam and modern science in Turkey. Discursively, the thinking and practices were based on the notion that Islam is the natural social philosophy, the true religion that has produced religious practices to regulate society and the lives of individuals.

The developments outlined above have been thoroughly studied by scholars of Islam and have also laid the foundation for various Muslim movements in the twentieth century. It would be natural to think that the contemporary discourse concerning the relationship between Islam and modern science rests on discussions among the early Muslim reformers such as the ones mentioned above. Their efforts to make sense of 'Islam' in changing circumstances and in the context of a political as well as philosophical challenge were important.[7] However, in today's discourse the relevance of interpretations and legal opinions produced in the late nineteenth and early twentieth centuries is not always clear. Current debates among Muslim stakeholders considering the Islamisation of modern science contain only a few references to the significant historical figures such as al-Afghānī, ʿAbduh, Khan and Riḍā. The exception is Nursi who is more referenced in the Turkish context.

Contemporary Discussion on Islam and Modern Science: the Aims of the Study

Instead of referring back to the arguments of the Muslim modernists of the nineteenth and early twentieth centuries, the current debate tends to invoke the time of the Prophet Muhammad and the history of science in a mainly Arab context in the period from 700 to 1400 CE. There are some references to more recent times and discussions among reformers in the late nineteenth century, but an overall preference is given to contemporary thought.[8] One possible reason for the lack of references to earlier thinkers is that contemporary discourse focuses on the Islamisation of modern science and claims that the Quran is compatible with modern science. Hence, in this paper I ask why contemporary Muslims who discuss the need to Islamise science from a confessional perspective are

---

[7] The period of the nineteenth and early twentieth centuries are covered in many scholarly contributions. For example, Corm 2020; Brown 1999; Hourani 1983.

[8] For a discussion on the role of these three periods in history and the discourse on Islam and modern science, see Stenberg 2004: 100–3.

reluctant to refer to the history of their own discourse.[9] Thus, I aim to examine the role and function of history in the contemporary discourse on Islam, the Quran and modern science in a Foucauldian sense.[10] A second aim involves analysing how the current production of Islamically founded ideas of the 'true' relationship between Islam, the Quran and modern science has been motivated and justified during the last decades. A third objective is to make brief remarks on the scholarship on Islam and science in the same period of time. The text has a chronological character and describes the discourse on Islam and modern science. Today the discourse is a vast field of ideas and I do not intend to cover it in its entirety.

Here I see religion as a broad and dynamic sociocultural phenomenon, and a set of diverse and evolving socially embedded discursive practices. This approach presents Islam as part of society and culture and the history of its ideas as a discursive practice. I discuss the meaning Muslims have given to Islam and its relation to modern science and the variety of resulting opinions that have appeared over time. In this context the discursive practice constitutes a tool to structure and describe the construction of meanings given to Islam, and I use it to examine how different opinions are involved in a power struggle about the correct or true conceptualisation of Islam. The successful contender appears momentarily in history as an established tradition.[11] Hypothetically, we can think of the current discourse on Islam and modern science as normative, that is, what creates a modern Muslimness, and aims to prevent the marginalisation of 'Islam' in the lives of Muslims globally.

Thus, the focus of this study is on the process of Islam-making. Discussion of the circumstances of a certain interpretation or practice is a constructive device in analysing Muslim experiences and creations of meaning. According to this understanding, the references to bygone moments in history are (whether the reference is to the 'Golden Age of Islam' or the late nineteenth or early twentieth century) contemporary constructions framed in a discourse of authenticity. Therefore, what happened in history is only important if it can be interpreted to legitimise an opinion in the present.

---

[9] In the following, it is necessary to think about regularities in the formation of what is considered knowledge in the contemporary discourse on Islam and modern science. This includes the expectations and notions that there are connections between what is stated in the current discourse and the thinking about Islam that existed in the nineteenth and early twentieth centuries.

[10] I am primarily influenced by Foucault 1972 and 1994. In the appendix (entitled 'The Discourse on Language') to Foucault 1972, he describes the production of discourse; see Foucault 1972: 216. Also, note Foucault's conceptualisation of the term 'episteme' as interactions that unite the discourse and create 'epistemological figures' that can, under certain circumstances, also turn into 'formalised systems'. This floating construction of knowledge is juxtaposed to the search for an eternal and constant meaning of Islam; see Foucault 1972: 191.

[11] For more on this form of approach and a method intended to form a text to present and analyse positions in a discourse on Islam and modern science, see Stenberg 1996 and 2004.

ISLAM AND MODERN SCIENCE: RAHMAN, NASR AND AL-ATTAS

I now turn to the discussion on Islam and modern science, beginning in the 1960s. The aim is not to give a general and complete picture of the discussions.[12]

Three key people in the establishment of the current discourse of Islam and modern science are Fazlur Rahman (d. 1988), Seyyed Hossein Nasr (b. 1933) and Sayed Muhammad Naquib al-Attas (b. 1931).[13] They were all born in Muslim societies, Rahman in today's Pakistan, Nasr in Iran and al-Attas in what later became Indonesia. All three were educated in the United States and the United Kingdom. Their education can be defined, broadly, as in humanities, language and Islamic studies, with the exception of Nasr who obtained an MA degree in geology and geophysics at MIT in 1956, but wrote his PhD thesis in the field of the history of science. In different ways they have pursued questions concerning Islam, philosophy, modernity, knowledge and tradition.[14] Their education in Muslim-majority countries and in North America and Europe stimulated their investigation of questions about knowledge production and the status of education and science in Muslim societies. From their various standpoints on what has from emic and etic positions been termed a discussion on the 'Islamisation of Knowledge' or the 'Islamisation of science', their positions in society, and their publications, they have become important references for Muslims seeking to understand the role of Islam in relation to modern science.[15]

Seyyed Hossein Nasr is an example of how historic circumstances appear in discussions on Islamising modern science.[16] Nasr, Muhammad Naquib al-Attas and others were inspired by Sufism and have stated that the process of secularisation and 'modernity' in Muslim societies is a threat to genuine Islamic values and norms. For Nasr, modern science and its philosophical consequences are

---

[12] A fourth person that could have been added is Ziauddin Sardar. He has been important in the discourse since the late 1970s. Sardar has published frequently on topics that could broadly be defined as under the umbrella of Islam and science, including questions on epistemology, future and cultural studies. See Stenberg 1996: 41–96 and https://ziauddinsardar.com/.

[13] Ismail al-Faruqi (1921–86) is another who can be mentioned. He arrived in the United States after 1948 and became an important figure in the discussion on Islam and modern science. He was also instrumental in the establishment of institutions in the United States, like the International Institute of Islamic Thought, the Muslim Student Association, and the Association of Muslim Social Scientists; see Stenberg 1996: 151–8 and https://ismailfaruqi.com/. Muhammad Iqbal's *The Reconstruction of Religious Thought in Islam* (1934) and Khurshid Ahmad's attempt to develop an Islamic economics are also forerunners to the current discourse.

[14] Early publications include those by al-Attas (1969) and Seyyed Hossein Nasr (from the 1960s). The conference in Mecca on Muslim Education (held in 1977), which included discussion on Islamic perspectives on knowledge, and the conference in Lugano, Switzerland (also in 1977) that laid the foundation for the International Institute for Islamic Thought (IIIT) were other milestones.

[15] For a study comparing discussions on Islam and knowledge in Malaysia and Egypt, see Abaza 2002.

[16] In the following, Nasr cannot be considered a scholarly reference. He is part of the empirical material and represents a specific position in the discourse on Islam, the Quran and modern science. He is a prolific author; for the positions attributed to Nasr in this text, see Nasr 1964, 1979 and 1981. See also Stenberg 1996: 95–148.

the engine of this destructive process. In his view, the profanation of nature by modern science has caused people to reject metaphysical truths.[17] For Nasr, re-Islamising knowledge and science involves subordinating human knowledge production to an absolute and divine knowledge.[18]

Nasr writes that humans have different spiritual abilities and qualities, and are ranked in a hierarchy in which sages are superior and of a higher standing than common individuals. According to his perspective, the sage par excellence is Muhammad: he is the complete and universal man. He is also the symbol of all positive things in the universe. Nasr's outline of the function of a sage is an example of an elitist perspective on humans linked to a genealogical model of history. In general, a sage is a historical prototype, a person who serves as an example to be imitated. Prominent people from Muslim history can be seen as sages. The description of the sage is often idealised and their biographies are narrated in a similar fashion. Nasr describes three examples: Ibn Sīnā (d. 1037), Shihāb al-Dīn Yaḥyā al-Suhrawardī (d. 1191) and Ibn ʿArabī (d. 1240). While these examples were Muslim, Nasr sometimes also refers to figures from ancient Greek stories or Christian traditions. In several works Nasr emphasises the unity of all world religions and, therefore, in order to underscore his ideas, he utilises 'sages' and a terminology from Islam, Hinduism, Christianity and Buddhism to present the idea of a common traditional wisdom present in all world religions.[19]

In Nasr's conceptualisation of history, he emphasises that schools and sages are the driving forces in the history and philosophy of Islamic knowledge and science. He utilises the sages to substantiate his standpoint, selecting them from a collective repertoire of Islamic prototypes. The ideal model for this is obviously Muhammad. In Nasr's view, this method is sanctioned by Islamic traditions. One of Nasr's aims, and the goals of those who share his ideas, is to curate a correct and authentic interpretation of history. This means establishing interpretations of historical and pseudo-historical personalities as prototypes for contemporary Muslims, whose ideas and actions substantiate and legitimate their statements on Islam, the Quran and modern science.

Finally, Nasr also projects his contemporary ideas onto these sages. The usage of the term 'sage' and the interpretation of the function of a sage reveals Nasr's view that sages share characteristic traits with Sufi masters, including the

---

[17] Nasr sometimes describes that which is lost as a traditional science and/or a *scientia sacra*; see Nasr 1993: 1f.

[18] Over the last decades Seyyed Hossein Nasr has influenced scholars, students and people in general concerning Islam. He belongs to a tradition called perennialism in which all religions share metaphysical truths and origin. It is an esoteric tradition critical of modernity and what they consider the loss of traditional knowledge. For an example, see http://sacredweb.com/. A prominent representative of this tradition is Osman Bakar; see Bakar 1998 and 2011. Also influenced by Nasr is Muzaffer Iqbal; see Iqbal 2002.

[19] See, for example, Nasr 1981, 1993.

ability to interpret the sources of Islam correctly. The choice of a sage, and the emphasis on aspects of the ideas of a sage, can vary in time and space. Thus, the interpretations of the ideas of Ibn ʿArabī are an ongoing process. It is a matter of unveiling different aspects of his ideas at different times. In the construction of a uniquely Islamic science, sages and schools are chosen carefully. They are the bonds between (and within) religious traditions. The aim is to form a normative concept of Islamic science and Islamic history in general – a history that continues to be relevant in the present. True knowledge can be grasped through an inner path, not through outward actions. This inner path is manifested in Sufi traditions. A contrasting view is represented by the physicist Abdus Salam and his thinking on the relationship between religion, the Quran and modern science.

ABDUS SALAM – SCIENCE AS UNIVERSAL AND RELIGION AS INSPIRATION

The Pakistani physicist and Nobel Prize laureate Muhammad Abdus Salam (d. 1996), and his compatriot and disciple Pervez Hoodbhoy (b. 1950), also a physicist, took a different approach.[20] According to these two scientists, science cannot be Islamised or, for that matter, Christianised. Science is a universal phenomenon. Yet, in their opinion, Islam is not intrinsically opposed to science. They usually emphasise that they are not against religion as such. Abdus Salam states that general references to the Quran support his views, but like Syed Ahmed Khan, he says that the Quran should not be read as a book of science. The statements of these scientists can be points of departure for criticism of the current situation of science and engineering in Muslim countries or can function as a source of inspiration for developing ideas of a universal ethics in science. He rarely criticises scientific theory and method, like, for example, creationists who explicitly criticise the theory of evolution.

Abdus Salam's and his followers position differ from that which persistently rejects Darwinism and the theory of evolution in favour of the Islamic narrative of creation. In his *Ideals and Realities: Selected Essays of Abdus Salam* (1987), which Abdus Salam wrote more or less in response to Seyyed Hossein Nasr's book *Ideals and Realities of Islam* (1966), some essays deal with Islam and science. Although Abdus Salam's position is not the same as that held by Muslim creationists, he explicitly states that Maurice Bucaille (see below) is correct in his remark that the Quranic verses on natural phenomena do not contradict what we know with certainty from discoveries in science.[21]

---

[20] Hoodbhoy 1991 is often referred to in studies on the discourse on Islam and modern science. Pervez Hoodbhoy is still active in the discourse and the discussion on the status of modern science in Muslim-majority countries, especially in his home country of Pakistan.

[21] The statements in this text attributed to Abdus Salam are from Salam 1987.

Abdus Salam outlines a number of steps to develop science education in Muslim countries. These steps are primarily concerned with education, organisation and funding. Yet, parts of Abdus Salam's *Ideals and Realities* concerning the implementation of the steps of how to acquire technology, are full of references to Islamic terminology (predominately terms drawn from the Quran and hadith) and to events in the idealised time of Muhammad. From a confessional perspective, Islamic terminology is understood as a reservoir of timeless terms that can be interpreted in multiple ways, and that represent an Islamic essence. In early Muslim history, Abdus Salam says, the use of *khandaq*, a word referring to ditches or trenches, specifically those built in preparation for a battle, shows that Muhammad himself was eager to use the latest technology of defence. Yet Abdus Salam does not use the reference to the Quran and the historiography of the early period to form the foundation for a specific Islamic science; rather, the references serve as a criticism of today's science policies. On the one hand, the governments of Muslim countries have failed to fill a supposed Quranic imperative, and, on the other hand, Abdus Salam's ideas could serve as the foundation for a strategy to legitimate the development of science and technology.

The ideas of Abdus Salam, and scientific worldviews in general, have not taken root in Muslim countries, according to his follower Pervez Hoodbhoy. His statement is referring to more popular understandings of the relationship between Islam and nature, and the scientific interpretations and miracles ascribed to the Quran, as well as the different academic projects to Islamise modern science.[22]

Popular Perspective on Science and the Quran – Dissemination of an Islamic Creationism

Many popular emic texts discussing modern science and Islam present the presumed scientific miracles of the Quran.[23] They aim to show that Islam is the final and absolute truth and sometimes reproduce examples similar to the ones given in a widely printed booklet published in the early 2000s entitled *A Brief Illustrated Guide to Understanding Islam* (printed in more

---

[22] See http://churchandstate.org.uk/2017/08/science-refuses-to-take-root-in-muslim-countries-dr-pervez -hoodbhoy/.

[23] In this paper I will use the terms 'Islamic creationism' or 'creationism' to describe what in Islamic terminology is described as *tafsir 'ilmī* and *i'jāz 'ilmī*. The Islamic terms are often used interchangeably. The former is a more popular one while the latter is used by Muslim scholars. For the historic origin of *i'jāz 'ilmī* and the scientific exegesis and eisegesis, see Daneshgar 2017 and a special issue of *Journal of Qur'anic Studies*, vol. 21, issue 3, 2019, devoted to modern science and approaches to Quranic hermeneutics.

than 800,000 copies).[24] This booklet illustrates a popular genre of Islam and modern science.[25]

This guide investigates Quranic suras and aims to explain (and translate) them in light of modern science. For instance, 23:12–14 is translated: 'We created man from an extract of clay. Then we made him as a drop in place of settlement, firmly fixed. Then we made the drop into an *alaqah* (leech/suspended thing/blood clot), then we made the *alaqah* into a *mudghah* (chewed-like substance) . . . .'[26] These verses are seen as expressions of a form of development in the process of creation. Therefore, the human embryo is understood as in an *'alaqa* stage. According to the author of the booklet, all three meanings of the word *'alaqa*, that is, 'leech', 'suspended thing' and 'blood clot' correspond accurately to the usual descriptions made (in medical textbooks) of the embryo at this early stage. The textbooks referred to here are primarily those by Keith L. Moore (d. 2019), professor in embryology at the University of Toronto, who spent time in Saudi Arabia in the early 1980s supporting a Saudi committee on embryology, comparing Islamic sources with current knowledge in the field of embryology. He collaborated in publishing texts on human development and the Quran and *Sunna* with the Yemeni-Saudi scholar and politician Abdul Majeed al-Zindani.[27]

Another example in the booklet is a statement on the construction of mountains, and the correspondence between modern geology and the Quranic text. Quran 78:6–7 says: 'Have we not made the earth as a bed, and the mountains as pegs?' And 16:15 says: 'And he has set firm mountains in the earth so that it would not shake with you . . .' These translations of the text are compared with academic textbooks saying that mountains have underlying roots. Hence, the author of the booklet states that modern science confirms the Quranic statement that mountains have a shape like a peg.

There are many other, similar, examples from the fields of anatomy, astronomy, biology and physiology.

Like other contributions to the genre, the booklet, printed on glossy paper,

---

[24] Golden 2002. This booklet was published by DarusSalam Publications, based in Riyadh, Saudi Arabia, with branches in a number of Muslim-majority countries, but also the United States, the United Kingdom and France. The booklet has been published in numerous languages with the objective, according to the publisher, to spread authentic Islam of a high standard, as it is explained by recognised Muslim scholars. The booklet is widely available and can be found at airports, mosques, museums and Islamic bookshops and is usually given away free.

[25] For other examples of the same emic genre, see more recent publications by Faisal Fahim, Gabriel Iqbal, Zakir Naik and Ibrahim Rather.

[26] The English translation of these verses can be compared to other translations of the Quran, many of which are available online. Some translations are closer to a scientific language, while others more closely reflect the Arabic of the Quran. See, for example, https://quran.com.

[27] See al-Zindani *et al.* 1994; Moore and al-Zindani 1982. For an introduction to al-Zindani and his many publications in Arabic, see Rahman and Razzak 2014. On al-Zindani's view on embryonic development and scientific miracles in the Quran, see Guénon 2019.

is full of pictures, figures and footnotes to underline the scientific character of the statements.[28] The footnotes refer readers to the statements of well-known scholars in the United States and western Europe on the similarity between the Quranic text and modern science. These scholars made some of these statements after participating in lavishly organised conferences that may well have impaired their ability or willingness to provide objective replies to their hosts, who asked questions about the similarities between the Quran and science.[29] Note too that the translations of the Quranic verses seem to be guided by discoveries in modern science. That is, irrespective of school or tradition, Sufi or Salafi, findings in science guide interpretations and translations of the Quran.

In this genre of literature, claims about the Islam, Quran and scientific writings produced by non-Muslims are also invoked to strengthen arguments. The statements attributed to Albert Einstein on the close and positive relationship between religion and science are one example. Another is when the truth of the final revelation, the authentic word of God, is 'proved' by the help of findings by non-Muslim and contemporary scientists.

The form of popular Islamic creationism presented above has been criticised by several Muslim scientists. They are formally trained in disciplines of natural sciences or medicine and through presentations of history and interpretation of Islam they present a harmonious relationship between Islam and modern science. One person who adopts this position is Nidhal Guessoum.

Nidhal Guessoum: a Scientist's View on the Harmony of Religion and Modern Science

During recent years, many Muslim scholars have discussed Islam and modern science, from a background in the natural sciences, medicine and engineering.[30] Most of them have no training in Islamic studies from a confessional or non-confessional perspective. Nidhal Guessoum is one example of this group of scholars. He is a professor of Physics and Astronomy at the American University in Sharjah.[31] In his book *Islam's Quantum Question: Reconciling Muslim Tradition*

---

[28] The booklet is part of a print culture that is very visible in publications connected to persons like Adnan Oktar, known under his pen name Harun Yahya. For a presentation of Harun Yahya, see Hameed 2014 and Ross Solberg 2013.

[29] See Golden 2002 for brief discussions with participating scholars and descriptions about the conferences organised in Saudi Arabia.

[30] It has been discussed whether more recent contributors in the contemporary discourse on Islam and modern science should be defined as a 'second generation' compared to an earlier generation, e.g. Nasr and Rahman; see Bigliardi 2014a, 2014c. After the initial discussion the idea has been revised and refined; see https://social-epistemology.com/2014/05/15/on-harmonizing-islam-and-science-a-response-to-edis-and-a-self-criticism-stefano-bigliardi/.

[31] Nidhal Guessoum received a PhD in Astrophysics from the University of California, San Diego in 1988.

and Modern Science (2011), he discusses the relationship between Islam and modern science, relying on Islamic and non-Islamic conceptions of philosophy and epistemology.[32] Guessoum makes a critical overview of interventions in the discourse by Abdus Salam, al-Faruqi, Nasr, Ziauddin Sardar and Muslim creationists who read science into the Quran. It is clear from the book that Guessoum is a scientist and he is critical of theologians untrained in science disciplines. However, his own limitations in regard to Muslim traditions and history as well as lack of training in the study of history and in Islamic studies, secular or non-secular, become evident in his presentation of a narrow number of Muslim scholars in history. His favourite is Ibn Rushd (d. 1198). Ibn Rushd is described in an idealised manner as a person that, in a Muslim context, can be a model for scientist and science in contemporary times.[33] This history of Islam is centred on a few selected persons of Andalusian and Arab origin, and the references to Muslims in history between Ibn Rushd and contemporary times are sparse.

Muslims need to recover a synthetic spirit that integrated scientific knowledge in their religion is the way forward, according to Guessoum. Serving this purpose, the historic example, Ibn Rushd, is described with the terminology of contemporary science. In the book, Guessoum engages thoroughly with science and its role in Muslim societies, but less with Islamic theology and theologians. Traditions of interpretations and the hadith are relatively unimportant. Topics discussed for centuries within branches of Islamic theology are at best briefly described. Beyond references to a few medieval models, the most important text appears to be the Quran. Under the heading 'educational and social issues' Guessoum seems to suggest a form of scientism in which modern science and nature should be the guiding principle for the understanding in society of Islam and Islamic theology.[34] In the end, the reconciliation of Muslim traditions and Islam with modern science expressed in the title of the book becomes vague. A key suggestion that Guessoum makes is that the reconciliation depends on how one reads religious texts: literal versus interpretative. A literalist reading of religious texts will make the harmonisation of science and religion problematic.[35]

Since the publication of the above-mentioned book, Nidhal Guessoum has engaged in the promotion of science, science education, and the idea that Islam and science harmonise. Guessoum has continued to discussed the challenges that Muslim scientists embracing science face and how they should engage

---

[32] See Guessoum 2011.
[33] It is apparent from his presentation of the Middle Ages that Guessoum is not trained in the discipline of history. For another and similar example of his way of presenting history, see https://www.youtube.com/watch?v=hFtTI8JHS-Q&t=511s.
[34] See Guessoum 2011.
[35] See Guessoum 2011.

with their religious traditions. That is, to integrate a theistic interpretation of modern science in 'the Islamic worldview' and to tackle challenges from other understandings of Islam, for example, creationism.[36] He has also published a book entitled *The Young Muslim's Guide to Modern Science* (2018). This book is directed to teachers and students to further explain the harmony between contemporary science and Islam. This is a harmonisation between knowledge founded on modern science and religious teaching without either of them being sacrificed. The book is published in several languages, English, Arabic, Malay and Urdu, in order to attract a large readership. The aim is that young Muslims should be able to maintain a Muslim identity while they also embrace modern science. It is more an introduction to the natural sciences than to social sciences or the humanities. It is a plea for an increased scientific literacy in Arab societies and, in a manner similar to his earlier book, he states that neither Muslim scholars in history nor the Quran are against science and scientific thinking. (Interesting that its title mirrors Seyyed Hossein Nasr's book, *A Young Muslim's Guide to the Modern World* (1993).)[37]

Guessoum's ambition to create a positive relationship between Islam and modern science contains, as has been stated above, a strong criticism of the tendency to ascribe the Quran with miraculous scientific content. One of the earlier proponents of this combined eisegesis and exegesis was the French medical doctor Maurice Bucaille and his approach to the Quran.

ISLAMIC CREATIONISM AND ITS ADVOCATES ON SOCIAL MEDIA

The last decades have witnessed the development of information and communication technology. This has also meant the appearance of a number of books, pamphlets, DVDs, CDs, films, YouTube clips, Facebook pages and websites concerned with the relationship between Islam and modern science, as part of an Islamic epistemology.[38] A prominent example of this is 'Islamic creationism', a genre of writing often linked to the French medical doctor, Maurice Bucaille

---

[36] See Guessoum 2015. In a critical overview and discussion of quantitative studies and qualitative studies on Muslim perceptions on evolutionary science and the theory of revolution it is stated that most existing studies have shortcomings. The most serious one is that the understanding among Muslims of evolution is founded on Islam in an essentialised form. The different contexts, diversity and socio-political environments in many Muslim-majority countries are not always taken into consideration, nor how these differences may affect the result of the research; see Carlisle *et al.* 2019.

[37] There are several books addressing young Muslims with the aim of guiding them in the modern world. As can be seen from examples above, they are published by different individuals with sometimes different interests and representing different interpretations of Islam. For another example, see Ghobash 2018.

[38] For a study that discusses online videos on Islam and science, especially contributions by Zakir Naik and how his videos clips are used, see Gardner *et al.* 2018. For a discussion on methodology studying videos online about natural sciences and Islam, see Gardner and Hameed 2017. For a video portal on Islam and science, see https://sites.hampshire.edu/scienceandislamvideoportal/.

(d. 1998), and his life story, as well as his statement that the Quran conforms with modern science.[39] Bucaille's book *The Bible, the Qur'an and Science: The Holy Scriptures Examined in the Light of Modern Knowledge* (1976) has become a classic in this genre.

A central point in Bucaille's book is that there is a conformity between the Quran and modern science and that the Quran mentions many scientific facts that have only been recently discovered. The Quran cannot be explained, according to Bucaille, if we assume that the text has a human origin. Bucaille's book has become a foundation for a position that is seen as an Islamic creationism sometimes called 'Bucaillism'. Bucaille often states that the Bible does not meet the rigorous standards of modern science. The Quran, on the other hand, does not comprise a single statement that is inconsistent with the established modern knowledge.

The Islamic creationism that has developed from the assertions of Bucaille has a presence on social media such as YouTube. For instance, Muslim scholars such as Yusuf Estes, Zakir Naik and Hamza Yusuf have all promoted their own conceptualisations of the relationship between Islam and modern science. Yusuf Estes' description of the life of Bucaille and his study of Egyptian mummies mirrors Zakir Naik's discussion on the Quran and modern science. Both Estes and Naik focus on the creation of the universe and arrive at the conclusion that the Quran is the word of God and the final revelation. Estes and Naik emphasise that the Quran stands the test of time and that it is, in the words of Zakir Naik 'the miracle of miracles'.[40] Estes and Naik state that the Quran gives humans signs. It is not a book of science in a direct sense, but as the word of God, the signs are still applicable in today's world. Although Naik practised medicine before becoming a Muslim preacher, and is aware of the history of ideas in science, his presentations are centred on the Quran as an eternal truth. He mixes references to the Quran with statements on science and the history of modern science.

Hamza Yusuf is rather different from Estes and Naik. He has maintained

---

[39] For discussions on Islamic creationism, see Hameed 2014; Riexinger 2008; Sayin and Kence 1999. On Maurice Bucaille, see Bigliardi 2012; Stenberg 1996: 217–62. See also the website dedicated to his legacy, http://bucaillelegacy.com/. For example, a film from 2010 entitled *Maurice & the Pharaoh* is based on the ideas of Bucaille, particularly his notions on the legacy of the Pharaohs of Egypt: https://www.youtube.com/watch?v=8Elan6Qplhc.

[40] On Yusuf Estes, see https://www.youtube.com/watch?v=mauWfnsWFR4. For Zakir Naik's argument, see https://www.youtube.com/watch?v=Oqa_ucuARn8. Among Muslims, the opinions of Estes and Naik are controversial. This is true not so much for their views on Islam and modern science, but more specifically on women, conversion, Islam and politics, terrorism, the criticism of other religions, and sharia. When Zakir Naik was accused by the Indian government of inspiring terrorism, he escaped to Malaysia. He was denied visas to the United Kingdom and Canada and today he is believed to live in Saudi Arabia. Talks by the three Muslim preachers Yusuf Estes, Zakir Naik and Ahmad Deedat (d. 2005) can be found on the Peace TV Network, see http://www.peacetv.tv/. For studies of their standpoints, see Mustapha and Abdul Razak 2019; Gardner *et al.* 2018; Bruk 2015.

that humans cannot understand God and therefore it is very difficult to make any statements on the creation of the universe.[41] He adds that the Big Bang did not occur *ex nihilo* and we do not know what existed at the time of the Big Bang. Ultimately, he is cautious of connecting the Quran to modern science, especially since the nature of science is its change.[42] Nevertheless, the fact that Hamza Yusuf makes these statements indicates that religious scholars feel a need to address matters concerning the creation of the universe, the laws of nature, and consequences of modern science, education and human knowledge in order to remain relevant.

The discussions of Naik, Yusuf and Estes on these topics mirror questions discussed by ordinary contemporary Muslims. These questions may be especially acute for Muslim minorities in Europe and America. This challenge can be observed in childrens' books published by the Islamic Foundation in Leicester, UK. Since the middle of the 1990s, the Foundation has published books dealing with nature and how to comprehend modern science. The aim appears to be to make sense of modern knowledge in relation to the Islamic story of creation. Moreover, they explain the truth about nature and provide children with a divine cosmology in a non-Islamic environment.[43] One reason for a socio-theological interest in modern science is that 'science' poses a very serious challenge to those who would like to see their religion as an all-encompassing order and the eternal truth. Other reasons may relate to strengthening the faith and identity of the minority community, emphasising that the Quran is the word of God, and explaining the implications of such a statement in daily life. The publication of books for children by the Islamic Foundation in the United Kingdom is also an example of how the discourse on Islam and modern science takes root in the pedagogical ambitions of British Muslims and how it becomes part of a media production within an Islamic institution.

---

[41] Hamza Yusuf's educational background is different from that of Yusuf Estes and Zakir Naik; he spent a number of years studying Islam in the United Kingdom, the United Arab Emirates and North Africa. Also, unlike Estes and Naik, he has a connection to Sufi traditions.

[42] See https://www.youtube.com/watch?v=ih5m2jo-AyY. Notably, all three persons referred to above, Yusuf Estes, Zakir Naik and Hamza Yusuf, have all experienced turning points in their lives, either through conversion or through personal decisions (e.g. Naik chose to leave medicine and become a preacher).

[43] See Janson 2003. For the idea of studying Islamic creationism beyond epistemologies of Islam and evolution or modern science, and that of studying notions among Muslims through the lens of migration, see Hameed 2014.

THE INSTITUTIONALISATION OF THE DISCOURSE ON
ISLAM AND MODERN SCIENCE

Educational programmes have been established to study Islam and modern science at, for example, the International University in Malaysia.[44] Curricula incorporate recent developments in contemporary science such as discussions about artificial intelligence, Islamic bioethics and biomedical ethics.[45] Efforts have also been made to integrate Islamic perspectives into various scientific disciplines, as well as the humanities and social sciences. In addition, there have also been several conferences organised to further discuss Islam and science. One example of the latter is the task force on Islam and science that was set up by the Islamic World Academy of Sciences. This organisation advises the Organisation of the Islamic Conference (OIC) and the two patrons are HRH Prince Hassan bin Talal of Jordan and the President of the Islamic Republic of Pakistan.[46]

Thus, we can stress that the discourse on Islam and modern science is not an epistemological island. It is linked to a broader discussion about other topics of public concern for Muslims and their co-citizens, such as the relationship between individual and collective identity, the role of religion in contemporary society, power and claims about the authentic Islam. In parallel to the various forms of statements and publications on the true relationship between Islam and modern science a number of specifically Islamic academies, institutes, schools and universities have been established.[47] Their ambition is to create a curriculum that incorporates what are defined as Islamic values with modern branches of learning, such as chemistry, physics and the social sciences.[48] Today, many universities in this category seek to integrate an idea of knowledge founded on Islam with modern academic disciplines.[49]

---

[44] See, for example, Dangor 2005 for the idea of Islamising disciplines and creating an indigenous educational system.

[45] See Ghaly (ed.) 2016.

[46] The task force produced a report in 2016 entitled *Muslim Responses to Science's Big Questions*; see https://www.iasworld.org/wp-content/uploads/2016/05/Task-Force-on-Islam-and-Science.pdf.

[47] The context and quality of science and scientists in the Middle East and Muslim-majority countries has been discussed for decades. A recent publication is a special issue of *Sociology of Islam* (2020, vol. 8, no. 2) on science and science production in the Middle East, edited by Ayman Shabana, The Center for International and Regional Studies at the Georgetown University Qatar.

[48] For one example, see the proceedings from a conference in Malaysia in 2016 discussing the integration of an Islamic perspective in education: https://www.researchgate.net/publication/329895788_E-PROCEEDING_OF_THE_3RD_WORLD_CONFERENCE_ON_INTEGRATION_OF_KNOWLEDGE_2016_E-PROCEEDING_OF_THE_3RD_WORLD_CONFERENCE_INTEGRATION_OF_THE_ISLAMIC_PERSPECTIVE_INTO_SCIENCE_SUBJECT_IN_MATRICULATION_CENTER_I.

[49] For example, Umm al-Qura University in Mecca; the International Islamic University in Islamabad, Pakistan; and the International Islamic University in Kuala Lumpur, Malaysia. The home pages of the three universities are: http://uqu.edu.sa/, http://www.iiu.edu.pk/, and http://www.iium.edu.my. For a study of the three universities with similar goals, see Bano and Sakurai (eds) 2015.

By contrast, in Muslim-minority contexts, Islamic educational institutions are not primarily large universities, but smaller institutes or universities offering students a limited number of programmes and courses.[50] Certainly, there are differences in terms of resources between full-scale universities in Muslim-majority countries and resource-poor institutes in western Europe. In North America and in Europe, the focus tends to be more on Islamic theology and practice than on natural sciences and technology. However, independent of location and links to specific traditions of interpretation, there is a common epistemology in these institutions. Shared premises are founded on the belief in transcendental values, the unity of God and humans, and the teleological purpose of knowledge. Five examples of institutes with limited economic and scientific or disciplinary resources are the International Institute of Islamic Thought (IIIT), Fairfax Institute, and Zaytuna College in the United States; the Cambridge Muslim College in the United Kingdom; and the Islamic University of Applied Sciences in the Netherlands.[51] Furthermore, these smaller institutes or universities often have a significant presence online. Independent of their majority or minority context, each of these institutions is usually connected to a particular interpretation and practice of Islam. In their understanding of Islam, the universities or institutes may be founded on Wahhabi or Salafi traditions, the Gülen movement, Sufi traditions, or the idea that Islam in a philiosphical sense is essential for the overall progress of humans and societies.

Though different, universities in Muslim countries and European and North American institutes have been inspired to a certain extent by ideas formulated by Muslim intellectuals in the discourse that has been charted above.[52] Among these are, in alphabetical order, Taha Jabir al-Alwani, Sayed Muhammad Naquib al-Attas, Maurice Bucaille, Ismail al-Faruqi, Mehdi Golshani, Nidhal Guessoum, Waqar Ahmad Husseini, Zaghloul El Naggar, Seyyed Hossein Nasr, Fazlur Rahman, Muhammad Abdus Salam, Ziauddin Sardar and Harun

---

[50] There are exceptions to this statement. For example, in the Indian context, more large-scale universities have been established, including the above-mentioned Aligarh University, as well as Jamia Millia Islamia, Jamia Hamdard, and the Islamic University of Science and Technology. For an analysis comparing evolution in biology textbooks in five Muslim-majority countries, see Asghar et al. 2014.

[51] The number of institutes in Europe and the United States is substantial. The websites give more information on their respective programmes: see http://www.iiit.org/, http://www.thefairfaxinstitute. org/, https://zaytuna.edu/, http://www.cambridgemuslimcollege.org/, and http://www.islamicuniversity. nl/. The Dutch state authorities accredited the masters' programme at the Islamic University in the Netherlands in 2010, and in 2015 Zaytuna College became the first accredited Muslim college in the United States. The bachelors' degree in Islamic studies offered by Cambridge Muslim College is awarded by the Open University in the United Kingdom.

[52] These figures are all men, and some belong to specific schools of thought. They are not just 'Muslims' representing views on Islam, the Quran and modern science, in fact, they sometimes hold diametrically opposing views. Disagreements are usually based on differences in interpretations of Islam, in combination with personal animosity.

Yahya.[53] (I cannot discuss all of these here.) Some of them have acted as educational advisors to organisations such as the Islamic World Academy of Sciences, governments and private institutes in Muslim countries, and to institutions of Islamic learning in western Europe and the United States.

We can study the connections between Islam, the Quran and modern science from a variety of perspectives and disciplines.[54] My own interest in relation to modern science and Islam primarily concerns the process in which the term 'Islam' and truth claims made in the name of the religion are conceptualised. In my perspective, the comprehension and conceptualisations of epistemological principles are key questions in attempts to create new ideas concerning the meaning and significance of what is termed 'Islam'. For example, the study of conceptualisations reveals the often mundane political or ideological foundation for statements on what Islam is. In other words, today's ideas on modern science and Islam are central elements in an ongoing process of Islam-making. Contemporary ideas on the relationship between Islam and modern science are linked to the development of new possibilities in global communication and exchange. Indeed, the current discourse on Islam, the Quran and modern science thrives on globalisation and new social media.[55]

THE DISCOURSE AND ITS CONTEXT FROM AN ISLAMIC STUDIES PERSPECTIVE

In a similar manner to how the positions and topics have developed in the discourse, the study of Islam, Muslims, evolution, knowledge and modern science has moved forward. Over the years, *Zygon: Journal of Religion and Science* and *Social Epistemology: A Journal of Culture and Policy* have been important; they have paid close attention to the discourse, publishing a number of articles and comments on Islam and science. Hence, the December 2020 issue of *Zygon* contains a section with five articles entitled 'Islam and Science in the Future'. Scholarship about the discourse is also broadening, with discussion space science, science fiction and astrobiology, as well as new ways of contextualising the discourse, such as migration.[56]

A first point discussing the discourse on Islam, Muslims, the Quran and modern science suggests that it can provide a Muslim scientist with an ethical

---

[53] For a discussion on the ideas of Harun Yahya, see Bigliardi 2014b; Ross Solberg 2013; Riexinger 2002. Notably, the discourse is dominated by male voices. The exception in this presentation is the Palestinian-Jordanian biologist Rana Dajani; see Dajani 2018.

[54] It should also be noted that the discourse is not unique to Muslims. Hence, in a Christian, Jewish or Hindu context one can find a number of individuals, institutes and universities that endeavour to create a connection between religion and modern science, and to some extent, to scientific epistemology.

[55] See Stenberg 2004.

[56] Two scholars that have developed the questions and broaden the discussion are Salman Hameed (see the articles referred in the bibliography) and Determann 2018 and 2021.

framework for his or her work, and a framework in dealing with modern technology. The values and norms attributed to Islam give the scientist a platform – an 'Islamic' consciousness – in which to use scientific results and technology. It can also make science indigenous in the sense that what are allegedly Islamic values guide research and the application of science. An idealised past can be an important tool in education and a means of strengthening a cultural heritage. It can also serve as a criticism of values and histories that are supposedly foreign, and assumed to be threatening to a local and Islamic culture. In both cases, history as well as education are fields of contestation in the current discourse.

Besides the criticism of Darwinism and the theory of evolution, another general topic in the current discourse concerns the control of interpretation. Many of the participants in the discourse on Islam, the Quran and modern science are not formally educated religious scholars. They are lay people and, in many ways, anti-clerical. To allow individuals to perform *ijtihād* ('reinterpretation') is important to most of these participants, but they still desire some restrictions. All these participants strive to appropriate the meaning of words such as *'ilm*, *ma'rifa*, *ḥikma* and *'aql*, that is, an Islamic terminology. The general trend is to refer directly to the Quran in search of solutions to perceived problems. The traditions of Muhammad (hadith and *Sunna*) and the interpretations made by the *'ulamā* (religious scholars) are referred to less frequently. In the early phases of the discourse, in the 1970s, 1980s and the 1990s, it was common to rhetorically describe the *'ulamā* as unable to deal with modern problems and they were not recognised as legitimate authorities. The *'ulamā* are, with some exceptions, still stereotyped as a negative and closed force in Muslim societies. However, there are formally trained religious scholars who are competent and trained in modern social sciences. Paradoxically, participants in the discourse desire a single principal religious authority, one who can make universally accepted judgements about 'Islam', even though such an authority would reduce their own ability to make claims on what is Islamic or not. Hence, history is used, perhaps selectively and intentionally, to underline the presence of multiple different interpretations of Islam and the ongoing search among practising Muslims for the eternal, objective, and inimitable Islam.

While formal religious scholars are often criticised by the Muslim intellectuals who shape the discourse, many recent contributors are academics in the sciences, medicine, natural sciences and engineering. They are not in confessional or non-confessional Islamic studies. They are not trained in the history of Islam or the interpretative traditions, nor are they educated in philosophy, history and the history of sciences, or informed about thinking in contemporary Islamic and religious studies. However, formal religious scholars and more recent contributors to the discourse do share the notion that the word of God is manifested in the Quran and Islam is the true revelation.

A common trend among these recent contributions involves focusing on the Quran and a selection of Muslims who are presented as scientists, and comparing their findings with more recent scientific inventions. In a way, they discuss the Quran in a circular and narrow sense, in which the Quran becomes Islam and Islam becomes the Quran, and figures from history are presented uncritically in order to legitimate the author's understanding of the Quran. 'Religion' becomes a single text, in this case the Quran, rather than a variety of texts, traditions, interpretations and practices. The aim here is not so much to achieve a science or production of knowledge guided in theory, method and ethics by Islam, but to reconcile Islam, primarily the Quran, with modern science.

The general impact of this discourse is difficult to judge. Umm al-Qura University in Saudi Arabia and the international Islamic universities in Pakistan and Malaysia are examples of Islamic universities established since the 1970s. As in the case of the Islamic University in Islamabad, their general objectives are to educate people who are imbued with Islamic ideology and who are 'capable to cater (sic) to the economic, social, political, technological and intellectual needs of the Muslim Ummah'.[57] Other aims include leading Muslims in various branches of knowledge, integrating Islamic values and worldview into their curricula, and creating students with a good character and morals in line with Islamic teachings.[58] The aims of the Pakistani and Indonesian universities are similar to most other Islamic universities. In practice, these objectives have been the foundation for the planning of the educational structure at Islamic learning institutions. The number of students at these universities, schools and institutes can be counted in the millions. Based on statistics in Saudi Arabia from 2000, Eleanor Doumato suggested that one-quarter of all university students in Saudi Arabia were studying at Islamic universities.[59] Organisations like the IIIT have been able – through liaison offices and cooperation with, for example, the Islamic Foundation – to distribute their books all over the world. Bucaille's *The Bible, the Qur'an and Science* has been printed in numerous languages and possibly in more than one million copies.

Yet the large number of texts and educational institutions are just indications of the importance of the discourse to Muslims in general. A person can attend a university or an institute for many reasons, not necessarily because he or she shares the ideological foundation of that particular university. To support the Islamisation of science or to claim that the Quran and modern science are compatible can be a politically correct statement in certain Muslim contexts and beneficial to an individual's career. It can qualify an individual for an

---

[57] See https://www.iiu.edu.pk/?page_id=11941.
[58] http://www.iium.edu.my/page/about-iium.
[59] Doumato 2003.

academic position at an Islamic university in a situation in which the failures of the national educational programmes are obvious, and the role of secular intellectuals are questioned.[60] Supporting the compatibility of Islam, the Quran and modern science can be part of a Muslim identity that copes with the challenge of modern science. Notably, the focus in higher education on medicine, engineering and the sciences in many Muslim-majority countries, in conjunction with shifts in economic opportunities for young Muslims at universities, can explain, in part, why university graduates are overrepresented in Islamist and jihadi groups.[61]

A state can establish and support Islamic universities not because the officials of the state want to promote the Islamisation of science or reconcile the Quran with modern science, but to reduce criticism from opposition groups for being un-Islamic. In a sense, the state strengthens its position by incorporating ideas from the opposition. Additionally, it seems that states like Malaysia, Indonesia, Pakistan and Iran, for example, take a pragmatic stance towards the discourse on Islam, the Quran and modern science. They all have Islamic and secular universities providing religious and non-religious education for young and growing populations.

IMPLICATIONS FOR ISLAMIC STUDIES

In the discourse on Islam, the Quran and modern science, the past is a source that can legitimise various views. A selective interpretation of history is an important part of this effort to present an essential Islam that can be defended from 'western' and 'traditionalist' critics alike. The history of the Middle Ages is mined for people who can be depicted as forerunners to later developments in Europe. The specific history and the individuals are selected and interpreted to fit into a discourse; the sources that are chosen, and their interpretation, often reveal a link to a specific tradition in Islam. It is not by chance that Nidhal Guessoum starts his book with a prologue about Ibn Rushd (d. 1198) named 'Averroes and I' or that Seyyed Hossein Nasr refers to al-Suhrawardī (d. 1191) on numerous occasions.

The reference to individuals in history or to a Quranic verse can be understood differently depending on the position of participants within the discourse. Participants strive to appropriate the 'true meaning' of a text or an individual. Indeed, the discourse is apologetic and one of its functions is to create a confidence among Muslims, not least those living in non-Muslim countries.[62] From

---

[60] For the status of academics in Arab countries in general, see Hanafi and Arvanitis 2015.
[61] See Gambetta and Hertog 2016 for the connection between higher education, engineering and the recruitment to jihadi groups.
[62] One example is the Exhibition of 1001 Inventions, which aims to reveal a golden age of Islam and

an analytical perspective, the discourse can also be understood as a search for a religiously based, alternative modernity that avoids the cognitive and social transformations that are usually attached to modernity, especially secularism and an individualistic conception of the self.[63] However, it can also be a form of polemic that provides new converts to Islam with a glorious past and redeploys modern natural sciences to legitimise Islam as the true revelation. Another aim involves creating a single, coherent idea of Islam, though, as this paper shows, the varied evolution of the discourse is itself an example of the multiple and ongoing interpretations of Islam. The discourse is not a critical investigation of the history of ideas, but a confessional discussion about how to make an Islam that is suitable for contemporary consumption and underline its status as an authentic revelation.

In this discourse, figures in recent history are not as present as we might expect. References to Muslim reformists like Riḍā or ʿAbduh are scarce, and so are references to Ali Abdel Razek (d. 1966) and his discussion of social and political science.[64] In the thought of Taha Jabir al-Alwani (d. 2016), for instance, the Muslim modernists of the early twentieth century were never able to solve the issues of their time and form a coherent Islamic alternative to a European modernity. Hence, al-Alwani wanted contemporary Muslim intellectuals to analyse various Muslim reform movements. This presupposes that the reform movements have not solved the predicaments of Muslims in Muslim countries. The key to success, according to al-Alwani, lies in the involvement of the intellectuals in the process, for example in interpreting the Quran, but also in breaking away from countries like Egypt or Saudi Arabia and establishing centres and institutes in western Europe and North America, institutions not bound by interpretative legacies and controlled by authoritarian states.[65]

In Islamic studies, questions of power concerning agency and interpretation play a significant role, as do etic or emic conceptualisations of Islam. In seeing Islam as a social phenomenon, confessional struggles about how to interpret and practice should be of scholarly interest. In this context, the term 'interpretation' represents the various processes in which a specific understanding of Islam is produced and how those interpretations are maintained and justified and sometimes translated into religious practices or more general notions of 'Islam'.

The discourse on Islam, the Quran and modern science provides important data for the field of Islamic studies. It displays how constructions of theology and

---

inspire Muslims for a better future. See https://www.1001inventions.com/. See also Brentjes *et al.* (eds) 2016, for criticisms of the Exhibition of 1001 Inventions and its presentation of the history of science.

[63] On alternative modernities, see the discussions in Gaonkar (ed.) 2001.

[64] See Abdel Razek 2012.

[65] See al-Alwani 1991, 1993. The idea to involve religious scholars, scientists and intellectuals in the interpretation of Islam is also proposed by Rana Dajani.

everyday realities structure understandings of Islam and how they are linked to political considerations, personal interests and local environments, and are not only formed in reference to a static and abstract theology. It exemplifies how the term 'Islam' becomes a subject in the sentence and is given agency. Muslims are given agency in the discourse when they are perceived as of the wrong opinion about Islam. If our interest in the discourse were to be on statements by Muslims (and not a search for the one and authentic Islam) it would reveal the many and different interpretations of the religion, and make the idea of a reconciliation of 'Islam' and contemporary 'science' problematic. From an Islamic studies point of view, the discourse reveals a dynamic, fluid and discursive Islam. For scholars in Islamic studies, one challenge is to study and analyse the process of Islam-making in this discourse, and comprehend if there are diachronic and synchronic patterns that can be revealed and allow analytical understandings of continuity and change.

Islamic terminology is a particularly important tool in the construction of a persuasive discourse. These terms are invoked in the discourse to find their 'true', objective, sacred and eternal meaning. The individuals in the discourse all use a form of realism in the philosophical sense of the term. Furthermore, they work with a teleological perspective and therefore there is a need to find the objective and eternal meaning of the Islamic terminology. Hence, all participants strive to appropriate the vocabulary of the Quran. But a significant feature of the discourse of Islam and science is the *reinterpretation* of the Quran's vocabulary through the influence of modern science. Consequently, if the true meaning of the Quranic terminology is established this will provide humanity with a deepened knowledge of God's creation. According to this understanding, modern science can also develop an understanding of Islam and, through the lens of modern science and the Quran, Muslims can understand nature. Earlier interpretations of the Quran are seen in terms of how they related to knowledge at a certain historical moment, and if Islam is understood as all-encompassing, modern science is a vehicle for new understandings that can lead humans closer to the eternal and authentic meaning of the divine revelation. In this perspective, God is still active in creation, and the observation of creation can lead the observer closer to God.

But an additional motivation for the employment of Islamic terminology involves evoking 'Islamic feelings', to call on common associations and collective memories to persuade Muslims to support a particular form of Islamic science. In this context, words and phrases from the sacred sources function as a link between an exponent of a specific position and groups of more loosely attached followers, mobilising the latter's support. Although the participants are affiliated with different traditions of Islam and adhere to a variety of ideological strands, they all share this presupposition concerning the significance of Islamic terminology.

Islamic terms are not the only terms whose meaning is contested in this discourse; 'the West', 'science' and 'knowledge' are also contested. The latter terms are also interpreted, given meaning, and are appropriated to strengthen a certain position on the relationship between Islam, the Quran and modern science. Thus, the terms 'science' and 'knowledge' are employed differently depending on context. If they describe Muslim scholars in medieval times, they are positive qualities, compared to descriptions of modern 'science' originating in Europe. The term 'the West' is utilised in a cognitive, geographic and political manner. Cognitive in the sense that it is a negative symbol. Geographic in that it points towards Europe and North America (even if the precise geographic location of 'the West' is unclear). From a political perspective, the term is understood negatively, and is founded on the notion that 'the West' seeks to dominate 'Islam'. However, as in many other cases, 'the West' is rarely defined. The point is to create a binary, where 'the West' and 'Islam' clarify the boundaries between evil and good.[66]

Finally, the discourse on Islam, the Quran and modern science is an example of how discussion, primarily among Muslims, develops and changes. The earlier attempts by Seyyed Hossein Nasr, Ismail al-Faruqi and Syed Muhammad Naquib al-Attas to formulate ideas about how to Islamise certain academic disciplines, science and understandings of knowledge are no longer in the forefront. The discourse has shifted in character and is now in the hands of new people, such as Nidhal Guessoum and Mehdi Golshani, who are trained in the sciences. It has also been popularised through figures like Hamza Yusuf and Zakir Naik, not least on social media. Today the focus is on a reconciliation between Islam in the form of the Quran, and to gain control of a lost social sphere, modern science.

CONCLUSIONS AND SUGGESTIONS

In conclusion, I would like to suggest a number of ways forward for the study of the discourse of Islam, Muslims, the Quran and contemporary science.

For scholars of Islam and science, one way forward may be to broaden the discussion on the varying significance of the discourse for Muslims in majority and minority contexts, rather than the current focus on Arab countries and the Middle East. Linked to this suggestion is also to pay more attention to the process of Islam-making with the aim to identify agency and interests concerning the relationship between Islam and contemporary science as well as the role of non-Muslims in forming views about the true relationship between Islam and science.

The discourse is linked to wider political ambitions and questions concerning gender, morality, migration, artistic expressions and radicalisation. The gender

---

[66] Also, see the discussion on 'Islam' and 'the West' in the Introduction of this book.

aspect, in particular, deserves more study, especially concerning the reception and redeployment of the discourse among women. Very few female Muslim scholars have touched on the topic of Islam and science in a broader understanding. The molecular biologist Rana Dajani is a scientist who discusses Islam and science and is an advocate of the biological evolution theory, but there are not many like her. Two earlier examples are the British convert Merryl Wyn Davies (d. 2021) and her ideas on an Islamic anthropology, and Mona Abul-Fadl (d. 2008) and her thinking about an Islamic social sciences in relation to 'western' thought built on Ismail al-Faruqi's ideas. The high number of female students in science disciplines in Muslim-majority countries may change the gender balance in the discourse in the future. However, a predicament to overcome is the male dominance in roles concerned with the interpretation and practice of Islam. A topic to study would be to analayse how female students, who are in the majority at universities in Muslim-majority contexts, understand the relationship between Islam and science, and if an involvement in the discussion by younger female scholars can open up for new developments concerning gender-related questions.

Scholars studying the discourse also need to pay more attention to the fluidity of Islam and its many interpretations and practices, and scrutinise the opposing conceptualisations of the term 'Islam' in the Islam and contemporary science discourse. The idea of one 'Islam' seems to sometimes join scholars studying the discourse and the individuals acting in it. But this is a case of scholars reproducing the emic terminology of their subjects, without recognising that this terminology is highly contested as well as being situated in specific contexts and serving specific interests. Also, the tendency to use a selected set of role models and the usage of history deserves more attention, as well as the neglect of theology and traditions of interpretations and practice in favour of a strong focus on the Quran.

Many scholars of the discourse also articulate their own position on the ideal relationship between Islam and modern science. They could be understood and studied as a form of activist and engaged scholars. The study of the discourse would benefit from a clearer distinction between those who propose something in regard to the relationship between Islam and science and those who study those proposals, that is, those who participate in the discourse and those who study it. The term 'science' is mostly conceptualised as natural sciences, and rarely social sciences and humanities (or new fields that bridge the perceived gap between the two, like Digital Humanities).

A final point concerns the reception. Few studies discuss the reception of this discourse among larger populations. From a scholarly point of view, it is a problem there is so little study of the *reception* of the discourse on Islam and modern science across several countries.

Bibliography

Abaza, Mona (2002), *Debates on Islam and Knowledge in Malaysia and Egypt: Shifting Worlds*, London: RoutledgeCurzon.

Abdel Razek, Ali (2012), *Islam and the Foundations of Political Power*, ed. Abdou Filali-Ansary, trans. Maryam Loutfi, Edinburgh: Edinburgh University Press/Aga Khan University-ISMC.

al-Alwani, Jabir Taha (1991), 'Taqlid and Ijtihad', *American Journal of Islamic Social Sciences* 8, no. 1: 129–42.

al-Alwani, Jabir Taha (1993), 'The Crisis of Thought and Ijtihad', *American Journal of Islamic Social Sciences* 10, no. 2: 234–7.

Asghar, Anila, Salman Hameed and Najme Kishani Farahani (2014), 'Evolution in Biology Textbooks: A Comparative Analysis of 5 Muslim Countries', *Religion and Education* 41, no. 1: 1–15.

al-Attas, Syed Muhammad Naquib (1969), *Preliminary Statement on a General Theory of the Islamization of the Malay-Indonesian Archipelago*, Kuala Lumpur: Dewan Bahasa dan Pustaka.

Bakar, Osman (1998), *Classification of Knowledge in Islam*, Cambridge: The Islamic Texts Society.

Bakar, Osman (2011), 'Islamic Science, Modern Science, and Post-Modernity: Towards a New Synthesis through a *Tawhidic* Epistemology', *Revelation and Science* Special Issue 1, no. 3: 13–20.

Bano, Masooda, and Keiko Sakurai (eds) (2015), *Shaping Global Islamic Discourses: The Role of al-Azhar, al-Medina and al-Mustafa*, Edinburgh: Edinburgh University Press.

Bigliardi, Stefano (2012), 'The Strange Case of Dr. Bucaille: Notes for a Re-Examination', *The Muslim World* 102, no. 2: 248–63.

Bigliardi, Stefano (2014a), *Islam and the Quest for Modern Science: Conversations with Adnan Oktar, Mehdi Golshani, M. Basil Altaie, Zaghloul El-Naggar, Bruno Guiderdoni, and Nidhal Guessoum*, Istanbul: Swedish Research Institute in Istanbul.

Bigliardi, Stefano (2014b), 'Who's Afraid of Theoscientography? An Interpretative Hypothesis on Harun Yahya', *Zygon Journal of Religion and Science* 49, no. 1: 66–80.

Bigliardi, Stefano (2014c), 'The Contemporary Debate on the Harmony between Islam and Science: Emergence and Challenges of a New Generation', *Social Epistemology* 28, no 2: 167–86.

Bod, Rens, Jaap Maat and Thijs Weststeijn (eds) (2014), *The Making of the Humanities: Volume III: The Modern Humanities*, Amsterdam: Amsterdam University Press.

Brentjes, Sonja, Taner Edis and Lutz Richter-Bernburg (eds) (2016), *1001 Distortions: How (Not) to Narrate History of Science, Medicine, and Technology in non-Western Cultures*, Würzburg: Ergon Verlag.

Brown, Daniel W. (1999), *Rethinking Tradition in Modern Islamic Thought*, Cambridge: Cambridge University Press.

Bruk, Selam (2015), *Missionarischer Islam auf YouTube. Argumente salafistischer Prediger kritisch untersucht*, Norderstedt: BoD – Books on Demand.

Carlisle, Jessica, Salman Hameed and Fern Elsdon-Baker (2019), 'Muslim Perceptions of Biological Evolution: A Critical Review of Quantitative and Qualitative Research', in Stephen H. Jones, Tom Kaden and Rebecca Catto (eds), *Science, Belief and Society:*

International Perspectives on Religion, Non-Religion and the Public Understanding of Science, Bristol: Bristol University Press, pp. 147–70.

Corm, Georges (2020), Arab Political Thought: Past and Present, London: Hurst & Company.

Dajani, Rana (2018), Five Scarves: Doing the Impossible – If We can Reverse Cell Fate, Why can't We Define Success? Hauppauge, NY: Nova Science Publishers.

Dallal, Ahmad (2010), Islam, Science, and the Challenge of History, New Haven: Yale University Press.

Daneshgar, Majid (2017), Tantawi Jawhari and the Qur'an: Tafsir and the Social Concerns in the Twentieth Century, London: Routledge.

Dangor, Suleman (2005), 'Islamization of Disciplines: Towards an Indigenous Educational System', Educational Philosophy and Theory 37, no. 4: 519–31.

Determann, Jörg Matthias (2018), Space Science and the Arab World: Astronauts, Observatories and Nationalism in the Middle East, London: I. B. Tauris.

Determann, Jörg Matthias (2021), Islam, Science Fiction and Extraterrestrial Life: The Culture of Astrobiology in the Muslim World, London: I. B. Tauris.

Doumato, Eleanor Abdella (2003), 'Education in Saudi Arabia: Gender, Jobs and the Price of Religion', in Eleanor Abdella Doumato and Marsha Pripstein Posusney (eds), Women and Globalisation in the Arab Middle East: Gender, Economy and Society, Boulder: Lynne Rienner Publishers, pp. 239–58.

Enayat, Hadi (2017), Islam and Secularism in Post-Colonial Thought: A Cartography of Asadian Genealogies, London: Palgrave Macmillan.

Foucault, Michel (1972), The Archaeology of Knowledge and the Discourse on Language, New York: Pantheon Books.

Foucault, Michel (1994), The Order of Things: An Archaeology of the Human Sciences, New York: Vintage Books.

Gambetta, Diego, and Steffen Hertog (2016), Engineers of Jihad: The Curious Connection between Violent Extremism and Education, Princeton, NJ: Princeton University Press.

Gaonkar, Dilip Parameshwar (ed.) (2001), Alternative Modernities. Durham, NC: Duke University Press.

Gardner, Vika, and Salman Hameed (2017), 'Science and Islam Videos: Creating a Methodology to find "All" Unique Internet Videos', CyberOrient 11, no. 1: 54–85.

Gardner, Vika, E. Carolina Maayes and Salman Hameed (2018), 'Preaching Science and Islam: Dr. Zakir Naik and Discourses of Science and Islam in Internet Videos', Die Welt Des Islams 58: 1–35.

Ghaly, Mohammed (ed.) (2016), Islamic Perspectives on the Principles of Biomedical Ethics: Muslim Religious Scholars and Biomedical Scientists in Face-to-Face Dialogue with Western Bioethicists, London: World Scientific Publishing.

Ghobash, Omar Saif (2018), Letters to a Young Muslim, London: Pan Macmillan.

Golden, Daniel (2002), 'Western Scholars Play Key Role in Touting "Science" of the Quran', Wall Street Journal, 23 January 2002.

Guénon, Melanie (2019), "'Abd al-Majīd al-Zindānī's i'jāz 'ilmī Approach: Embryonic Development in Q. 23:12–14 as a Scientific Miracle', Journal of Qur'anic Studies 21, no. 1: 32–56.

Guessoum, Nidhal (2011), Islam's Quantum Question: Reconciling Muslim Tradition and Modern Science, London: I. B. Tauris.

Guessoum, Nidhal (2015), 'Islam and Science: The Next Phase of Debates', *Zygon Journal of Religion and Science* 50, no. 4: 854–76.

Guessoum, Nidhal (2018), *The Young Muslim's Guide to Modern Science*, Oldham: Beacon Books.

Halevi, Leor (2019), *Modern Things on Trial: Islam's Global and Material Reformation in the Age of Rida, 1865–1935*, New York: Columbia University Press.

Hameed, Salman (2014), 'Making Sense of Islamic Creationism in Europe', *Public Understanding of Science* 4, no. 4: 388–99.

Hanafi, Sari, and Rigas Arvanitis (2015), *Knowledge Production in the Arab World: The Impossible Promise*, London: Routledge.

Hoodbhoy, Pervez (1991), *Islam and Science: Religious Orthodoxy and the Battle for Rationality*, London: Zed Books Ltd.

Hourani, Albert (1983), *Arabic Thought in the Liberal Age 1798–1939*, Cambridge: Cambridge University Press.

Iqbal, Muhammad (1934), *The Reconstruction of Religious Thought in Islam*, Oxford: Oxford University Press.

Iqbal, Muzaffar (2002), *Islam and Science*, Aldershot: Ashgate.

Issawi, Charles (1988), *The Fertile Crescent 1800–1914: A Documentary Economic History*, Oxford: Oxford University Press.

Janson, Torsten (2003), *Your Cradle is Green: The Islamic Foundation and the Call to Islam in Children's Literature*, Stockholm: Almqvist and Wiksell International.

Moore, Keith L., and Abdul Majeed al-Zindani (1982), *The Developing Human, with Islamic Additions*, Philadelphia and Jeddah: Saunders and Dar al-Qiblah for Islamic Literature.

Motadel, David (ed.) (2016), *Islam and the European Empires*, Oxford: Oxford University Press.

Mustapha, Maziah, and Mohd Abbas Abdul Razak (2019), 'A Contrastive Analysis of Yusuf Islam and Zakir Naik's Styles of Religious Propagation (or Preaching)', *Al-Itqan* 4, no. 2: 65–85.

Nasr, Seyyed Hossein (1964), *Three Muslim Sages: Avicenna, Suhrawardi, Ibn 'Arabi*, Cambridge, MA: Harvard University Press.

Nasr, Seyyed Hossein (1979), *Ideals and Realities of Islam*, London: Mandala Books.

Nasr, Seyyed Hossein (1981), *Knowledge and the Sacred*, The Gifford Lectures, Edinburgh: Edinburgh University Press.

Nasr, Seyyed Hossein (1993), *The Need for a Sacred Science*, London: Curzon Press.

Rahman, Tazli sham Ab., and Monika Munirah Abd Razzak (2014), 'Contributions of Shaykh 'Abd al-Majid Alzindani to al-I'jaz al-'Ilmi', *Online Journal of Research in Islamic Studies* 1, no 2: 45–62.

Riexinger, Martin Thomas (2002), 'The Islamic Creationism of Harun Yahya', *ISIM Newsletter* 11, December.

Riexinger, Martin Thomas (2008), 'Propagating Islamic Creationism on the Internet', *Masaryk University Journal of Law and Technology* 2, no. 2: 99–112.

Ritzer, Georg (1983), *Sociological Theory*, New York: Alfred A. Knopf.

Ross Solberg, Anne (2013), 'The Mahdi Wears Armani: An Analysis of the Harun Yahya Enterprise', Doctoral Dissertation, Södertörns högskola, Huddinge.

Salam, Abdus (1987), *Ideals and Realities: Selected Essays of Abdus Salam*, ed. C. H. Lai, Singapore: World Scientific.

Sayin, Ümit, and Aykut Kence (1999), 'Islamic Scientific Creationism: A New Challenge in Turkey', *Reports of the National Center for Science Education* 19, no. 6.

Stenberg, Leif (1996), *The Islamization of Science: Four Muslim Positions Developing an Islamic Modernity*, Stockholm: Almqvist and Wiksell International.

Stenberg, Leif (2004), 'Islam, Knowledge and the "West": The Making of a Global Islam', in Birgit Schaebler and Leif Stenberg (eds), *Globalization and the Muslim World: Culture, Religion, and Modernity*, Syracuse: Syracuse University Press, pp. 93–110.

al-Zindani, Abdul Majeed, *et al.* (1994), *Human Development as Described in the Qur'an and Sunnah: Correlation with Modern Embryology*, Bridgeview, IL: Islamic Academy for Scientific Research.

CHAPTER 7

Paradigms of Religion and the Swift Birth of Islam: Wilfred Cantwell Smith Revisited

PHILIP WOOD

Wilfred Cantwell Smith commented that, of modern world religions, Islam alone is conscious of the world being divided into many religions. He argues that Islam launched itself into a world that already had religious traditions, but did so with a developed self-consciousness that allowed it to be conceived of as a closed system. In this sense, he argued, it was quite unlike a movement like Manichaeism, which emphasised its continuity with and inheritance from other traditions.[1] Moreover, Islam was also different from Christianity, in that the Gospels have little sense of Christianity as a distinct religion: following Jesus was a new form of discipleship, but it was unclear how this related to earlier forms of communal membership or scripture. 'Muhammad seems to know what he was speaking of when he spoke of Islam, but it is hazy thinking to speak of Guru Nanak or Jesus or Lao Tzu as founders of religions.'[2]

Smith wrote some sixty years ago, so we might wish to issue several caveats regarding his statements. We are now much more wary of speaking of a single Islam, or equating it so straightforwardly with Muhammad's 'revelation'. Instead, we might separate the thought-world of the Quran from the traditions that grew from it (or claimed to grow from it) in Kufa, Basra and Damascus, and then in Baghdad and a host of other centres of scholarship.[3]

Fred Donner has proposed that Muhammad presided over a much more heterogenous community than was hitherto thought, one in which Jews and Christians co-operated with former pagans who were all united by belief in one

[1] Smith 1962: 81–6, 93–4.
[2] Smith 1962: 106.
[3] Calder 1993: 196.

God and the last days.[4] He stresses that much of the content of the Quran is addressed towards believers (in the One God) and that references to Muslims are a minority in the text. He links this ambiguity in the Quran to the inclusion of Jews into Muhammad's *umma* (community) in Medina and the patronage of Christian Arabs by the caliph Muʿāwiya at his court in Damascus. He argues that it was only under ʿAbd al-Malik in the 690s that we really see firm lines drawn between Muslims on one hand, and Jews and Christians on the other.[5]

Donner's argument would seem to undermine Smith's claim that Muhammad was unlike other prophets in being conscious of founding a discrete new religion. I do feel that Donner's book makes a significant point about the importance of the imminence of the end of days in the Quran and his point about a community of believers holds true for some sections of the Quran.[6] Nevertheless, parts of the Quran contain barbed polemics against central Christian and Jewish beliefs and institutions. I would use these to argue that a disenchantment with Jews and Christians occurred in Quranic time. Nor do contemporary Christian sources in Syriac or Armenian identify their conquerors as a kind of Christian: they are descendants of Abraham and Ishmael who are monotheists, bound by distinctive laws given by a new prophet, who have inherited the promises that God made to Abraham and who pray towards a shrine located in Arabia.[7]

I would understand Muʿāwiya's patronage of the Banū Taghlib or the continued presence of groups of Jews in Medina as acts of pragmatism by Muslim rulers, rather than indications of the uncertain boundaries of the Muslim community.[8] None of this is to deny that uncertain cases could arise, cases in which individuals seem to adhere to multiple worldviews in different contexts (i.e. religious code switching), as when Christians referred to Muhammad as a prophet, or to Jesus as merely one of the prophets, or prayed alongside Muslims.[9] But these cases do not disprove the existence of relatively discrete religious communities with their own scriptures which, while related, were still distinct.[10]

---

[4] Donner 2010.

[5] For Muʿāwiya's patronage of the Christian poet al-Akhṭal, who wrote scathing invectives against the Anṣār, as well as the Banū Tamīm, see Stetkeyvetch 2002: 132, 140–1.

[6] Cf. Shoemaker 2018.

[7] Sebeos chap. 42; *Khuzistan Chronicle* 38. Sebeos stresses that Jewish informants played a role in making the 'Ishmaelites' aware of their heritage and their claim to Palestine. Sebeos observes that Muhammad's call to monotheism and moral conduct was linked to the restoration of the covenant between God and the descendants of Abraham. The *Khuzistan Chronicle* refers to the Dome of Abraham as an ancient site of worship for the Ishmaelites.

[8] Donner 2010: 72–4, 181, 212–14. The eighth-century jurist Abū Yūsuf explains early attitudes to the Banū Taghlib as a pragmatic attitude because they still bore arms and the early caliphate faced a threat from Byzantium. Al-Akhṭal threatened to withhold Taghlibī support from Muʿāwiya if he failed to protect Christians: Stetkeyvetch 2002: 145.

[9] Chrysostomides 2017.

[10] Note the comments of Tannous 2018: 274 and 396 on Donner 2010 and Penn 2015. Also see Friedmann 2003: 33 for an earlier critique of Donner's position.

If I am right, then 'Islam' acquired its distinctiveness much more quickly than Christianity emerged from the Jesus movement. The volume edited by Annette Reed and Adam Becker, *The Ways that Never Parted* (2003), charts the continued existence of groups who, until the late fourth century, considered themselves both Jewish and Christian; it also addresses the transfer of ideas, often unacknowledged, between Jews and Christians. How then could Islam emerge so quickly as a distinctive tradition?

In part, we can answer this question with reference to the Arabian peninsula's previous exposure to Roman and Persian statecraft. Skills learnt at the courts of the Nasrid and Jafnid phylarchs not only allowed the Arabian conquerors of the seventh century to run the conquered lands efficiently, but also to distribute an officially approved version of the Quran. Likewise, the courts of the phylarchs were likely to have been important centres for the dissemination of Arabic poetry. This helped to generate the notion of Arabic as a prestigious language with established aesthetic norms, a notion which the Quran takes for granted.[11]

But we can also add that the Roman Empire had already produced a categorisation of 'religion' into which the Quran could insert itself. The prior experience of the Christian Roman Empire with the Jews was significant both for the way that the Quran conceptualised a world divided into religious communities and the way that the nascent caliphate managed different communities and put Quranic principles into practice. Muhammad preached in a world where communal divisions based on religion were taken for granted as the predominant means of identifying individuals and their loyalties.

THE LATE ROMAN CATEGORISATION OF RELIGION

Recent work in the study of religion has observed that religion is not a neutral term of analysis. For commentators like Talal Asad (1993) and Tomoko Masuzawa (2005), the term 'religion' is rooted in nineteenth-century political structures that took Protestant Christianity as a norm for religion.[12] Religion is presumed to be based on interior belief and on a canon of written scriptures that are entirely separable from politics or culture and are also sealed off from other religions. Implicitly, this marked movements such as Islam or Buddhism as substandard versions of religion because they overlapped with other belief systems or did not possess a religious canon or because belief and politics were too deeply intertwined.[13]

---

[11] Wood, forthcoming; Fisher and Wood, forthcoming. Van Putten 2019 makes a convincing argument for the compilation of the Quran by the caliph 'Uthmān.

[12] Asad 1993; Masuzawa 2005.

[13] Nongbri 2013. Also note Bayly 2004, chap. 8 for his account of the spread of 'liberal' attitudes

The strand of scholarship represented by Asad and Nongbri has focused on the 'etic' side of this observation: their aim has been to produce better tools for scholars to use to describe the phenomena they encounter. But there is also an emic implication to their model (especially in Nongbri's case): what was it about nineteenth-century European imperialism that allowed it to forge the category of 'religion' for other societies?

The Talmudic scholar Daniel Boyarin has further probed this emic side of the question. He proposed that the nineteenth-century invention of 'religion' is but one example of an imperial power redefining 'religion' to suit their own interests and their own presumptions of what religion ought to be. That is, based on the experience of a single privileged belief system, it classifed and made judgements about other belief systems.[14]

Boyarin argued that the fifth-century Roman Empire saw the creation of a typology of 'religion' that framed Christianity and Judaism as comparable religions. While pagan institutions were systematically stripped of all institutional rights, the situation for the Jews was much more complicated.

In spite of their differences in belief, Jewish religion was often seen as in a category comparable to Christianity, because of its focus on specific books in a distinctive language. Before the Quran coined the phrase, Judaism and Christianity were both religions of the book.[15] Jerome studied Hebrew with a rabbi in Palestine to gain a closer knowledge of the Hebrew Bible, rather than reading the text in Greek.[16] And even when rioters destroyed a synagogue in Minorca they preserved the books kept in it, presumably recognising that they shared a scripture with the Jews even if they disagreed on how to interpret it.[17] Perhaps the clearest recognition of the sharing of scripture appears in Justinian's Novel 146, in which the emperor responds to a group of Jews who petition for the Bible to be read in Greek rather than Hebrew. The emperor responded by prescribing the translation to be used and banning the recitation of the Midrash or public interpretation of any kind, to allow the 'clear meaning' of the text to bring Jews to Christianity.[18]

In law, Jews are sometimes referred to as possessing a 'religio', and the codes conceive of them as belonging to a community that is universal and defined

---

to religion after the French Revolution and the effects of industrial printing and pilgrimage on disseminating canons and religious doctrine.

[14] Boyarin 2004. He has later questioned the appropriateness of using the term 'religion' for late antiquity *in toto*: Boyarin 2018. Whether or not the fifth century witnessed the 'first' invention of 'religion' falls outside our field of enquiry here.

[15] Stroumsa 2015: 105–9. For the centrality of the Torah in rabbinic Judaism, see Halbertal 1997: 13 and Schwartz 2001: 59–61, who stress that recitation became an act of prayer; and note the prominence of the Torah in the layout of the synagogue.

[16] Millar 2010.

[17] Stroumsa 2015: 111.

[18] De Lange 2005: 421; Stroumsa 2015: 184.

by belief: it is this that makes them distinct from Christians.[19] Laws also stress that Jewish 'clergy' are equivalent to Christian clergy and bear the same rights of exemption from curial service; have the free use of public transportation (the *cursus*); and have the right to convene law courts and excommunicate dissidents.[20] A Jewish patriarch was also permitted to levy taxes from synagogues, at least until the office was last attested in 429.

This respect for the Jews was rooted, in part, in the respect Christian legislators had for the Jews as precursors to Christians, and in part to the older legacy of Roman law, which had already framed Jewish religion as an honoured 'religio'. But this respectful tone, in which Jews held a licit but inferior 'religio', coexisted with a more polemical attitude in which Jews, like pagans, held a mere 'superstitio'. Constantine refers to the Jews' evil deeds (*nefaria*) and calls them 'bestial' (*feralis*). Constantine's successors banned Jews from government service, from bearing arms, from building new synagogues, or acquiring non-Jewish slaves.[21]

In theory, Roman law granted Jews the same protections that were granted to all citizens. Laws forbade discriminating against Jews by illegally confiscating their grain, destroying their places of worship, and injuring individual Jews.[22] However, in contrast to this periodic admission of Jews as co-citizens in the legislation, it is striking to read fifth- and sixth-century Christian fantasies about the violent elimination of Jews, as justified by Jews' alleged collaboration with outside enemies, such as the Persians.[23]

One of the most exclusive versions of the Christian conceptualisation of the category of religion is heresiology, which stands in marked contrast to the categorisation used in Roman law. The stereotypical language that had once been applied to external barbarians (e.g. that they were vain, irrational, inconsistent, disorderly and divided) was increasingly applied to non-orthodox groups in the Roman world (Jews, Manichees and Christian heretics).[24] For Epiphanius of Salamis, whose heresiological catalogue, the *Panarion*, was copied and extended by many later figures, Judaism was one of four archetypal heresies (alongside Barbarism, Hellenism and Scythianism). The remaining heresies in his list of eighty are all permutations or combinations of the original four. The original meaning of heresy is a choice (*hairesis*); Epiphanius employs it to mean

---

[19] Terms like *natio*, *populus* and *gens* were used for Jews in the legislation, but only occasionally. There is no indication here that Jewish converts to Christianity retained their 'Jewishness' in any sense.

[20] Lindner 1987: 70–6. Also, see Rabello 1987, who treats the evidence in great detail. For the role of bishops in law courts, and the state's endorsement of canon law, see Humfress 2007; Rapp 2005: 242–9, 290.

[21] Lindner 1987: 56, 65, 74, 82–5. In practice new synagogues were built; for examples, see De Lange 2005: 406–7.

[22] Lindner 1987: 64–5.

[23] Wood 2010: 101–10.

[24] Maas 2003; Schott 2008; Berzon 2016. For earlier ethnographic representations of 'barbarian' peoples, see Dauge 1981; Chauvot 1998.

the false, promiscuous choices that, since the creation, have led mankind away from orthodoxy. Epiphanius' schema implies that orthodoxy is something that pre-existed the incarnation of God in Jesus, and could also be found in the faith of Adam and the Old Testament prophets.[25]

THE QURAN'S ATTITUDE TO MONOTHEISTS

Late Roman Christians had two coexisting models in which to categorise Jews: first, as inferior members of the category 'religion'; or second, as archetypes of false belief, whose influence will spawn other forms of heresy by corrupting the orthodox. Both of these models have analogues in the way the Quran categorises non-Muslim monotheists.

One model for groups in the Quran seems to be the Israelites of the Torah. However, the Quran removes any sense of the Israelites' continuing covenant with God: their significance is as an example of a people who persecuted and ignored the prophets who had been sent to them. The Quran shares this attitude towards the Old Testament with a strand of Christian patristic writing, especially the West Syriac tradition.[26] And this model, in which a people receives a 'warner' from God and ignores him, is also used to describe the extinct civilisations of ancient Arabia, whose ruins served as reminders of God's power.[27] We may be intended to see the audience of the Quran as a people analogous to the Israelites and to the ancient Arabian peoples, who have now received their own Arabic-speaking prophet and who are asked to surpass the Israelites by accepting him and following his message.[28]

But this image of the Jews as persecutors of the prophets coexists with a second model of group identity, in which different peoples of the book (*ahl al-kitāb*) are named as an *umma* (religious community). These *ummat* are Jews and Christians, and sometimes Sabians, who appear in the Quran as analogous to Muslims.[29] In this second model, scriptures define religious communities; and

---

[25] On heresiology, see Cameron 2003; Kim 2015; Boyarin 2004: 24–6. Later authors, such as Theodoret of Cyrrhus, John of Damascus and Theodore Bar Koni, continued to develop and elaborate Epiphanius' schema. John of Damascus' classification of Islam as a Christian heresy fits into this Epiphanian discourse, which had already presented Judaism and Hellenism as 'heresies' (cf. Schadler 2018).

[26] Hayman 1985; Reynolds 2010.

[27] Cook 1983: 35.

[28] It is possible that Roman Christian ethnography paved the way for a common Arab identity, by presenting the inhabitants of the Arabian Peninsula as being all from the descendants of Ishmael: Cook 1983: 35–8; Millar 2005; Fisher and Wood 2015: 289–90, 304–6, 367–71. The key texts are Sozomen 6.38; Cyril of Scythopolis, *Life of Euthymius* 14. Sebeos and the *Khuzistan Chronicle* give very early accounts of Islamic ritual practice (see above, note 7). Webb (2016) argues that the common Arab identity was a product of the Marwanid caliphate and earlier (here he follows Donner's (2010) dating for the appearance of a Muslim identity). I would rather see some elements of a shared ethnic identity appearing in the generation before Muhammad.

[29] See, in general, Karamustafa 2005.

religious communities, rather than ethnicities, are the main means of classifying humanity. To return to Wilfred Cantwell Smith's formulation, the author(s) of the Quran already had a paradigm of multiple monotheistic religious communities into which he could place a new example.

DISCRIMINATION

Analysts of early Islam have often stressed that it lies within late antiquity. But they mean different things by this: some have in mind the production of the Quran in a sectarian milieu in Arabia;[30] others are referring to the creation of Islamic norms in the cities of the Fertile Crescent in the centuries that followed the conquests.[31] Both points are correct, but we should note that the influence of Roman, Persian and Arabian (and of Christian, Jewish and Zoroastrian) sources differed according to time and place. So, if the Quran inherited a late Roman paradigm of classification that divided humanity into religious communities (each following a scripture), the Quran did not provide a blueprint for how to operationalise these divisions in an Islamic empire. Instead, models for how to delineate the boundaries between communities and the hierarchy between them were generated through a dialogue with the political thought of earlier empires, the ideas of the Quran and ad hoc inventions by men on the spot.

The initial relationship between Muslims and non-Muslims was (allegedly) based on a series of distinct treaties between different communities and their conquerors. Over time they became standardised into a single set of arrangements that were attributed to the caliph 'Umar b. al-Khaṭṭāb, but were probably only fully promulgated in the mid ninth century. In this text (the shurūṭ 'Umar), the non-Muslims petition the caliph for protection in exchange for a series of restrictions, which include the renunciation of bearing arms and riding horses, and agreeing not to build any new religious buildings.[32] At the same time, Muslim jurists promulgated hadith that banned non-Muslims from positions of leadership over Muslims in the caliphate.[33]

It is hard to know to what extent these restrictions were actually put into place. Certainly, Christians continued to build churches in the Abbasid period and beyond and continued to occupy prominent positions in the administra-

---

[30] Neuwirth 2010.
[31] Calder 1993: 196. Also note Marsham 2009: 161–4, 200, 300, 313 for Sasanian influence on Umayyad court culture; Morony 2005: 158–9 for Sasanian assumptions that different religious communities merit different laws; Gariboldi 1999 on the possible Sasanian origins of a poll tax used to differentiate status.
[32] Levy-Rubin 2011.
[33] Yarbrough 2019.

tion.[34] But I would stress that non-Muslims undertook such banned activities by grace of the caliph, and they remained vulnerable to any changes in regime.

The restrictions of the *shurūṭ ʿUmar* all bear a marked resemblance to the Theodosian Code's treatment of the Jews, who were similarly banned from civil and military service, or from constructing new religious buildings (though in fact they too continued to do so). Andrew Jacobs has argued that the Jews of Palestine were rendered into harmless trappings for Christian pilgrims, who might admire the beautiful Jewesses of Nazareth as part of their 'sensory experience' of the Holy Land.[35]

Like the Jews in the Roman Empire, Christians were forbidden from the kinds of military displays that had been an important facet of the identity of male Roman elites. The restrictions on bearing arms and riding horses may have helped to maintain a sense of Muslims as a martial population, the descendants of conquerors, in contrast to groups that had been rendered subordinate to them.[36]

Albrecht Noth argued that the *shurūṭ ʿUmar* did not, in fact, curtail the rights of *dhimmīs* (non-Muslims) but simply canonised a situation that was already present. Christians, he argued, simply gave up fields of activity that were of no interest to them and left them to the conquerors.[37] But his argument presents the *effects* of the *shurūṭ ʿUmar* as a natural and permanent condition of Christians in the Middle East: a glance at Procopius and sixth-century Roman history, or the accounts of Christian banditry in the eighth-century *Chronicle of Zuqnin* would indicate that Christians were perfectly capable of belligerence.

The *shurūṭ* can, in part, be read as a restriction of Christian male display; we can press this analysis further if we turn to the *Kitāb al-diyārāt*, the poetry that celebrates wine-drinking in Christian monasteries. These are striking for their celebration of drunken parties. In part they depict Muslim elites escaping the censorious gaze of pious critics. But Tom Sizgorich has also described them as 'Muslim imperial fantasies', in which claims to Christian celibacy and piety are shown to be false and Christian men are incapable of fending off the sexual conquests of the Muslim elite.[38] Even in a quintessentially Christian space like a monastery, Muslim elites are able to seduce young men and women and prove their own power and the impotence and effeminacy of the Christians.[39]

---

[34] Schick 1995; Cabrol 2012.
[35] Jacobs 2004: 127–30, discussing the late sixth-century Piacenza Pilgrim
[36] Other aspects of the *shurūṭ ʿUmar* may owe more to Sasanian precedent, such as the *ghiyār* rules that distinguished non-Muslims by obliging them to wear different forms of clothing (Levy-Rubin 2011, chap. 3). The extent to which the *shurūṭ* drew on earlier forms of discriminatory legislation is a matter of debate: Sahner 2017; Levy-Rubin 2016; Yarbrough 2016.
[37] Noth 2004.
[38] Sizgorich 2012.
[39] Cf. El-Rouayheb 2005: 15.

We might read the sexual submission of the Christians that is described in the *Kitāb al-diyārāt* in the context of the prohibition of marriage between Muslim women and non-Muslim men and the permission of marriage between Muslim men and non-Muslim women that is made in Quran 5:5 and elaborated in the *Sunna*.[40] In a patriarchal society, this prohibition was presumed to lead to the spread of Islam, but it also asserted the distinctive value of Muslim women and their male protectors, over and above *dhimmī* women, whose disarmed and unmanly fathers could not protect them.

The visit of the caliph al-Mutawakkil to a monastery near Homs to view ruins is a case in point. He was greeted by a monk, who introduces him to his daughter Saʿānīn. Instead of protecting her from male visitors, he allows her to drink with them. As the caliph becomes enraptured, she leads them to an upper room that overlooks the church, brings them food, and sings them a Christian song on the lyre. Ultimately, the caliph convinces her to convert to Islam and marries her.[41]

The anecdote presents the Christian girl as exotic, indulging in behaviour that would be impossible for a Muslim woman (singing, drinking and being alone in male company). But this exoticism also allows the caliph to demonstrate his sexual and religious victory: he shows his own moral superiority and that of Islam by converting the girl and marrying her, two actions that tame both her unguarded behaviour and her inferior religion.[42]

SUPERSESSIONISM

A second feature that Muslim thought under the caliphate shares with Christian thought in the Roman Empire is a condemnation of innovation and the definition of a single path of orthodoxy (often coterminous with the faith of the rulers). In principle, this orthodoxy stretches back to the creation. Thus, Eusebius of Caesarea imagines Abraham as a proto-Christian:

But although it is clear that we are new and that this new name of Christians has really but recently been known among all nations, nevertheless our life and our conduct, with our doctrines of religion, have not been lately invented by us, but from the first creation of man, so to speak, have been established by the natural understanding of divinely-favoured men of old.[43]

---

[40] Friedmann 2003: 112, 114, 148, 161–2.

[41] Campbell 2009: 147–8.

[42] Al-Jāḥiẓ complains about Byzantine women being 'unveiled and uncircumcised' and hence free and wanton in a way that threatens the order of Islamic morals and society: el-Cheikh 2015: 83–4. Also note that al-Muʿtasim's conquest of the Byzantine city of Amorium in 838 was also celebrated in terms of a sexual conquest: el-Cheikh 2015: 91.

[43] Eusebius HE I.4.4.

The ancient prophets, such as Noah and Abraham, were true Christians before the name 'Christian' existed, both because of their virtuous lives and because they shunned circumcision and dietary laws, which were only adopted by the Israelites under Moses.[44]

Andrew Jacobs has argued that fourth-century Christians appropriated the Old Testament past in order to claim its prestigious antiquity while silencing the use of the Old Testament by contemporary Jews.[45] He argued that Eusebius in particular invited his readers to see Palestine as a repository of artefacts from the Old Testament, rather than the home of real Jews.[46] Likewise, Jerome's efforts to translate Hebrew frame the Jews as a source of authoritative knowledge about a useful, Christian, past, but also as a group who deserve denigration and derision in his own day.[47] Jacobs tellingly evokes Edward Said to describe the effects of Roman imperialism in this context: 'to know a thing is to dominate it, to have authority over it . . . and to have authority means for us to deny it autonomy'.[48]

A similar intellectual strategy exists in the identification of other Abrahamic religions as forms of false innovation by Muslim theologians. Muslims too claimed Abraham as a proto-Muslim (ḥanīf), and with him the prestigious antiquity that the Christians and Jews had also contested. Here the tension between non-Muslims as bearers of a proto-Islam and non-Muslims as corrupters of pre-Muhammadan Islam is resolved by an accusation of taḥrīf – the wilful alteration of scripture – to remove references to Muhammad's prophecy.

In the case of Christians, this strategic accusation of taḥrīf occurred when Muslim polemicists targeted those parts of Christian scripture and history that are not endorsed in the Quran. Thus, the apostle Paul is accused of corrupting Jesus' message (to allow the consumption of pork and the abandonment of circumcision). And the emperor Constantine, who was venerated by churches for his role in convening the council of Nicaea and the establishment of 'orthodoxy', was blamed by Muslims for blending Christianity with Roman paganism. In other words, the expansion of Christianity involved fatal compromises that transformed Christians from being ḥanīf (pre-Muhammadan true believers), to being mushrikūn, who had adopted polytheistic beliefs because of the temptations of power.[49]

This Muslim construction of the Christian past allowed Muslim writers to explain the positive references to Christians in the Quran as references to those pure Christians, such as Waraqa and Baḥīrā, whom Muhammad had

---

44 Eusebius HE 1.4. 2–8.
45 Jacobs 2004: 29–30, 62.
46 Jacobs 2004: 35, 110–12.
47 Jacobs 2004: 56–7.
48 Jacobs 2004: 59 quoting Edward Said's Orientalism.
49 Reynolds 2004; Griffith 1993.

encountered in the Hijaz, as atypical Christians who had preserved a pure version of Christianity, far from the corrupting influence of the churches of the Roman and Persian empires.[50] By implication, any true Christians would have already converted to Islam, since true Christianity prophesied Islam, while those who remained Christians were simply *mushrikūn*, who deserved their subordinate status as a conquered population.[51]

The Quran has a complex image of the *ahl al-kitāb*: sometimes Christians are *mushrikūn*, like the Quraysh, because they (allegedly) worshipped beings alongside God. But sometimes, they are fellow believers in one God and the last days, together with the Muslims and Jews, and are called 'the closest to the Muslims in affection'.[52] But none of this complexity is preserved in the *futūḥ* accounts (the stories of the Muslims' divinely mandated conquest of the Middle East under Abu Bakr and Umar): here the Christians are simply dismissed as *mushrikūn* or *kuffār* (unbelievers), and the wars of conquest in Syria are simply continuations of Muhammad's wars against the *mushrikūn* of Mecca. Indeed, for the tenth-century poet Ibn Ḥazm, the military defeat of the Byzantines was a consequence of their false belief in the Trinity and the power of the Cross, which mark them as intellectually feeble and deserving of defeat. Their fate serves as a cautionary message for Muslims, who might also be threatened by military defeat if they abandon true Islam.[53]

RELIGION, ETHNICITY AND ACHIEVEMENT

One feature of late Roman heresiology emphasised above is the transformation of stereotypes of barbarians into stereotypes of heretics and the increasing salience of 'religion' as a way of characterising peoples. This tendency is developed even further for Arab Muslim writers. We find a good example of the prioritisation of religion in the polemic of the Abbasid belle-lettriste al-Jāḥiẓ. Al-Jāḥiẓ condemned the affection extended to Christians in ninth-century Baghdad and complained that they were given credit for all the scientific achievements of the ancient Greeks. Furthermore, he argues that the ancient Greeks are different from the contemporary Byzantines or the Christians of the caliphate (*Rūm*). Crucially, he states that by adopting Christianity they lost their scientific heritage:

---

[50] Ibn Isḥāq's *Sira* mentions Baḥīrā, the monk who foretold Muhammad's prophetic status (Guillaume 1955: 80) and Waraqa, Khadīja's Christian relative (Guillaume 1955: 83). Ibn Isḥāq also describes the successive conversions of Salmān al-Fārisī, one of Muhammad's Companions, from Zoroastrianism to Christianity to Islam. This seems to set out a hierarchy of religions in which Christianity is a step on the way to true religion, superior to the alternatives but still inferior to Islam (Guillaume 1955: 95–7)
[51] See Gibson 2015: 100 for this logic in al-Jāḥiẓ.
[52] Griffith 2005.
[53] Hermes 2009: 56.

But if our masses knew that the Christians and Byzantines are not men of science and rhetoric, and are not people of deep reflection, (and possess nothing except iron working . . .) they would remove them from the roll of men of culture, and would strike their names off the list of philosophers and scientists. For the books of Logic . . . were composed by Aristotle, and he was neither Byzantine nor Christian. And the book *Almagest* was written by Ptolemy, and he was neither Byzantine nor Christian . . . All these authors belong to a race that has perished, but whose intellectual impress has endured, and they were the Greeks. Their religion was unlike the religion of the Christians, and their mode of living was totally different. The Greeks were savants, and these are mechanical manipulators. It was by chance of geographical proximity that they got hold of the Greek books. Either the authorship of some of the books they falsely ascribed to themselves or tampered with their contents so as to make them appear Christian. And if the work was too popular and the contents too well known, so that they could not change the name of the book, they would tell us that the Greeks were a group of Byzantine tribes, and would boast of the superiority of their religion over that of the Jews, Arabs, and Indians. They even went so far as to assert that our scientists were the followers of the Byzantine writers, and our philosophers their imitators. Such is the state of affairs.[54]

Al-Jāḥiẓ stresses that the Byzantines' only merit is therefore as transmitters of this ancient wisdom, because they know Greek; Arab Muslims need feel no inferiority. He alleges that they claim that Aristotle and Plato were one of their own, whereas in fact they were neither Byzantine nor Christian.[55]

Scholarship on the later Roman Empire and Byzantium has stressed that its population never ceased to think of themselves as Roman, even after the conversion of most of the empire's population to Christianity.[56] And the study of Aristotle in particular continued to flourish in Christian circles in the caliphate.[57] But al-Jāḥiẓ was operating with a different criterion, one that defines a population by their religion. Based on this criterion the Byzantines were fundamentally different from the Greeks because they changed their

---

[54] Al-Jāḥiẓ, *Refutation of the Christians*, section 4.8. I am grateful to James Montgomery for allowing me to use his forthcoming translation of al-Jāḥiẓ, which will be published as part of the Library of Arabic Literature.

[55] Cf. the discussion and translation of this text in Gutas 1998: 86–8. However, in another text, the *Kitāb al-akhbār*, al-Jāḥiẓ argues that the ancient Greeks and the Byzantines are the same people (Gutas 1998: 85–6). Here al-Jāḥiẓ stresses that the Byzantines represent a cautionary tale for al-Jāḥiẓ's audience: even a people like the Greeks who boast such great intellectual achievements can become weak and corrupted if they start believing in a fundamentally irrational concept like the Trinity.

[56] Brown 1971. The extent to which a Roman identity was significant in late antique and medieval Byzantium remains debated; see Kaldellis 2019; Stouriatis 2014.

[57] Tannous 2013; Fowden 2014: 143.

religion. They are compared to three other ethno-confessional groups (Jews, Arabs and Indians) and found to be fraudulently claiming civilisational superiority.

The caliphate was, like the Roman Empire, a state that was endorsed by God and led by men who were especially close to God. In this order, the faith of the emperor or caliph was rendered public through material culture and law-making. And in texts like the Theodosian Code or the *shurūṭ 'Umar*, Christianity and Islam became imperial religions by denigrating the faiths that they superseded – Judaism in the first case, and Judaism and Christianity in the second.

AN ISLAMIC PARADIGM FOR RELIGION

So far, I have argued that the Quran emerged in an environment where the existence of multiple religious communities built around various scriptures was taken for granted, and the hierarchical relationship between these communities was organised using a number of discourses and practices that developed out of fifth- and sixth-century Roman precedent. But if the late Roman Christian imagination of 'religion' was important for the Quran's conceptualisation of Islam, then eighth- and ninth-century Muslims also exerted a substantial influence on how other groups came to present themselves. The most striking of these requirements is the notion that true religions must have a prophet. As Patricia Crone noted, Muslim intellectuals like al-Jāḥiẓ believed that prophets were necessary to have any kind of 'civilisation' or social order, since they inhibit humankind's anti-social tendencies with divinely approved laws.[58] Here I take the examples of the Sabians and the Christians and their transformation under the caliphate into 'Islamicate religions'.

The term Sabian is used in the Quran to distinguish a third group of *ahl al-kitāb*, alongside Jews and Christians. But in practice, early Muslims seem to have found it hard to identify this group. One group of polytheists from the city of Harran in Mesopotamia were successful in presenting themselves as Sabians. Kevin Van Bladel has charted how they emphasised their veneration of Hermes Trismegistos, who was promoted from being a holy man to being a monotheistic prophet, and was sometimes identified with Enoch. He was presented as the founder of the *milla al-ḥanifiyya* (a monotheistic community), who provided a *sunna* (ideal acts worthy of imitation) that formed the basis for a *sharia* (a divinely-approved law based on this *sunna*). All of the moral teachings attributed to him would have been quite unobjectionable to Muslims. In the

---

[58] Crone 2018a, esp. 188. One eccentric intellectual, Ibn Khābiṭ, even argued that animals, as well as humans, must have prophets since they enjoyed their own social orders.

tenth century, a number of Harranian Sabians achieved fame as astrologers and physicians in Baghdad.[59]

The Mandeans, a group from the marshlands of southern Iraq, are another group that claimed the name 'Sabian' and along with it the protections that came with the status of being *ahl al-dhimma*. The Mandean scripture, the *Book of Yaḥyā*, speaks of harassment by Muslims on the specific issue of prophecy and on suspicions that they were really idolaters: 'Who is your prophet? Tell us who is your prophet? And tell us, what is your book? Tell us, who do you bow down to?'

The stakes here were high: the same book complains that Muslims seized Mandaic temples and turned them into mosques. As Van Bladel persuasively argues, the attribution of the text to 'Yaḥyā son of Zachariah' implies a point of composition in the early Islamic period (640–900), when Mandeans were trying to establish their credentials as holders of a prophecy.[60]

Christians were obviously in a safer position that the Harranians or the Mandeans because their status as *ahl al-kitāb* was defined much more clearly in the Quran. Nevertheless, we should note that groups like the Manichees and Marcionites would have called themselves Christians but were not accorded the rights of *ahl al-kitāb* by the Muslims. Indeed, under the Abbasids the Manichees were identified as a particularly disruptive force and were subject to the death penalty.[61]

The Muslim authorities accepted three major Christian confessions, the Chalcedonians (Melkites), the Miaphysites (Jacobites) and the Church of the East, and their patriarchs were given access to the courts in Baghdad and Raqqa. In the Abbasid period, Christian patriarchs were endorsed by the caliphs, who occasionally intervened in their elections and employed them as intermediaries with the Byzantines or Christian rebels. This caliphal endorsement included the right for the higher clergy to raise tithes from their co-religionists and to use caliphal troops to imprison priests or monks who denied patriarchal authority.[62]

The higher clergy justified their proximity to caliphal power by claiming to petition the caliph for tax relief and for a suspension of discriminatory laws (such as bans on church construction). Therefore, in a sense, the existence of restrictions on Christians – restrictions that the caliph could suspend – encouraged the development of institutions to represent all Christians or all Christians of a given confession. One consequence was that smaller Christian confessions were prompted to seek union with larger ones.[63]

---

[59] Van Bladel 2009, esp. 88–9, 107–8, 234–7; Roberts 2017.
[60] Van Bladel 2017: 55–6.
[61] Friedmann 2003: 7, 140; Kristo-Nagy 2015.
[62] Wood 2019.
[63] Wood 2019. On the proposed union between the Jacobites and Julianists, see Draguet 1941. Also see Mikhail 2016: 161 on the union between the Miaphysite church in Egypt and the Barsanuphians in the early ninth century.

There was an expectation that Quranic prophets should be lawgivers. This expectation was true for Muhammad and for Moses, but less so for Jesus, to whom explicit instructions are rarely attributed in the Gospels. The eighth-century (?) Syriac forgery, the *Testament of Our Lord*, in which church canons were attributed to Jesus himself to fill this gap, seems to have been a response to this expectation.[64] At any rate, church leaders became legislators for laypeople, roles that they had never enjoyed in the Roman Empire. In the Abbasid world, religious leaders were expected to provide laws for entire religious communities.[65]

The Christian use of the term imam is a good example of how Muslim expectations helped shape the development of clerical authority. In a famous address by the Jacobite patriarch Dionysius of Tel-Mahre to the caliph al-Ma'mūn, Dionysius tells al-Ma'mūn that he is like the caliph in the sense that he too is an imam: his authority comes from the will of his people and he leads his people in prayer and ensures their good order. The subtext here is that he wants the caliph to promise to support his right to excommunicate clergymen who challenge his authority.[66]

This idea of a Christian imam is made even more forcefully by the Takriti Jacobite theologian Ibn Jarīr in the eleventh century. According to Ibn Jarīr, because prophets will leave the earth one day, it is necessary to write their commandments and prohibitions in mens' souls. It is necessary for people to transmit their books without alteration and to establish a successor to the prophet, and this successor is an imam. This imam is the priest who guards the commandments of the religion created by its inventor for the benefit of mankind; the imam causes them to obey the commandments by persuasion or force. It is the imam's duty to obey the prophet's commands and to oblige others to obey them, and because of this he receives the 'charisma' of priesthood, which is not just for his own benefit but for the benefit of the whole community.[67]

Ibn Jarīr's formulation is extraordinary because it forms part of a discussion of Christian theology. His prime motivation seems to be to establish an analogy between Christian and Muslim practice: both religions have an imam who keeps belief pure for the people. He assumes the Islamic precept of the imam as an ideal believer and as the man responsible for commanding right and forbidding wrong (Q. 3:104).[68] Here religion as a general category is modelled after Islam, with a scripture, a prophet, and a succession of imams. Indeed, one could add that the Islam that Ibn Jarīr uses as a model is an imam-centred Islam that

---

[64] Drijvers 1994. David Taylor has challenged Drijvers' attribution of the text to Jacob of Edessa (quoted in Tannous 2018: 89).

[65] Edelby 1950–1; Simonsohn 2011, 2016; Weitz 2016. Summaries of the legal material are provided in Kaufhold 2012.

[66] The scene is described and analysed in Harrak 2015.

[67] Khoury-Sarkis 1967: 430–1, sections 16–17.

[68] In general, see Cook 2001.

might appeal to an Abbasid loyalist or to an Alid.[69] There is no sense that the community at large is responsible for commanding right or forbidding wrong or that knowledge of hadith and *Sunna* has any privileged role, as it would for Aḥmad b. Ḥanbal and his followers.[70]

This formulation of the patriarch as an imam may have been attractive because it enlisted caliphal approval for a Christian priestly hierarchy. But this articulation of an Islamicate Christianity also makes a substantial concession: it implicitly reduces Jesus to the status of prophet, rather than incarnate God. Such ideas were not unprecedented, but they tended to occur among laymen.[71] Here a theologian, for whom clerical hierarchy seems to have been more significant that traditional soteriology, makes the case.

CONCLUSIONS

Historians of religion have rightly observed that the nineteenth century was a very important threshold in which many religious traditions were re-imagined along the lines of Protestant Christianity. This process delegitimised some traditions as mere superstition, and in other traditions it amplified the voices of chosen native informants. Richard King has argued that the nineteenth century saw the creation of a single Hinduism out of a multitude of different (though related) belief systems. This was modelled on Judaeo-Christian assumptions, with a central role given to belief in God, a scriptural canon, ecclesiastical structures, conversion between mutually exclusive belief systems, and claims of historicity for Hindu deities. And Hindu reformers and Indian nationalists, as well as British colonial officials, embraced this paradigm for what religions should be.[72]

I have argued here that other empires, before those of the nineteenth century, also disseminated their own paradigms for classifying humanity, and that these earlier paradigms also provided an important framework for 'subaltern' groups to reimagine themselves.[73] I have argued that the late Roman period saw an increased salience for religion as a way to characterise groups and that Jews and Christians were sometimes, but not always, seen as comparable religious groups. This paradigm of multiple licit religions helps us explain the relatively swift rise of Islam, since the author(s) of the Quran already had access to a model of multiple religions, each with its own scripture. Finally, I have proposed that Islam,

---

[69] Crone 2004, chaps. 8 and 10 on the role of the imam in Abbasid and Alid thought.
[70] Melchert 2006; Hurvitz 2002.
[71] Compare Thomas of Marga III. 3 (Wallis-Budge 1893, ed. 151/ tr. 310).
[72] King 1999.
[73] Jacobs 2004 and Schott 2008 in particular have drawn on postcolonial theory for their analysis of the Roman world, but also note Crone 2006, 2012, 2018b.

in turn, influenced the development of subordinate religions in the caliphate, especially through its expectations that true religions ought to be founded by a law-giving prophet.

My argument here has been focused on late antiquity, but in conclusion, it is worth noting that Islam has continued to provide a model for other world-views to present themselves as 'religions' worthy of the name (and therefore also worthy of the material advantages that might come with this status, such as the right to construct religious buildings or receive tax breaks). Protestant Christianity is not the only belief system that provides a paradigm by which other worldviews are judged worthy of the name 'religion'. A good example is Confucianism in Indonesia. Confucianism in China is often presented as a philosophy, rather than a religion, and its adherents often also follow aspects of Daoism and Buddhism. By contrast, in Indonesia, the government has asserted the existence of five licit religions: the 'Pancasila' of Islam, Buddhism, Catholicism, Protestantism and Hinduism. Chinese Confucians in Indonesia have been wary of being classified as atheist communists who may pose a danger to the state, and hence become the targets of violence or the expropriation of property. Here, in order to conform to Islamicate expectations of true religion, they have begun to speak of Confucius as a prophet with his own revelation.[74]

BIBLIOGRAPHY

Primary sources

Al-Jāḥiẓ, *Refutation of the Christians*, ed. and trans. J. Montgomery (forthcoming).

Cyril of Scythopolis, *Life of Euthymius*, ed. E. Schwartz, *Kyrillos von Scythopolis* (Leipzig: Hinrichs Verlag, 1939); trans. R. Price, comm. J. Binns, *The Lives of the Monks of Palestine* (Kalamazoo: Cistercian Publications/Liturgical Press, 1991).

Eusebius, *Ecclesiastical History*, ed. and trans. H. Lawlor and J. Oulton (Cambridge MA: Loeb, 1928).

Khuzistan Chronicle, ed. and trans. I. Guidi, *Chronicon anonymum*, in *Chronica Minora* (Paris: CSCO, 1903), pp. 15–39.

Sebeos, *The Armenian History attributed to Sebeos*, trans. R. Thomson, comm. J. Howard-Johnston (Liverpool: Liverpool University Press, 1999).

Sozomen, *Ecclesiastical History*, ed. J. Bidez and G. Hansen (Berlin: Deutsche Akademie der Wissenschaften, 1960).

Secondary sources

Asad, Talal (1993), *Genealogies of Religion: Discipline and Reasons of Power in Christianity and Islam*, Baltimore: Johns Hopkins University Press.

Bayly, C. (2004), *The Birth of the Modern World, 1780–1914: Global Connections and Comparisons*, Oxford: Blackwell.

---

[74] Sutrisno 2017.

Berzon, T. (2016), *Classifying Christians: Ethnography, Heresiology and the Limits of Knowledge in Late Antiquity*, Oakland: University of California Press.

Boyarin, Daniel (2004), 'The Christian Invention of Judaism: The Theodosian Empire and the Rabbinic Rejection of Religion', *Representations* 85: 21–57.

Boyarin, Daniel (2018), 'Why Ignatius invented Judaism', in L. Baron, J. Hicks-Keeton, and M. Thiessen (eds), *The Ways that Often Parted: Essays in Honor of Joel Marcus*, Atlanta: Society of Biblical Literature Press, pp. 309–23.

Brown, P. (1971), *The World of Late Antiquity: From Marcus Aurelius to Muhammad*, AD 150–750, London: Thames and Hudson.

Cabrol, C. (2012), *Les secrétaires nestoriens à Bagdad (762–1258 AD)*, Beirut: Université de Saint-Joseph.

Calder, Norman (1993), *Studies in Early Muslim Jurisprudence*, Oxford: Oxford University Press.

Cameron, A. (2003), 'How to Read Heresiology', *Journal of Medieval and Early Modern Studies* 33: 471–92.

Campbell, E. (2009), '"A Heaven of Wine": Muslim-Christian Interactions at Monasteries in the Early Islamic Middle East', PhD dissertation, University of Washington.

Chauvot, A. (1998), *Opinions romains face aux barbares: au IVe siècle ap. J.-C.*, Paris: De Boccard.

Chrysostomides, A. (2017), '"There Is No God But God": Islamization and Religious Code Switching 8th–10th Centuries CE', in A. Peacock (ed.), *Islamisation: Comparative Perspectives from History*, Edinburgh: Edinburgh University Press, pp. 118–33.

Cook, Michael (1983), *Muhammad*, Oxford: Oxford University Press.

Cook, Michael (2001), *Commanding Right and Forbidding Wrong in Islamic Thought*, Cambridge: Cambridge University Press.

Crone, Patricia (2004), *Medieval Islamic Political Thought*, Edinburgh: Edinburgh University Press.

Crone, Patricia (2006), 'Post-Colonialism in Tenth Century Islam', *Der Islam* 83: 2–38.

Crone, Patricia (2012), *The Nativist Prophets of Early Islamic Iran: Rural Revolt and Local Zoroastrianism*, Cambridge: Cambridge University Press.

Crone, Patricia (2018a), 'What Are Prophets For? The Social Utility of Prophets in Islamic Thought', in P. Crone and H. Siurua (eds), *Islam, the Ancient Near East and Varieties of Godlessness*, Leiden: Brill, pp. 186–99.

Crone, Patricia (2018b), How the Field Has Changed in My Lifetime', in P. Crone and H. Siurua (eds), *Islam, the Ancient Near East and Varieties of Godlessness*, Leiden: Brill, pp. 239–46.

Dauge, Y. (1981), *Le barbare: recherches sur la conception romaine*, Brussels: Latomus.

De Lange, N. (2005), 'Jews in the Age of Justinian', in M. Maas (ed.), *The Cambridge Companion to the Age of Justinian*, Cambridge: Cambridge University Press, pp. 401–26.

Donner, Fred (2010), *Muhammad and the Believers*, Cambridge, MA: Belknap.

Draguet, R. (1941), 'Le Pacte de l'union de 797: Entre les Jacobites et les Julianistes du patriarcat d'Antioche', *Le Muséon* 54, 91–100.

Drijvers, H. J.-W. (1994), 'The Testament of Our Lord: Jacob of Edessa's Response to Islam', *Aram* 6: 104–14.

Edelby, N. (1950–1), 'L'autonomie législative des chrétiens en terre de l'Islam', *Archives d'histoire du droit oriental* 5: 307–51.

El-Cheikh, N.-M. (2015), *Women, Islam and Abbasid Identity*, Cambridge, MA: Harvard University Press.

El-Rouayheb, K. (2005), *Before Homosexuality in the Arab-Islamic World, 1500–1800*, Chicago: University of Chicago Press.

Fisher, G., and Philip Wood (2015), 'Arabs and Christianity', in G. Fisher (ed.), *Arabs and Empires Before Islam*, Oxford: Oxford University Press, pp. 276–322.

Fisher, G., and Philip Wood (forthcoming), 'The Arab Peninsula and the Great Powers'.

Fowden, G. (2014), *Before and After Muhammad: The First Millenium Refocused*, Princeton: Princeton University Press.

Friedmann, Y. (2003), *Tolerance and Discrimination in Islam: Interfaith Relations in the Muslim Tradition*, Cambridge: Cambridge University Press.

Gariboldi, A. (1999), *Il regno di Xusraw dall'nima immortale: riforme economiche e rivolte sociali nell'Iran sasanide del VI secolo*, Milan: Mimesis.

Gibson, N. (2015), 'Closest in Friendship? Al-Jāḥiẓ' Profile of Christians in Abbasid Society in "The Refutation of the Christians" (*al-Radd ʿalā al-Naṣārā*)', PhD dissertation, Catholic University of America.

Griffith, S. (1993), 'Muslims and Church Councils: The Apology of Theodore Abū Qurrah', *Studia Patristica* 25: 270–99.

Griffith, S. (2002), *The Beginnings of Christian Theology in Arabic: Muslim-Christian Encounters in the Early Islamic Period*, Aldershot: Variorum.

Griffith, S. (2005), 'Christians and Christianity', in J. D. MacAuliffe (ed.), *The Encyclopedia of the Qur'an*, Leiden: Brill.

Guillaume, A. (1955), *The Life of Muhammad: a translation of Ibn Ishaq's Sirat Rasul Allah*, Oxford: Oxford University Press.

Gutas, Dimitri (1998), *Greek Thought, Arab Culture: The Graeco-Arabic Translation Movement in Baghdad and Early Abbasid Society (2nd–4th/8th–10th Centuries)*, Princeton, NJ: Princeton University Press.

Halbertal, M. (1997), *People of the Book: Canon, Meaning and Authority*, Cambridge MA: Harvard University Press.

Harrak, A. (2015), 'Dionysius of Tell-Maḥrē: Patriarch, Diplomat, and Inquisitive Chronicler', in M. Doerfler, E. Fiano and K. Smith (eds), *Syriac Encounters: Papers from the Sixth North American Syriac Symposium, Duke University, 26–29 June 2011*, Leuven: Peeters, pp. 215–35.

Hayman, A. (1985), 'The Image of the Jew in Syriac Anti-Jewish Polemical Literature', in J. Neusner and E. Frierichs (eds), *To See Ourselves as Others See Us*, Chico, CA: Scholars' Press, pp. 423–31.

Hermes, N. (2009), 'The Byzantines in Medieval Arabic Poetry: Abu Firas' "al-Rumiyyat" and the Poetic Responses of al-Qaffal and Ibn Hazm to Nicephore Phocas' "al-Qasida al-Arminiyya al-Malʿuna" (The Armenian Cursed Ode)', *Byzantina Symmeikta* 19: 35–61.

Humfress, C. (2007), *Orthodoxy and the Courts in Late Antiquity*, Oxford: Oxford University Press.

Hurvitz, N. (2002), *The Formation of Ḥanbalism: Piety into Power*, New York: Routledge.

Jacobs, A. (2004), *The Remains of the Jews: Imperial Christian Identity in the Late Ancient Holy Land*, Stanford: Stanford University Press.

Kaldellis, A. (2019), *Romanland: Empire and Ethnicity in Byzantium*, Cambridge, MA: Belknap.

Karamustafa, A. (2005), 'Umma', in J. MacAuliffe (ed.), *Encyclopaedia of the Qur'an*, Leiden: Brill.

Kaufhold, H. (2012), 'Sources of Canon Law in the Eastern Churches', in W. Hartmann and K. Pennington (eds), *The History of Byzantine and Eastern Canon Law to 1500*, Washington, DC: Catholic University of America Press, pp. 215–342.

Khoury-Sarkis, G. (1967), 'Le livre du Guide de Yahya ibn Jarir', *L'Orient syrien* 12: 303–54, 421–80.

Kim, Y. R. (2015), *Epiphanius of Salamis: Imagining an Orthodox World*, Ann Arbor: University of Michigan Press.

King, R. (1999), 'Orientalism and the Modern Myth of Hinduism', *Numen* 46: 146–85.

Kristo-Nagy, I. (2015), 'Denouncing the Damned Zindīq! Struggle and Interaction Between Monotheism and Dualism', in C. Adang, H. Ansari, M. Fierro and S. Schmidtke (eds), *Accusations of Unbelief in Islam: A Diachronic Perspective on Takfīr*, Leiden: Brill, pp. 56–81.

Levy-Rubin, M. (2011), *Non-Muslims in the Early Islamic Empire: From Surrender to Coexistence*, New York: Cambridge University Press.

Levy-Rubin, M. (2016), ''Umar II's *Ghiyār* Edict: Between Ideology and Practice', in A. Borrut and F. M. Donner (eds), *Christians and Others in the Umayyad State*, Chicago: University of Chicago Press, pp. 157–72.

Lindner, A. (1987), *The Jews in Roman Imperial Legislation*, Detroit: Wayne State University Press.

Maas, M. (2003), 'Delivered from Their Ancient Customs: Christianity and the Question of Cultural Change in Early Byzantine Ethnography', in A. Grafton and K. Mills (eds), *Conversion in Late Antiquity and the Early Middle Ages*, Rochester, NY: University of Rochester Press, pp. 152–88.

Marsham, A. (2009), *Rituals of Islamic Monarchy: Accession and Succession in the First Muslim Empire*, Edinburgh: Edinburgh University Press.

Masuzawa, T. (2005), *The Invention of World Religions: Or, How European Universalism Was Presented in the Language of Pluralism*, Chicago: University of Chicago Press.

Melchert, C. (2006), *Ahmad ibn Hanbal*, Oxford: Oneworld.

Mikhail, M. (2016), *Byzantine to Islamic Egypt: Religion, Identity and Politics after the Arab Conquest*, London: I. B. Tauris.

Millar, F. (2005), 'The Theodosian Empire (408–450) and the Arabs: Saracens or Ishmaelites', in E. Gruen (ed.), *Cultural Borrowings and Ethnic Appropriations in Antiquity*, Stuttgart: Franz Steiner Verlag, pp. 297–314.

Millar, F. (2010), 'Jerome and Palestine', *Scripta Classica Israelica* 29: 59–79.

Morony, M. (2005), 'History and Identity in the Syrian Churches', in T. Van Lint, H.-M. Murre-Van der Berghe and J. Van Ginkel (eds), *Redefining Christian Identity: Cultural Interaction in the Middle East since the Rise of Islam*, Leuven: Peeters, pp. 1–35.

Neuwirth, A. (2010), *Der Koran als Text der Spätantike. Ein europäischer Zugang*, Berlin: Verlag der Weltreligion.

Nongbri, B. (2013), *Before Religion: A History of A Modern Concept*, New Haven: Yale University Press.

Noth, A. (2004), 'Problems of Differentiation between Muslims and non-Muslims: Re-reading the "Ordinances of 'Umar" (*al-Shurūṭ al-ʿumariyya*)', in R. Hoyland (ed.), *Muslims and Others in Early Islamic Society*, Aldershot: Ashgate, pp. 103–24.

Penn, M. P. (2015), *Envisioning Islam: Syriac Christians and the Early Muslim World*, Philadelphia: University of Pennsylvania Press.

Rabello, A. (1987), *Giustiniano, Ebrei e Samaritani alla luce delle fonti storico-letterarie, ecclesiastiche e giuridiche*, 2 vols, Milan: Giuffre.

Rapp, C. (2005), *Holy Bishops in Late Antiquity: The Nature of Christian Leadership in an Age of Transition*, Berkeley: University of California Press.

Reed, A., and A. Becker (eds) (2003), *The Ways that Never Parted: Jews and Christians in Late Antiquity and the Early Middle Ages*, Tübingen: Mohr Siebeck.

Reynolds, G. (2004), *A Muslim Theologian in the Sectarian Milieu: ʿAbd al-Jabbār and the Critique of Christian Origins*, Brill: Leiden.

Reynolds, G. (2010), 'On the Qurʾānic Accusation of Scriptural Falsification (*taḥrīf*) and Christian anti-Jewish Polemic', *Journal of the American Oriental Society* 130: 1–14.

Roberts, A. (2017), 'Being a Sabian at Court in Tenth-Century Baghdad', *Journal of the American Oriental Society* 137: 253–77.

Sahner, C. C. (2017), 'The First Iconoclasm in Islam: A New History of the Edict of Yazid II (AH 104/AD 723)', *Der Islam* 94: 5–56.

Schadler, P. (2018), *John of Damascus and Islam: Christian Heresiology and the Intellectual Background to Earliest Christian-Muslim Relations*, Leiden: Brill.

Schick, R. (1995), *The Christian Communities of Palestine from Byzantine to Islamic Rule: A Historical and Archaeological Study*, Princeton, NJ: Darwin Press.

Schott, J. (2008), *Christianity, Empire and the Making of Religion in Late Antiquity*, Philadelphia: University of Pennsylvania Press.

Schwartz, S. (2001), *Imperialism and Jewish Society, 200 BCE to 640 CE*, Princeton, NJ: Princeton University Press.

Shoemaker, S. (2018), *The Apocalypse of Empire: Imperial Eschatology in Late Antiquity and Early Islam*, Philadelphia: University of Pennsylvania Press.

Simonsohn, U. (2011), *A Common Justice: The Legal Allegiances of Christians and Jews under Early Islam*, Philadephia: University of Pennsylvania Press.

Simonsohn, U. (2016), 'The Introduction and Formalization of Civil Law in the East Syrian Church in the Late Sasanian–Early Islamic Periods', *History Compass* 14: 231–43.

Sizgorich, T. (2009), *Violence and Belief in Late Antiquity: Militant Devotion in Christianity and Islam*, Philadelphia: University of Pennsylvania Press.

Sizgorich, T. (2012), 'Monks and Their Daughters: Monasteries as Muslim-Christian Boundaries', in M. Cormack, *Muslims and Others in Sacred Space*, Oxford: Oxford University Press, pp. 193–211.

Smith, Wilfred Cantwell (1962), *The Meaning and End of Religion: A New Approach to the Religious Traditions of Mankind*, New York: Mentor.

Stetkeyvetch, S. P. (2002), *The Poetics of Islamic Legitimacy: Myth, Gender and Ceremony in the Classical Arabic Ode*, Indianapolis: University of Indiana Press.

Stouriatis, Y. (2014), 'Roman Identity in Byzantium: A Critical Approach', *Byzantinische Zeitschrift* 107: 175–220.

Stroumsa, G. (2015), *The Making of the Abrahamic Religions in Late Antiquity*, Oxford: Oxford University Press.

Sutrisno, E. (2017), 'Confucius Is Our Prophet: The Discourse of Prophecy and Religious Agency in Indonesian Confucianism', *Sojourn: Journal of Social Issues in South-East Asia* 32: 669–718.

Tannous, J. (2013), 'You Are What You Read: Qenneshre and the Miaphysite Church in the Seventh Century', in P. Wood (ed.), *History and Identity in the Late Antique East*, Oxford: Oxford University Press, pp. 83–102.

Tannous, J. (2018), *The Making of the Medieval Middle East: Religion, Society and Simple Believers*, Princeton, NJ: Princeton University Press.

Van Bladel, K. (2009), *The Arabic Hermes: From Pagan Sage to Prophet of Science*, Oxford: Oxford University Press.

Van Bladel, K. (2017), *From Sasanian Mandaeans to Ṣābians of the Marshes*, Leiden: Brill.

Van Putten, M. (2019). '"The Grace of God" as Evidence for a Written Uthmanic Archetype: The Importance of Shared Orthographic Idiosyncrasies', *Bulletin of the School of African and Oriental Studies* 82: 271–88.

Wallis-Budge, E. (1893), *The Book of Governors: The Historia Monastica of Thomas Bishop of Maraga* AD 840, London: Kegan Paul.

Webb, P. (2016), *Imagining the Arabs: Arab Identity and the Rise of Islam*, Cambridge: Cambridge University Press.

Weitz, L. (2016), 'Shaping East Syrian Law in Abbasid Iraq', *Le Muséon* 129: 71–116.

Wood, P. (2010), *We Have No King But Christ: Christian Political Thought in Greater Syria on the Eve of the Arab Conquest (c. 400–585)*, Oxford: Oxford University Press.

Wood, P. (2019), 'Christian Elite Networks in the Jazira, c. 730–840', in S. Heidemann and H. Hagemann (eds), *Transregional and Regional Elites – Connecting the Early Islamic Empire*, 359–383, Berlin: De Gruyter.

Wood P. (forthcoming), 'Christian Contexts for the Qur'an'.

Yarbrough, L. (2016), 'Did ʿUmar b. ʿAbd al-ʿAzīz Issue an Edict Concerning Non-Muslim Officials?', in A. Borrut and F. Donner (eds), *Christians and Others in the Umayyad State*, Chicago: Oriental Institute, pp. 173–206.

Yarbrough, L. (2019), *Friends of the Emir: Non-Muslim State Officials in PreModern Muslim Thought*, Cambridge: Cambridge University Press.

Chapter 8

Prospects for a New Idiom for Islamic History[1]

Shahzad Bashir

History is a treacherous word. I say this in the kindest of spirits and with an eye toward the word's pronounced polysemy. In this short reflection, I high-light three meanings that, interlaced, relate to the problem of how history frames discussions of Islam. I suggest that attending to history is a baseline for methodological reflection on Islam. As an object of academic attention, Islam is a predicate of time and space, which are aspects of human lives. As the generic name for narrative structures that interrelate between times and spaces, history is evoked directly or is presupposed in all scholarly discussions of Islam. Therefore, wherever it is encountered in academic contexts, the term 'Islam' is imbued with presumptions or arguments pertaining to history. In the essay, I lay out the three relevant meanings, identify issues that arise from thinking critically about established usage, and, briefly suggest some ways to look beyond the current horizons.[2]

Three Meanings of History

First, I focus on the way we use the term history today; namely, to designate a modern method for deciphering data from the past. Institutionalised in univer-sity departments around the world, the historical method subjects evidence to

---

[1] A preliminary version of this essay was presented at the Workshop 'Religious Diversity and the Secular University' at the Centre for Research in the Arts, Social Sciences and the Humanities at the University of Cambridge in January 2019. I am grateful to Theodor Dunkelgrün, Simon Goldhill and Faridah Zaman for their inciteful comments.
[2] Given the brevity of this essay, the prescriptive aspect of my presentation will remain a gesture. My forthcoming book on this topic consists of interpretive essays that expand on issues pertaining to the past that I find most compelling (Bashir, forthcoming).

principles of contextualisation and material causality. Although encompassing much diversity and nuance, the historical method is rooted in an overall commitment to a stance that one perceptive interpreter calls 'ontological realism'.[3] This deserves a brief unpacking. It denotes the underlying presumption that allows us to project that, when provided adequate sources, we have the ability to reconstitute events of the past as they must have happened. Very few historians working today would claim that this can be done in an absolute way. Even the founders of the modern discipline, such as the German historian Leopold von Ranke to whom this view is often ascribed, had a nuanced understanding of the matter.[4] And most historians writing now see their discipline as based on a softer version, that reconstitution can only happen in the form of perspectives on events that may be mutually irreconcilable. This makes room for ambiguity and allows for a variety of explanations. While acknowledging that the past is knowable variably and only in part, this view retains a commitment to the past as a set of facts that can be related in forms of language authorised by the discipline.

My second concern is with the way history matters as the root underlying 'historicism'. This word 'historicism' has its own wide variety of uses, including as a name for the contextualist method associated with ontological realism. That is, the imperative to historicise, to critically appraise sources as effects that emerge from specific backgrounds and then to use them to create persuasive accounts of the past, or to interpret literary works as effects of the world in which they were composed.[5] My current interest in historicism is for a more differentiated purpose, namely, its identification as the basis for deriving universal principles out of disparate data about and from the past. Famously, this is the kind of historicism that was critiqued by Karl Popper, who was then criticised severely for the idiosyncrasy and inconsistency of his usage.[6] I am not interested in defending Popper or restating the critique in detail. Rather, I want to make use of what Popper calls historicism as a philosophical attitude to the past that is imbricated in such practices of the modern social sciences that attempt to systematically understand the past for purposes of solving social problems and predicting and controlling the future. Understood in this way, historicism remains an important academic as well as popular discourse. It authorises the use of the past for making political policy. It is also reflected in phrases taken as truisms, such as that those who do not know history are doomed to repeat it. In recent years, this perspective has received prominent attention with respect

---

[3] Kleinberg 2017.
[4] Toews 2019.
[5] Iggers 1995; Hamilton 1996; Beiser 2011.
[6] Popper 2002; Keuth 2005; Keaney 1997.

to Islam in fields such as radical politics and economic development.[7] More generally, the Islamic past as an antidote to the present has loomed large in many influential attempts at defining and redefining Islam.[8]

The third significant meaning of history is the elision through which understandings of the past that are neither historicist nor fruits of work undertaken according to the modern historical method are assimilated into modern discourses. That is, we take a work written about the past in the past (e.g. in tenth-century Baghdad, or thirteenth-century Isfahan, or fifteenth-century Delhi) and call it *history* even though we would not call a narrative like it history if someone were to write it today. This use of history is an interpretive sleight of hand since it obfuscates the quite different epistemological bases and sociopolitical purposes of chronographic works written in different sociohistorical contexts. Indeed, an appreciation of this difference is supposed to be a cardinal principle in the modern historical method. Modern readers are usually aware that narratives about the past written in premodern contexts are not history in the modern sense. But this distinction is obscured to make the works legible in our categories. The elision conceals the facts that human beings objectify the past in diverse ways and that the modern historical method is hardly a transhistorical universal. Most often, modern readings of past understandings of the past overlook framing narratives. Instead, they focus on declarative descriptions that are seemingly meaningful in the ontological realist paradigm that underlies current practice.[9]

'Islamic history' as it exists in the modern academy corresponds to a braiding together of the three senses of history I have outlined. Of these, the first two are second-order concerns since they relate to disciplinary method (the historian's profession) and the theoretical basis for undertaking certain kinds of work (the purpose of history). The third is a first-order issue in that it pertains to the initial encounter that makes it possible to make any claims about the past at all. The last is foundational also because the vast majority of what we refer to as Islamic history is a partial rendition of events described in premodern chronographic texts. The field began in the nineteenth century with the work of self-proclaimed orientalists who projected authority on the basis of their ability to read texts about Islam and Muslims from past centuries. Working philologically, they took works in Arabic, Persian, Turkish, and so on, as statements of contested facts, which they subjected to comparison and rationalisation to produce a presumably critical historical account of Islam consisting of a string of events running from Muhammad to their present. In this undertaking, framing

---

[7] E.g. Wasserstein 2017; Kuran 2011.
[8] See Hughes, Kersten, Enayat, Olsson and Stenberg, and Wood in this volume.
[9] Fasolt 2004; Grafton 2007; Tanaka 2019.

arguments that contained intense theoretical contestation on the nature and knowability of the past were given little attention. Further, modern understandings of material causality provided the criteria for highlighting or overlooking what was found in the vast original literature. Claims of miracles, for example, were deemed inadmissible whereas descriptions of administrative practices were understood to be historical, despite the fact that statements pertaining to both could be found side by side in the same original source. The field did include the sub-category 'Islamic historiography'. However, this subject area consists of schematic or developmentalist descriptions of how Muslims have discussed history along the presumed unified vector that is Islamic history.[10] Rare examples notwithstanding,[11] conceptual issues invoked in the sources as problems regarding representation of the past were given scant attention. For example, authors' introductions that spoke at length about the difficulty of determining the value of written or oral evidence, and variant moral purposes that led authors to narrate the past in particular ways, were not treated as essential to understanding the representations contained in the works. When heeded, such concerns can place us in a conversation with the authors around issues that matter in writing about the past today as much as they did in premodern contexts.

The sources were also treated as 'primary' material, although these were all 'secondary' rhetorical projections on the past embedded within the circumstances of various points of composition. As a result, the classics of Islamic history as a modern subject enshrine severely truncated representations of what is in the originals. This is partly due to shrinkage from thousands of volumes to schematised, hugely abridged treatments. More significantly, the modern historiographic method compelled the invention of a streamlined, intellectually impoverished, Islamic history that underplayed the great diversity and contention about the basis for talking about the past found in the cited sources.

Over the course of the twentieth and twenty-first centuries, Islamic history has retained much of what accrued to the field at its origins. Philological expertise – not linguistic ability as such, but the more particular processing of linguistic data according to modern philological principles[12] – remains the predominant way to measure competence to speak on the subject. But since the middle of the twentieth century, philology has become increasingly entwined with historicism as the basis of modern social sciences in the understanding I have discussed above. This was especially the case in the vogue for social history that sought to process sources into aggregated assessments of society. Since the Cold War period, even the premodern past has been made to speak to contemporary

---

[10] E.g. Rosenthal 1968; Khalidi 1994.
[11] Waldman 1980; Laroui 1999.
[12] Olender 2009.

political concerns, subject to perspectives ranging between Marxism(s), cultural or economic determinism, and the effort to portray Muslims as being fundamentally medieval even when living contemporaneously.[13] In the social scientific use of the past, the key has been to make Islam into a constant, a force that is either understood as being unchangeable or is presumed to be caught in a cycle that can be determined and plotted to predict the future on the basis of the past. Prominent examples for this include appeals to sectarian theological arguments found in premodern texts as explanations for the rise of radicalism, revolutionary movements, and the slow pace of economic development.

Through the accumulation of critical mass on various topics – and partly due to the critique of orientalism common since the 1980s – current scholarship in the field of Islamic history has tended to become more nuanced. Scholars in the field read materials sensitively, try to avoid unwarranted assumptions, and present their work in sophisticated, multi-level arguments. But this work is carried out in piecemeal fashion, through specialised studies of individuals, movements, regions, and so on. To project value, such studies must adhere to the established sense of Islamic history that continues as a legacy from the nineteenth century. For premodern topics, this is necessary in order to make one's work legible to the scholarly community. One has to place the topic in grids of periodisation established on the basis of regional differentiations and names of dynasties (Abbasid, Mamluk, Timurid, Ottoman, Mughal, etc.) tied to chronology.[14]

Works on the modern history of societies that involve Islam and Muslims identify on the basis of nation states, which have created their own identities by presuming stable premodern contexts as their sources. Crucially, history is the key ingredient in the politics, social policies and public performance of modern states.[15] As a consequence of the intertwining of various intellectual and historical factors, Islamic history as we know it today constitutes an authoritative temporality. That is, it is a packaged account of the relationship between Islam and time that is presented as the 'truth' in educational settings and is instrumentalised in situations where the past matters for current political purposes. Contrary to what is often projected in its instantiations, this history is tenuously derived from a vastly diverse source base. Modern ontological realist presumptions – which compel scholars to ignore much of what is in the original sources and to treat certain statements as material 'facts' without attention to the rhetorical contexts in which they occur – have tended to strip the material of complexity in order to fixate on narrower intellectual and political imperatives.

---

[13] See Otterbeck, Stenberg, and Hammer in this volume.
[14] Bosworth 1996.
[15] E.g. Di-Capua 2009; Vejdani 2014.

A CORRECTIVE

My portrayal of Islamic history above is admittedly overly broad and expresses my impatience with the status quo. However, I should emphasise that this is not meant as moral criticism. I am not suggesting that scholars who created the field in the nineteenth century were intellectually unsophisticated or ethically suspect. Nor am I contending that work since the nineteenth century reflects a conspiracy or consistent bias against Islam and Muslims. Good reasons are available to explain the field's trajectory, reasons involving intellectual as well as political developments that can be understood sympathetically in context. The purpose of my critique is to identify analytical shortcomings that deserve to be addressed in order to refine the way we treat Islam as an object of historical interest.

I suggest that the streamlined, unidirectional understanding of history that sees Islam as being born in the sixth century and continuing to the present deserves to be jettisoned on the basis of new ways to read the original sources. From this perspective, all the introductory books on Islamic history available today are problematic and counterproductive. They perpetuate a constrictive framework that forces the use of a (sectarian Sunni) theological vision of Islam as the basis of thinking about Islam and Muslims. Sociointellectual limitations pertaining to orientalists who created the field in the nineteenth century are easily visible today. There is little reason to continue being constrained by them while interpreting the texts and other materials at our disposal. We should hope that those who come after us do the same with respect to the work we do today.

The first crucial step in my prescription involves changing the way we see Islamic history: it is not something 'out there', waiting to be unveiled on the basis of ontological realism. Islam is not a corporate being whose existence can be plotted over the ages. To think of Islam in this way – as is done across much work pertaining to the history of Islam – is to misapprehend the very nature of the object under study. Islam is, rather, a collective name given to certain aspects of thought and behaviour of certain human beings. Islam is not 'real' aside from the circumstances in which it is invoked. From this perspective, Islamic history must be seen as a discursive field subject to imaginative generation of stories made viable through playing with ambiguous evidence. We should permit ourselves to rethink and invent new frameworks that match the intensively varied senses of Islam that we can gather from the sources. This history should be treated as a field of contention suspended between different types of perspectives, academic and otherwise. Islam as a historical object should also be decoupled from the issue of Muslim self-representation. Moreover, when assessing Muslim projections, the past should be understood as a site of constant problematisation and reinvention, tied to interpersonal and inter-community negotiation.

When attempting to understand Muslim contexts, treating Islam as an explanation for conduct amounts to misdirection stemming from a historicist perspective. This approach turns Islam into an ahistorical force that is then used problematically to explain and predict matters in a social scientific vein. To describe Islam as having a trajectory in time is a reification that is a root cause for thinking that certain modes of thought and practice are religious constants that propel Muslims' observable behaviour. Dismissing this approach, we should presume that Islam is created when it is invoked; it ought not to be seen as an actor independent of human agency. References to Islam are ideological postures that we have no reason to regard to be coherent across different times and places on a universal scale. Removing Islam as a *sui generis* historicist category means that connections and possible coherences amongst various Muslim contexts must be argued for analytically, not presumed beforehand.

The ontological realism that characterises modern historiographical practice is an inefficient and misleading way to process materials pertaining to Islam. It forces us to ignore much of what is projected about the past in literary sources. Moreover, descriptive sections culled and turned into 'facts' to be made believable in the realist paradigm can distort when sheered from their rhetorical moorings. Stepping away from this mode, the commonality surrounding Islam should be understood nominally. Islam is a discursive realm in the process of being made and unmade through the agency of those who invoke it in specific circumstances.[16]

Islamic history cannot be the temporal progress of a set of religious roles and behaviours since a historical understanding shows that these are subject to constant and unlimited change. It must be the ever-evolving story of discussions about an abstraction we name Islam, which is endowed with ideological and sociological potency but acquires shape only in the context of localised human circumstances. Our evidence for this history consists of objects, 'not just things, but whatever we individuate and allow ourselves to talk about . . . not only "material" objects but also classes, kinds of people, and, indeed, ideas'.[17] These objects are carriers of varied, often mutually antagonistic and unrecognisable ways of creating the past. When Islam is put in conjunction with history, the continual invention of the past should be a core concern. Although possibly unsettling, such an attitude to the subject is also freeing and an invitation to construct new stories. This is a creative approach to Islamic history that involves paying acute attention to the available materials in order to think about Islamic pasts and futures.

---

16 Thum 2019: 9–11.
17 Hacking 2002: 2.

POSSIBLE FUTURES

To render the view of Islamic history I am advocating concrete, it is necessary to suggest topical arenas that are ripe for thematisation in new ways. In this vein, issues pertaining to rhetoric, temporal structures, and voice in literary materials are especially significant. I first lay these out generally and then speak to the details of one historical account from the nineteenth century that illustrates new ways to think about such materials.

Representations of the Islamic past in literary sources are all rhetorical exercises. By rhetoric I do not mean that these are sophistic, intellectually and morally fallow creations meant for elite entertainment. Rather, these are elaborate works that require careful parsing to go from words to imagining worlds to understand the pictures in words about the past they describe. Citing reports in these works as sources of fact without attention to overall and immediate framing can be misleading. To become attuned to the rhetoric requires that languages be understood as being subject to constant change and manipulation. Some rhetorical underpinnings can be gleaned from formal discussions of rhetoric, such as prescriptive and idealising works on *balāgha* in Arabic, Persian, and so on. However, to my reading, in works pertaining to the past, rhetorical postures usually do not follow formalised principles and must be excavated from the literary works themselves. Quite often, prefaces to chronicles and other works contain autobiographical notes on authors' methods and circumstances. Self-representation need not be taken at face value, but it can orient us toward richer understandings of events presented in words.

Rhetoric is also discernible when we pay attention to narrative as a mode of practice. This requires thinking comparatively, since what may be peculiar to one author becomes visible only through knowledge of how others might write. Rhetorical features vary greatly between as well as within languages. For example, the same event narrated in Arabic versus Persian comes across as quite different, even when a text purports to be a translation from one language to the other. And Persian chronicles written in, say, the eleventh century, have a flavour utterly different from what one finds in the same language two centuries later. Overall, we can presume that, to represent the past, words and tropes used by authors constitute self-conscious choices tied to ideological and stylistic purposes. These matters are not mere embellishments or screens that we must look through to get to the facts. Rhetorical differences index varying views on the relationship between language and facticity, including positions on what is to be regarded as real or unreal. Rhetoric is an existential matter and a major source for us to understand the past.

In the words of a theoretician whose work has done much to sensitise us to conceptual problems pertaining to the past, 'when one seeks to form an intuition of time as such, one is referred to spatial indications'.[18] These may be a clock's surface, a written calendar, the wrinkles and scars on a human body, ruins and new buildings, and the movement of celestial bodies. This insight is especially fruitful for analysing literary works concerned with the Islamic past. For example, the fact that chronicles written in the identical time and place spatialise the past differently indexes ideological variability. Some narratives tie Islam to a single timeline (with internal cycles), connected to a calendar. Others insist on a multiplicity of timelines that preserve competing community identities. Some attempt to coordinate between calendars, while for others, calendars are repositories of communal memory that relate separate forms of authority.

Besides timelines and calendars, it is common to represent time as a series of gardens, with events deemed worthy of description being treated as paradisiacal reality made manifest in earthly terms. Or time is rendered into a multi-story building, gaining height as one adds years and centuries. The passage of time can be organised cyclically through correlation with planetary conjunctions, signifying both explanation for what has come to pass and what can be predicted by reading the stars. All this diversity regarding the spatialisation of time is not reducible to a determined pattern, such that we could speak easily of evolution or linear development. Rather, the variety is most often simultaneous, indicating that authors competed with each other in the way they created their pictures of time. Given that we can find alternative understandings in the same settings, we can presume that the audiences for these works were also well aware that time can be represented in multiple ways. Creativity pertaining to the representation of the past was thus expected, and attending to variation can help us understand the works with greater sophistication.[19]

Literary evidence pertaining to the past is often a congress of different voices under an author's curatorial control. Authors can be autobiographical to varying degrees, depending on personal predilection as well as relationships to the subjects and sponsors of their narratives. As elaborate rhetorical exercises, chronicles and other chronographic works are formalised texts that instantiate conventions of genres. In such material, the first-person voice has specific possibilities and limitations. Moreover, works also convey the voices of others through the citation of alleged dialogues, commands, emotions, and so forth. Authorial choices convey the interplay of voices through formal features, such as chains of authority. Attention to the use of voices is a major source for us to understand how authors make the past authoritative for their present circumstances.

I exemplify the significance of this attention to rhetoric, temporal structure

---

[18] Koselleck 2002: 103.
[19] E.g. Bashir 2014.

and voice in works about the Islamic past by describing a Persian chronicle completed in India in 1863. The description I provide would seem like an ordinary summary of a work of the type found in many modern scholarly works. My key suggestion here is that we should *not* read the work I am describing as a minor production that deviates from better known examples of the genre. Rather, I insist that this and all similar works on the Islamic past should be taken as equally authoritative expressions for representing the Islamic past. There is no Islam 'out there' except as can be found in works such as these, written in particularised circumstances for specific purposes. Islamic history in this view amounts to the everchanging vision of the Islamic past that was as unfixed in the ninth century CE as it may appear in a work produced in the nineteenth century.

The work I describe aims to be a universal history and survives in a unique manuscript that has received little to no attention in the scholarship. In the ontological realist paradigm of Islamic history, this work is largely useless since it repeats information from other sources. As the sole scholarly assessment of the work indicates, in this mode only the information it provides about the recent history of Bengal may be considered valuable.[20] However, I believe, its exceptionality is a resource for appreciating the potentialities of Islamic history as a creative arena ensconced within inherited genres and specific sociohistorical circumstances. When we pay attention to its conceptual content rather than regarding it as a repository of facts, it becomes a valuable exemplum for the way I am suggesting we should re-invent Islamic history as an academic field.

Sayyid Ilāhī Bakhsh Angrēzābādī's *Khūrshīd-i jahān-numā* (The sun that displays the world) is 583 folios (1116 pages) of a manuscript now in the National Library of India in Kolkata.[21] The author was born in a small town in Bengal in 1824 and died in the same place in 1892. The work appears, upon first encounter, as a narrative in standard literary Persian studded with familiar salutations, idioms and turns of phrases one can find elsewhere in abundance. In fact, if reading in the volume at random, without looking at the work systematically, one may think it could be a chronicle written at any time in the early modern period. However, delving deeper dispels this possibility. The author's last name indicates his residence at Angrēzābād (English Bazar) in Bengal, British India; this fact helps us understand the work's contents. Contrary to general appearances, this work is thoroughly indebted to the presence of European persons and ideas. This fact should not be taken as an instance of contamination; works produced in centuries prior to it were equally indebted to knowledge stemming from contexts relevant for them.

---

[20] Beveridge 1895.
[21] 'Abd-ul-Muqtadir 1921: 77–8.

The author begins with the praise of God, Muhammad and the Twelve Shii imams, followed by his intention to share his knowledge of history. A spatial metaphor then provides an overview of the work's contents. It is named a sun (khūrshīd) and is divided into twelve chapters that the author calls by the term burj. This last word has many meanings whose simultaneous invocation provides us with a sense of the kind of splicing between space and time that happens in writing history. Burj means, first, a tower, by which token the narrative is a spacialisation, as if by reading it we would traverse a territory marked by twelve towers that give distinctive spaces their identities. Second, burj also means star or planet, or the celestial houses in which astral bodies reside during different times. This meaning indicates that the narrative is an account that foregrounds time as an abstraction measured by the movement of celestial bodies. And third, burj is the generic term for the constellations in the sky, the subject of the influential art and science of astrology. In this sense time is a factor that connects cosmic movement to the lives of individual human beings in horoscopes. Between the title and the organisation, then, Angrēzābādī's conceit is that his narrative is like a sun that makes manifest the earth, the sky, and the life histories of individuals and groups that derive from the contingency of circumstances.[22] Saying that the work is a history, then calling it a sun, and finally organising it around the complex multiple meanings associated with the word burj are deliberately creative ways to present the past. The crucial point being that the creative spirit exhibited here is entirely the norm, rather than an exception, when it comes to the chronicle tradition associated with Islam. Yet, conceptual creativity has seldom been the subject of academic attention because of overarching presumptions regarding the contents of Islamic history.

Let us now move from the rhetorical posture and the abstract structure underlying the work to its specific content. Its narrative table of contents describes the twelve burj as follows:

1. Cosmography (various Islamic and European perspectives on geography and history) [pp. 3–5]
2. Americas (North and South) [pp. 5–12]
3. Africa [pp. 12–20]
4. Europe [pp. 20–51]
5. Asia (including most of what is usually identified as 'Islamic' history, and Indian geography and history to the beginning of British empire) [pp. 51–815]
6. Australasia and Polynesia [pp. 815–28]

---

[22] Angrēzābādī 1863: 1–3.

7. Prophets (biblical figures according to an Islamic understanding) [pp. 828–66]
8. Ancient philosophers [pp. 866–8]
9. Important persons (biblical, ancient Indian sages, Sufis, contemporary Hindus, and British officials, etc.) [pp. 868–1054]
10. Sufi genealogies [pp. 1054–73]
11. Varia (architecture in India; arithmetic; the inhabited world; royal genealogies, lunar and solar calendars) [pp. 1073–99]
12. The author's personal history (born 1824, completed the work in 1863 after a labour of eleven years) [pp. 1099–107]

The first element to note is the sheer volume of information that is being conveyed here by a resident of a small town in the middle of rural Bengal in the middle of the nineteenth century. Perfectly self-conscious as both a Muslim and a historian, the author cannot be called a parochial intellect by any stretch of the imagination. The work's table of contents is an eclectic mix of categories involving space, time and topic put into chapters of vastly different lengths. Following a pattern found in earlier works of the same type in Persian, it has an accordion-like structure that has expanded to provide space for absorbing new knowledge available to someone living in India with access to Europeans. Between the multiply signifying term *burj* and the shape of the narrative, this work fits well in patterns for writing a chronicle that were nearly five centuries old by the time Angrēzābādī took up the pen. But unlike the chronicles of old, he provides extensive information about countries and regions in Europe, the Americas, Australia, and elsewhere.

Even more significantly, in cosmographical sections, he describes views from the 'people of Islam' (*ahl-e Islām*), non-Muslim Indians, and the English and Europeans more generally (Angrēzhā, *ahl-e Farang*). The contrast between different perspectives on such issues is presented without preference or prejudice for any party. This gives the narrative a tone of intellectual ecumenism that does not seem to contradict the use of heavily Islamic nomenclature, benedictions, and so on, that also pervade the work's language throughout. We might say that the contents of this work present a compelling instance of the proverbial new wine in old bottles. The author has retained taxonomic, rhetorical and aesthetic paradigms that he inherited from the Indian-Persian teachers he recalls in various passages with great reverence. But narrative shells created from these orientations have been made hospitable to new opinions and knowledge. The example provides evidence for the extreme malleability of the form in use, which accommodates new content with the same degree of flexibility we usually presume for modern understandings of history.

One further aspect of Angrēzābādī's work hints at the fact that this may be a new historical subjectivity conveyed in an old language. When I first came across the *Khūrshīd-i jahān-numā*, quite accidentally in the microfilm collection of the Sinor Research Institute for Inner Asian Studies at Indiana University, I presumed that the work would contain the author's explanation for the circumstances that had led him to undertake this huge labour. Such explanations are a standard feature of earlier works in the genre to which it belongs. The prospect seemed all the more likely because the last section of the work (the twelfth *burj*) is entitled 'The author's personal history'. What I found, however, is that the author only provides a long chronology of his family, the content of which consists of names, places of domicile, and death dates given in both the Hijri and the Gregorian calendars.

The author's description of the space of Angrēzābād, his birthplace and continuing residence, is entirely devoid of personal reminiscences of any kind (pp. 547–54). In the twelfth *burj*, he tells us about an ancestor who had moved from the area around Dhaka to Angrēzābād, the hub of silk production for the English East India Company, in the late eighteenth century. This is then followed by a long list of names of male and female relatives, including ancestors, coevals, and his own children and others in later generations (pp. 1099–117). The clinical nature of the information provided here is quite unusual for a work in the genre. Circumstantially, I am inclined to interpret the presentation of self in dates alone, rather than through the more usual recourse to sentiment, as a novel way to think about the valuable past, which the author would have absorbed from his reading of European materials. This seems especially so because Angrēzābādi is punctilious about giving Gregorian era dates for his family, perhaps adopting a pattern that he observed in the practices of his European associates. I find this line of interpretation appealing but a fully compelling case requires going into more depth with this and other comparable works than the space available at present.

Between rhetoric, structure and voice, Angrēzābādī's *Khūrshīd-i jahān-numā* both affirms and defies the genre of universal Islamic history written in Persian. This is an Islamic chronographic work that operates under a non-Muslim aegis and relies extensively on non-Islamic sources, seemingly without a sense of contradiction. It also absorbs new understandings of the past even as it sticks to indigenous narrative forms. My point in using this *unusual* source to clarify my perspective on Islamic history is that what we see here is in fact utterly *usual* once we start paying attention to the conceptual issues present in the vast source base available to us for exploring the conjunction between Islam and history. Some such work already exists in the form of fine studies that have highlighted important sources earlier excluded from the field.[23] But even well-

---

[23] E.g. Florida 1995; Sajdi 2013.

known works that have been read for decades by multiple scholars readily yield new understandings.[24]

The kinds of issues I have highlighted using the example of a Persian chronicle apply equally well to works in other languages and genres. The present context is insufficient to address the many other issues that remain, which are taken up in earnest in my forthcoming book on this topic. Within current constraints, I hope I have made an adequate case for the overarching suggestion that we need to evaluate all sources we utilise on the basis of a "first principles" approach, rather than being guided by the established pattern of what is considered Islamic history. When attending to issues such as rhetoric, structure and voice, one primary concern should be understanding what Islam means to, or meant to, the authors. This goes against the established pattern, in which we presume that Islam exists outside these sources such that, when we read, our effort is geared toward contextualising on the basis of the presumed facticity of a certain timeline of Islamic history. If actualised, the fundamental shift of approach and perception I am advocating will lead to a new idiom for Islamic history that better accounts for what is to be found in the original sources. The stakes of the reorientation I am prescribing become evident if I say that we should treat the *Khūrshīd-i jahān-numā* as the truest possible understanding of Islam. To do this would mean that, for instance, the great classics for Islamic history (such as the ancient chronicles of Ṭabarī and Masʿūdī) should be dethroned from their priv-ileged place for understanding the Islamic past. The replaceability is the crux of my point since it is only through accepting this proposition that we radically rethink the possibilities of Islamic history.

I end with the suggestion that we understand the field of Islamic history as a non-exclusive domain in a radical sense. My intensive focus on certain themes aims to encourage analytical probity with respect to sources that pertain to the Islamic past. All understandings of the past can be understood in this way. Much, if not all, of what I have said is relevant to the consideration of other histories, religious and otherwise. On this account, the attempt to free Islamic history from ontological realism, historicism, and the problematic slippage between modern history and diverse premodern chronographies is relevant for historiographical theorisation at the most general level.

BIBLIOGRAPHY

ʿAbd-ul-Muqtadir (1921), *Catalogue of the Persian Manuscripts in the Buhar Library*, Calcutta: Imperial Library.

Angrēzābādī, Sayyid Ilāhī Bakhsh (1863), *Khūrshīd-i jahān-numā*, MS. Buhar 102, National Library of India, Kolkata.

---

[24] E.g. Bashir 2018.

Bashir, Shahzad (2014), 'On Islamic Time: Rethinking Chronology in the Historiography of Muslim Societies', *History and Theory* 53, no. 4: 464–519.

Bashir, Shahzad (2018), 'Everlasting Doubt: Uncertainty in Islamic Representations of the Past', *Archiv für Religionsgeschichte* 20: 25–44.

Bashir, Shahzad (forthcoming), *A New Vision for Islamic Pasts and Futures*, Cambridge, MA: MIT Press.

Beiser, Frederick (2011), *The German Historicist Tradition*, Oxford: Oxford University Press.

Beveridge, Henry (1895), 'The Khurshid Jahan Numa of Sayyad Ilahi Bakhsh ak-Husaini Angrezabadi', *Journal of the Asiatic Society of Bengal* 64, no. 3: 194–236.

Bosworth, Edmund C. (1996), *The New Islamic Dynasties: A Chronological and Genealogical Manual*, New York: Columbia University Press.

Di-Capua, Y. (2009), *Gatekeepers of the Arab Past: Historians and History Writing in Twentieth-Century Egypt*, Berkeley: University of California Press.

Fasolt, Constantin (2004), *The Limits of History*, Chicago: University of Chicago Press.

Florida, Nancy (1995), *Writing the Past, Inscribing the Future: History as Prophesy in Colonial Java*, Durham, NC: Duke University Press.

Grafton, A. (2007), *What Was History? The Art of History in Early Modern Europe*, Cambridge: Cambridge University Press.

Hacking, Ian (2002), *Historical Ontology*, Cambridge, MA: Harvard University Press.

Hamilton, Paul (1996), *Historicism*, London: Routledge.

Iggers, Georg (1995), 'Historicism: The History and Meaning of the Term', *Journal of the History of Ideas* 56, no. 1: 129–52.

Keaney, Michael (1997), 'The Poverty of Rhetoricism: Popper, Mises and the Riches of Historicism', *History of the Human Sciences* 10, no. 1: 1–22.

Keuth, Herbert (2005), *The Philosophy of Karl Popper*, New York: Cambridge University Press.

Khalidi, Tarif (1994), *Arabic Historical Thought in the Classical Period*, Cambridge: Cambridge University Press.

Kleinberg, Ethan (2017), *Haunting History: For a Deconstructive Approach to the Past*, Stanford: Stanford University Press.

Koselleck, Reinhart (2002), *The Practice of Conceptual History: Timing History, Spacing Concepts*, trans. Todd Samuels Presner *et al.*, Stanford: Stanford University Press.

Kuran, Timur (2011), *The Long Divergence: How Islamic Law Held Back the Middle East*, Princeton, NJ: Princeton University Press.

Laroui, Abdallah (1999), *Islam et histoire: Essai d'épistémologie*, Paris: Flammarion.

Olender, Maurice (2009), *The Languages of Paradise: Race, Religion, and Philology in the Nineteenth Century*, trans. Arthur Goldhammer, Cambridge, MA: Harvard University Press.

Popper, Karl (2002), *The Poverty of Historicism*, London: Routledge.

Rosenthal, Franz (1968), *A History of Muslim Historiography*, Leiden: Brill.

Sajdi, Dana (2013), *The Barber of Damascus: Nouveau Literacy in the Eighteenth-Century Ottoman Levant*, Stanford: Stanford University Press.

Tanaka, Stefan (2019), *History Without Chronology*, Amherst, MA: Lever Press.

Thum, Rian (2019), 'What is Islamic History', *History and Theory* 57, no. 4: 7–19.

Toews, John (2019), 'Historicism from Ranke to Nietzsche', in W. Breckman and P. E. Gordon (eds), *The Cambridge History of Modern European Thought*, vol. 1, Cambridge: Cambridge University Press, pp. 301–29.

Vejdani, Farzin (2014), *Making History in Iran: Education, Nationalism, and Print Culture*, Stanford: Stanford University Press.

Waldman, Marilyn Robinson (1980), *Toward a Theory of Historical Narrative: A Case Study in Perso-Islamicate Historiography*, Columbus: Ohio State University Press.

Wasserstein, David (2017), *Black Banners of ISIS: The Roots of the New Caliphate*, New Haven: Yale University Press.

Chapter 9

Constructing Islamic Studies: Gender, Power and Critique as Ethical Tools

Juliane Hammer

I see the academy, especially the humanities and social sciences, as a dia-logical project; a project in which scholars explore the world around them, analyse it in all its complicated structures, institutions, practices, discourses, histories and dynamics, and then communicate and discuss the findings with other scholars, and sometimes even the broader society. In this formation, scholarship, rather than being produced from a place of personal detachment and from a distance, is both inherently positional and political. This claim holds true even when scholars, as many have done and still do, claim objec-tivity, impartiality, or detachment from their research subjects and topics of enquiry.

In the invitation to the workshop that became the foundation of this current volume, scholars in Islamic studies (broadly conceived) from Europe and North America were tasked with exploring how to see 'Islam as a discourse that is reproduced in each generation and context according to a changing paradigm'. The invitation continued:

> Thus our interests lie in how Muslimness and Islam intersect with other forms of identitarian politics (class, gender, and nation); how different bodies of evidence illustrate the different ways in which Muslimness and Islam are con-structed and how the construction of Islam responds to the construction of other traditions and concepts. In an intellectual environment that thrives on binary constructs, our hope is to provide complications to these narratives, not just by demonstrating the complexity of categories, but also undermining the significance of the political use of ethnic and religious categorisation itself.

In response to that invitation, I propose that, rather than engaging in the deconstruction of Islam and Muslimness – a project that has many followers in Islamic studies – I invest in a constructive approach to the study of Islam and Muslims. This approach recognises my scholarship as intentionally political and engaged in a project of world-changing rather than world-accounting. There is of course room for diverse approaches to Islamic studies and I do not claim that the approach I follow is the only acceptable path or indeed the only methodo-logical and ethical possibility. I have, however, encountered frequent dismissal of my scholarship as valuable or even scholarship at all because I acknowledge the normative commitments that undergird my contributions to knowledge production. I also lay claim to a community of scholars in the academy, and in Islamic studies specifically, that have built and continue to build the momentum for a necessary and critical rethinking of our field. In other words, I am not alone in this endeavour and not the first or last to take on rigid notions of academic discipline or the purported need to distinguish scholarship from activism.[1]

I write this essay from my own location in Islamic studies, as part of religious studies in the specific context of the United States, where the field of the study of religion has a long history of Protestant and white Christian hegemony as well as an equally long history of debates about religious normativity versus analytical distancing (that is, theology versus 'real' religious studies). The study of Islam and Muslims sits somewhat uncomfortably at the margins of that debate but has also acquired a particular flavour of exceptionalism that implicates it even fur-ther and more deeply in 'too much' religious normativity (also sometimes called theology) or demands even more vigorous self-distancing from scholars so as to not be labelled apologists for Islam and Muslims. I am neither a theologian nor a detached observer of Muslim communities and societies. As a self-identified Muslim feminist scholar of Islamic studies, I recognise that my ethical, religious and political convictions and commitments have always been the inspiration for my work as a scholar and as an activist.

Over the past fifteen years my career has focused, in a variety of ways, on the work of Muslim scholars and activists who strive to change Muslim communities

---

[1] I continue to be inspired by the work of members of this community. For example, Justine Howe wrote in 2017, in her essay, 'What is Scholarship Good For?': 'To bridge this gap, we need more than just explanations that satisfy the terms of academic conversations. For all my attention to fluid subjectivities, I simply cannot ignore that religious designations matter all the more today – specifically religious identities within human bodies. Within human flesh. These everyday practices are still embodied, still emanate from and through bodies, and "religion" – a sometimes fixed and involuntary demarcation – is increasingly the basis for physical exclusion and violence. Prayer groups executed at point blank. Car hoods smeared with human flesh. Streets lined with broken bodies. Bombs detonated just minutes before dawn prayer. It is relatively easy for me to understand such violence within the frameworks of critical theory that line the bookshelves of my office. Can I also accept my role in enabling, if not producing, these traumas by obviating the practices of excess in favor of nuance?' See Howe 2017.

and societies. In several projects, on feminist *tafsir*, on woman-led prayer, on efforts against domestic violence, and on marriage equality and the rights of LGBTQI+ Muslims, I have engaged with the works of scholars who are also activists and I have argued for the recognition of grassroots advocates as exegetes of foundational Islamic texts. Therein lies another blurry boundary (if one exists at all) between what is scholarship and what is activist discourse, not to mention the important question of how discourses are related to practices and vice versa.

To take the boundary negotiation (or perhaps erasure?) even further, many of the Muslim scholars whose works I have analysed and engaged would lay claim to being Islamic studies scholars and many hold teaching positions in Islamic studies, in religious studies departments, though mostly in private colleges and universities. In the context of the United States in particular, there is a recurring debate about what constitutes authentic Islamic studies scholarship, especially among scholars who participate in the American Academy of Religion. The debate is usually framed as a question of methodology as well as scholarly authenticity and inevitably aims to separate the analytic study of Islam from prescriptive (or unfortunately named 'theological')[2] approaches to Islam and Muslims.[3] A similar debate continues to take place in the context of the German government project to establish institutes for Islamic theology in Germany.[4] In short, this chapter not only concerns my own position as a scholar of Islam; rather, I participate here, with fellow scholars, in an ongoing exploration of the politics of Islamic studies knowledge production that informs our work and our participation in constructing the field of Islamic studies.

In what follows, I focus on gender, power and critique as three of the numerous tools I see at my disposal in my contributions to Islamic studies scholarship. I describe them as ethical tools, thereby upholding my claim that knowledge production is political. This claim and commitment hold us, as scholars, responsible for seriously and deeply considering the ethical implications of our work. As discursive concepts, they frequently and organically interact with each other in my work and, naturally, with other theoretical and methodological tools. My goal is to discuss each, in its relationship to the other two, by offering specific examples from my work, in conversation with other scholarship.

---

[2] I admit to some difficulty with transferring the Christian notion of theology to Muslim contexts. The religious studies debate in general is so invested in protecting religious studies from the notion of the theological as prescriptive that any attempt to argue that there may be broader notions of religious normativity and prescription ends up being dismissed as obfuscation.

[3] See, for example, the original provocation by Aaron Hughes 2012 and responses to it by Berg 2012; Kelsay 2012; Martin 2012; Mas 2012; Rippin 2012. There is also a series of blog posts on the *Religion Bulletin*, entitled 'Reflections on Islamic Studies', from 2014, including my piece; see Hammer 2014, and contributions by Vernon Schubel, Edward Curtis IV, James Crossley, Ruth Mas and Philip Tite. I am thus no stranger to these debates and have participated in several over the past five years.

[4] See, for example, Khorchide and Möller (eds), 2012; Engelhardt 2016, 2017.

GENDER

Despite decades of robust scholarship on gender issues and dynamics in Muslim texts and contexts, Islamic studies scholars seem to be divided between those who focus on gender as an analytic and those who do not engage in gender theory at all. My own interest in gender theory comes from my early investment in feminist activism, an investment that preceded my academic engagement with and eventual commitment to feminist methodology as the foundation of my work.[5] As a feminist scholar, I embrace the dynamic relationship between what Saba Mahmood has described as the 'diagnosis' of patriarchal structures in societies past and present, and the inherent commitment to feminism also offering a 'prescription' (or more than one) for the dismantling of patriarchy as a hierarchical and oppressive societal structure.[6]

Gender, like race, but historically older and not fully attached to capitalism and modernity, is a social construction linked to historically contextual forms of patriarchy as a hierarchical social structure that has been justified by various ideological frameworks affirming the power of men over women, some women over other women, and so on. Its social construction provides, for feminists, the foundation for our argument for the possibility and necessity of change. If something is not uniform across space and time, and has in fact changed, then it could also be changed again. However, anti-feminist backlash in many societies around the world points to the fact that social construction does not equal easy deconstruction or flexibility because human beings are invested in stable constructs and because men (and some women) are loath to give up the privileges bestowed on them by these forms of patriarchal hierarchies.[7]

In my project on the 2005 woman-led, mixed gender congregational Friday prayer, I also more broadly explored women's Quranic exegesis, negotiations of mosques as gendered spaces, the search for historical role models, and precedents for gender equality from Muslim histories and interpretations as well as the politics of Muslim women's media representations. The resulting book, *American Muslim Women, Religious Authority, and Activism: More Than a Prayer*, captured and narrated more than a decade of American Muslim women's negotiations of gender hierarchies and their struggles for gender justice. In the

---

[5] Many things can and should be said here about the complex relationship between feminism and Muslims, including Muslim women who identify as feminists and those who reject the label. The discussion of 'Islam and feminism' is ongoing and productive and rather than attempting to summarise it, here I reference the outstanding work of Fatima Seedat who has surveyed the debates and argued for a complex relationship between the two constructs. See Seedat 2013, 2016.

[6] Mahmood 2006: 10. Mahmood describes it as 'both an analytical and a politically prescriptive project'.

[7] As Deniz Kandiyoti has argued, in addition to men's access to power, women can also access limited power in a patriarchal system, namely by what Kandiyoti calls 'bargaining with patriarchy'. See Kandiyoti 1988, 1998. For a very compelling study of women in the Nation of Islam, see Taylor 2017.

book, I argue that Muslim women scholars and activists focus their efforts on interpretations of the Quran and *Sunna* that support their claim that God's intention for Muslim societies, and indeed all human societies, is the achievement of gender justice.

Amina Wadud[8] has described gender jihad as 'a struggle to establish gender justice in Muslim thought and practice. At its simplest level, gender justice is gender mainstreaming – the inclusion of women in *all* aspects of Muslim practice, performance, policy construction, and in both political and religious leadership.'[9]

In this particular gender justice project, based on the argument that equality in ritual leadership is a reflection of gender equality in all other social interactions, Muslim scholars and activists have relied on a construction of Islam (i.e. divine intent) as inherently 'gender-just' which necessitates explaining why Muslim societies are diagnosed by the same scholars and activists as patriarchal and oppressive to women if not outright misogynistic. In other words, where does the discrepancy between divine will and social reality come from? Sometimes, this construction of a gender-just Islam juxtaposes Islam as God's intent with Muslim practices which differ from that intent; at other times, Islam is juxtaposed with culture, especially Muslim cultures past and present, as the problem. Amina Wadud has recognised that the claim to gender justice from within 'Islam' requires a productive engagement with varying definitions of that 'Islam' while also attending to the dynamics of authority and power over discourses in Muslim communities and contexts.[10] In a chapter titled, 'What's in a Name?', she writes:

> Despite numerous definitions, historical and current, whether explained or not, knowingly or unknowingly, each user assumes some authority that justifies him or her to determine when others would be considered adherents to their understandings, practice, and limitations of 'Islam'. From the multiple parameters of these understandings of 'Islam', the discussions with diverse presumptions, the social-cultural climate, and the positions of authority, others could be accused of heresy, deviance, or even blasphemy or *kufr*, disbelief or infidelity to Islam. Meanwhile if one intends to work from 'an Islamic perspective', he or she does not want to forfeit Islamic legitimacy. One of the most intimidating strategies used to deter women from working openly on

---

[8] Dr wadud has preferred her name spelled with lower case letters, amina wadud, like bell hooks did before her, to shift attention from her identity to her ideas. I want to acknowledge and honour that commitment even if the academy and publishing industry do not, including the editors of this volume.

[9] Wadud 2006: 10.

[10] I see interesting parallels to Wadud's discussion in the chapters by Aaron Hughes and Carool Kersten in this volume.

reforms within an Islamic framework is the powerful force of techniques that accuse others of denying or going against 'Islam'.[11]

More recently, Wadud has described 'Islam' as dynamic and living, thereby further emphasising that all claims to legitimacy are relative to those making such claims and the interpretive communities that support them. The significance of interpretive communities, the role of critique, and the generational stratification of feminist scholarship on Islam can all be demonstrated in the responses to Aysha Hidayatullah's 2014 book, *Feminist Edges of the Qur'an*. The book is a careful and critical study of the work of Muslim feminist Quran scholars; it created serious controversy among Muslim feminist scholars because she suggests that there may be limits to what Muslim feminists can ask the Quran to say for them in support of gender justice.[12] She argues that Muslim feminist exegesis has reached an impasse at which we have to ask ourselves whether the sacred text does indeed advocate for the abolition of social hierarchies including slavery, patriarchy and economic inequality. Hidayatullah's book (begins and) ends with the cautious suggestion to look elsewhere for divine self-disclosure and acknowledge that the Quran as a historical document and a product of its time may have limits that cannot be transcended by more and better interpretation.[13] In the preface, an unflinching and honest discussion of the potential fallout from the book, she writes:

> I have become only further convinced that if Muslim women are to come fully to terms with cases in which the Qur'anic text lends itself to meanings that are detrimental to them, we must begin to confront those meanings more honestly, without resorting to apologetic explanations for them, or engaging in interpretive manipulations to force egalitarian meanings from the text. Furthermore, I have also come to believe firmly that we must begin to radically reimagine the nature of the Qur'an's revelation and divinity.[14]

It was Amina Wadud who argued, even before Hidayatullah's book was published, that the struggle for social justice has to be rooted in personal experience, thereby allowing forms of God's self-disclosure to emerge from sources other

---

[11] Wadud 2006: 21.
[12] The controversy following the publication of *Feminist Edges of the Qur'an* appears to me to be based both on an ungenerous misreading of her central arguments and frustration on the part of the previous generation of Muslim feminist scholars for being engaged critically and moving beyond their ideas. See contributions to a roundtable in the *Journal of Feminist Studies in Religion* (32:2, Fall 2016): Barlas 2016a, 2016b; Ali 2016; Bauer 2016; Wadud 2016; Hidayatullah 2016; Seedat 2016; Rahmaan 2016.
[13] Hidayatullah 2014, esp. chap. 9.
[14] Hidayatullah 2014: viii.

than the Quran.[15] Kecia Ali has suggested, in a somewhat different vein, that texts other than the Quran could yield insights into divine intent.[16] Rethinking the centrality of the Quran as the exclusive access point for Muslims from which they make meaning and define themselves is but one arena, albeit an important one, in which attention to gender and to gender justice has contributed to the formation of Islamic studies as an academic field. I am well aware that Wadud's work in particular has intentionally transcended the boundaries of the academy, Euro-American or otherwise. Instead, Wadud has located her purpose, through her work with Sisters in Islam and Musawah, and through intentionally writing and publishing beyond the confines of the academic book market, in a broader engagement with Muslims as experts in analysing and changing the world.

I share some of these arguments here to demonstrate that Muslim scholars and activists engage in the construction and deconstruction of Islam – and that they are well aware of the constructedness of their exegetical projects, and are still committed to a gender-just Islam as a blueprint for a better society. It is possible, but in my view unethical, to judge further academic deconstruction, in the form of judging these scholars and activists as less than sincere in their engagement with their Islam, or, perhaps worse, to judge them insufficiently rational because of their religious commitments. Such a project would also need to be acknowledged as explicitly political in its uses: the dismissal of Muslims' agency in producing scholarly discourse echoes earlier orientalist scholarship that catalogued Muslim thought and practice for the purpose of colonial control and domination; and/or it denied Muslims, as colonial subjects, the ability to be modern, secular, and thus in control of religion as a limited and private domain, or it denied Islam the status of a religion altogether.

In my scholarship on American Muslim religious practice, exegetical projects and activism, the introduction and application of gender as a feminist analytical tool has organically led to my recognition and critique of gender hierarchies and gendered forms of systemic oppression. I share with many of the scholars and activists I have studied and written about the commitment to recognising injustices, including gendered injustice and oppression in society, and the desire to offer a vision for society that embraces and strives for social justice.

POWER

The feminist movement, in both theory and practice, is not and has never been a unified or homogenous one. Here it is important to distance myself from versions of feminist critique that simply blame religion as irrevocably patriarchal,

---

[15] For a discussion of this aspect of Wadud's work, see Majeed 2012.
[16] Ali 2009.

as this would necessitate the liberation of women from religion altogether, in order to destroy the patriarchy. A particularly insidious and early version of such feminist critique can be found in those who single out 'Islamic patriarchy' as uniquely oppressive. Leila Ahmed and others have discussed the complicity in and active support of European feminist movements for colonial projects in the nineteenth and early twentieth centuries. Saba Mahmood and Megan Goodwin describe, quite powerfully, how this particular form of anti-Muslim hostility not only survived but thrives in the American public square and US foreign policy. While there are differences between colonial feminisms and those of the late twentieth and twenty-first centuries, the historical connection between them needs to be acknowledged. For Mahmood and Goodwin, feminist complicity in neocolonial projects such as the 'War on Terror' and US imperial domination in the Middle East is linked to domestic policies that identify Muslim men as (potential) terrorists at the worst, and as oppressors of Muslim women at the least.[17]

In a constructive approach to Islamic studies, we need to ask, where is the power to define our subjects of study and our concepts located? As an advisor to PhD students in Islamic studies, I am all too aware of the genealogy of the field of Islamic studies, and of its roots in orientalist scholarship. Edward Said and many others after him have demonstrated in great detail and very convincingly that power is unevenly distributed in the project of knowledge production. Those with the power to define the field and its objects of study are able to assert their theoretical and academic superiority and secure higher positions in political and institutional hierarchies. In addition to recognising and describing the hierarchical binaries of Europe and the Middle East, of Europeans and Middle Easterners, Said's *Orientalism* made another important contribution when he argued that such binary representations are powerful tools for shaping/changing the very societies and people they purport to objectively and dispassionately describe.[18]

In several research projects, I have aimed to capture the gendered nature of anti-Muslim hostility in the US context of the early twenty-first century. I reluctantly waded into the murky depth of anti-Muslim media content, especially post-9/11, and wrote about the ways in which Muslim women, as objects of anti-Muslim (and often feminist) discourse take 'center stage' while not being recognised as agents in the deliberations about their supposed need for 'liberation' from Islam and Muslim men. I analysed the utilisation of the trope of oppressed and silent Muslim women in white and liberal feminist discourse

---

[17] Ahmed 1992: 150–5; Mahmood 2008; Goodwin 2018.

[18] See Said 2003. The literature that engages with orientalism is expansive, both laudatory and critical. Said's most influential work continues to inspire such engagement more than forty years after its original publication.

in the service of US Empire, and the othering of Muslim men and Islam as foreign to the United States and as a threat. Politicians as well as pundits have described American Muslim women as a demographic fifth column that aims to overwhelm US society with Muslims.[19]

These works, published in 2013, were relatively quickly overtaken by a new dynamic in the construction and application of gendered anti-Muslim discourse. No longer in need of saving by white imperial feminists, more recently, Muslim women have acquired notoriety as potential terrorists themselves, rather than as victims of the men in their families, as, for example, in the cases of the San Bernardino attackers in 2015 and the heinous attack on the Pulse Club in Orlando in 2016. The presidential executive orders of 2017, dubbed 'Muslim Bans' for good reason, have not distinguished between men, women and children, and have denied all of them shelter, asylum and safety. Not least, outspoken Muslim women activists who engage in intersectional social justice work, most prominently Linda Sarsour, have been viciously attacked by mainstream and Islamophobic news outlets and the Islamophobia industry. I have argued that an increasing number of women in these latter categories are now beyond even the pretense of being savable and have fallen beyond the boundaries of a benevolent, if deeply hierarchical, feminist and liberal project of saving Muslim women.[20]

The power dynamic in the above seems clear. In my studies of American Muslim approaches to gender and sexuality, in both discourse and practice, I have also found that, in line with Edward Said's argument, American Muslims are acutely aware of the ways they are perceived and treated in American society. This awareness of perceptions (as evidenced in public scrutiny) and of government surveillance, and even government infiltration and entrapment (both with a long history in the twentieth century),[21] plays an important role in how American Muslims engage in discursive production, religious and social practices, and even more so, in any kind of activism.

This is especially evident in intra-communal conversations and debates about gender and sexuality. First, every intra-Muslim conversation already takes place under, and conscious of, the gaze of the broader American public. Second, the many forms and faces of anti-Muslim hostility are frequently used as an argument by those in relative power and authority in Muslim communities to shut down or curb internal critique of gender injustice. Muslim religious scholars and authority figures (mostly male) have accused activists for gender justice who are critical of gendered hierarchies and oppression in Muslim communities

---

[19] See some of my work on gendered anti-Muslim hostility: Hammer 2013a, 2013b.
[20] See Hammer 2019a.
[21] See Johnson 2015; Curtis 2013.

of being feminists, being agents of US imperialism out to destroy Islam and Muslim communities, and more recently, of being representatives of liberalism, respectively. Clearly, there is power in labelling one's opponent in this way; the result is a marginalisation of gender justice activists, their ideas, and their activist projects in Muslim communities.

Yet, a public critique of such tactics inevitably plays into the rampant anti-Muslim sentiments in the public sphere and Muslim gender-justice activists have found themselves in an untenable situation. They navigate these challenges in a variety of ways and build alliances in different directions in order to emerge from the corner that they have been manoeuvered into. Some find allies in other religious feminist scholars and activists; others benefit from a somewhat patronising but also more protected space in academic institutions; yet others build national and global networks and coalitions with other Muslim women (and men) grassroots activists; and yet others participate in intersectional social justice movements, such as the Black Lives Matter movement, the movement for migrant rights and protections, and struggles for climate justice. In all these and other grassroots movements, and in the scholarship produced by and about these struggles, critique plays an important and productive role as an ethical tool for self-reflection, improvement and accountability.

CRITIQUE

In reflecting on the possibilities of critique I return to the 2015 debate over Islamic studies generated by Aaron Hughes' provocation, all published in *Method and Theory in the Study of Religion*. More particularly, I invoke here Ruth Mas's constructive contribution to that conversation, aptly titled, 'Why Critique?'. Early on, Mas distinguishes between critique and criticism, and then writes:

> Not only has the use of criticism been propped up by the authority of the secular in the socio-political arenas of the modern state, it has also functioned to shape the concept of the humanities in the West as a project that originated within the enlightenment and from which it inherited its critical intentions and tendencies.[22]

According to Mas, in asking the question 'why critique(,) can therefore lead to either an acceptance or dismissal of critique or, as is the intention here, to an interrogation of its historical situatedness and the functions that are being established therein'.[23] I take from Mas both the possibility of constructive

---

[22] Mas 2012: 391.
[23] Mas 2012: 405.

critique and the necessity for a critical self-interrogation of the purpose of our critique.

I add to Mas's framework the contribution of Middle East studies scholar Miriam Cooke who much earlier had advocated for the possibility of 'multiple critique', specifically in the work of writers and advocates she described as Islamic feminists.[24] And to expand and deepen my own understanding of critique I also call on political scientist Rochelle Terman's notion of responsible critique.[25] Terman recognises the weight of navigating the dual pressures of engaging in critique of imperialist and anti-Muslim modes of representing Muslim women on one hand and patriarchal limitations from within Muslim contexts on the other. She concludes:

> In order to engage in the 'productive undoing' of the double bind, I propose we shift the paradigm of responsible critique from recruitability to one based on openness. A responsible critique is one that opens the widest analytic space in which a double critique can take place, qualifies the most voices, and allows for the greatest creativity in producing new political imaginaries.[26]

Critiquing someone or something as patriarchal, oppressive and unjust is not too difficult and within the ethical boundaries of my project of Islamic studies. A feminist analysis of gender dynamics in Muslim communities and the accompanying critique which, in turn, would form the foundation for an alternative and more just vision provides the tools for such a project. As I have argued above, such responsible critique does not require the deconstruction of 'Islam' as a frame of reference for social and gender justice projects, even when that 'Islam' is explicitly recognised as a construction. The political goals of the scholar of Islam can indeed align with those of the Muslims they are studying and I see no reason to not support a more just vision of society, one that does not necessitate the complete deconstruction of religion, or the detachment from religious commitments or religiously informed ethical visions.

In my work on American Muslim efforts against domestic violence (DV), however, I encountered a different challenge. The Muslim advocates at the frontlines of the work to raise awareness of DV in Muslim communities and provide services to DV victims, unlike those in the mainstream anti-DV movement in the United States, did not frame their work in feminist terms, namely as a critique of patriarchy and the attendant familial hierarchies that feminists argue have created the power and control dynamics typical for DV situations.

---

[24] Cooke 2002.
[25] Terman 2016.
[26] Terman 2016: 24.

Rather, the majority of the DV advocates I worked with for my book on the topic were engaged in a different project, which I describe as protective patriarchy.

I do not embrace protective patriarchy as an alternative to the replacement of patriarchal hierarchies with gender justice and equality. But I did have to admit that the arguments for deploying protective patriarchy can be in the best interest of DV victims whose suffering and endangered bodies and minds cannot wait for the liberation of all society from patriarchal oppression. These considerations form an important part of my book and are framed there as a continuous respon-sibility to reflect on our methods and the ethical implications of certain critiques. And the proponents of protective patriarchy certainly recognise that 'Islam' can be a resource, as well as a roadblock, in the fight against domestic abuse. I say much more in *Peaceful Families* about the ways in which grassroots activists intentionally and carefully navigate between their own ethical vision of society and the realities on the ground. Meeting Muslim communities where they are at in their negotiation of rapidly changing gender norms and practices has proven to be one effective strategy for raising awareness of the issue of domestic violence, and arguing that DV is 'un-Islamic' accomplishes something where framing DV as patriarchal violence and oppression of women may have not yet succeeded, at least in US Muslim contexts. The book also contains ample evidence that Muslim feminist activists and scholars, while not the mainstream of Muslim communities, have made important discursive and practical contributions to the fight against domestic abuse.[27]

CONCLUSION

In his groundbreaking book, *The Idea of the Muslim World*, Cemil Aydin identi-fies the notion of the Muslim world as a nineteenth-century construct with deep roots in the European colonial and expansionist agenda. Aydin also chronicles how Muslim intellectuals and politicians participate in the perpetuation and redefinition of the idea of a Muslim world that echoes older notions of a unified Muslim *umma*, but also rebirths that very notion of the *umma* as a unifier of Muslims in the face of European colonialism. While Aydin does not take up gender as an analytic at all (it is a men's history, so to speak), he recognises very clearly the impact of his analysis of the Muslim world as a geopolitical construct. A good portion of the critical engagement with his book has pointed out the political dynamic at work in scholarship that seems to deconstruct the foundation of global Muslim solidarity. In his conclusion, Aydin aptly writes:

---

[27] Hammer 2019b.

The dispiriting trajectory of the idea of the Muslim world does not entail that contemporary Muslims are beyond their rights in imagining their own humanitarian or political solidarity. On the contrary, Muslims of all kinds have every right to be concerned about the current conditions and future of their coreligionists and to resist their racialized treatment, and they have the right to act on their internationalist and humanitarian visions to create a more just world. The religious and spiritual traditions of Muslims will continue to inspire them in their struggle for justice and dignity.[28]

As a scholar of Islam, and as a Muslim feminist, I take such inspiration seriously, and I am committed to a project that explores Muslim negotiations of Islam and Muslimness in all their complexity, and recognises such scholarship as an intentional and critical contribution to a world in need of change.

BIBLIOGRAPHY

Ahmed, Leila (1992), *Women and Gender in Islam: Historical Roots of a Modern Debate*, New Haven: Yale University Press.

Ali, Kecia (2009), 'Timeless Texts and Modern Morals – Challenges in Islamic Sexual Ethics', in Kari Vogt, Lena Larsen and Christian Moe (eds), *New Directions in Islamic Thought*, London: I. B. Tauris, pp. 89–100.

Ali, Kecia (2016), 'On Critique and Careful Reading', *Journal of Feminist Studies in Religion* 32, no. 2: 121–6.

Aydin, Cemil (2017), *The Idea of the Muslim World: A Global Intellectual History*, Cambridge, MA: Harvard University Press.

Barlas, Asma (2016a), 'A Response', *Journal of Feminist Studies in Religion* 32, no. 2: 148–51.

Barlas, Asma (2016b), 'Secular and Feminist Critiques of the Qur'an: Anti-Hermeneutics as Liberation?', *Journal of Feminist Studies in Religion* 32, no. 2: 111–21.

Bauer, Karen (2016), 'In Defense of Historical-Critical Analysis of the Qur'an', *Journal of Feminist Studies in Religion* 32, no. 2: 126–30.

Berg, Herbert (2012), 'The Essence of Essentializing: A Critical Discourse on "Critical Discourse in the Study of Islam"', *Method and Theory in the Study of Religion* 24, nos. 4–5: 337–56, https://doi.org/10.1163/15700682–12341235.

Cooke, Miriam (2002), 'Multiple Critique: Islamic Feminist Rhetorical Strategies', in Laura E. Donaldson and Kwok Pui-Lan (eds), *Postcolonialism, Feminism, and Religious Discourse*, New York: Routledge, pp. 142–60.

Curtis, Edward (2013), 'The Black Muslim Scare of the Twentieth Century: The History of State Islamophobia and Its Post-9/11 Variations', in Carl Ernst (ed.), *Islamophobia in America: The Anatomy of Intolerance*, New York: Palgrave, pp. 75–106.

---

[28] Aydin 2017: 236–7.

Engelhardt, Felix (2016), 'On Insiderism and Muslim Epistemic Communities in the German and US Study of Islam', *Muslim World* 106, no. 4: 740–58.

Engelhardt, Felix (2017), *Islamische Theologie im deutschen Wissenschaftssystem. Ausdifferenzierung und Selbstkonzeption einer neu etablierten Wissenschaftsdisziplin*, Wiesbaden: Springer.

Goodwin, Megan (2018), '"They Do That to Foreign Women": Domestic Terrorism and Contraceptive Nationalism in *Not Without My Daughter*', *Muslim World* 106: 759–80.

Hammer, Juliane (2013a), 'Center Stage: Muslim Women and Islamophobia', in Carl Ernst (ed.), *Islamophobia in America*, New York: Palgrave, pp. 107–44.

Hammer, Juliane (2013b), 'Gendering Islamophobia: (Muslim) Women's Bodies and American Politics', *Bulletin for the Study of Religion* 42, no. 1: 29–36.

Hammer, Juliane (2014), 'Changing the World: Reflections on Islamic Studies', http://bulletin.equinoxpub.com/2014/06/changing-the-world-reflections-on-islamic-studies/.

Hammer, Juliane (2019a), 'Muslim Women, Anti-Muslim Hostility, and the State in the Age of Terror', in Mohammad Khalil (ed.), *Muslims and Contemporary US Politics*, Cambridge, MA: Harvard University Press, pp. 104–26.

Hammer, Juliane (2019b), *Peaceful Families: American Muslim Efforts Against Domestic Violence*, Princeton, NJ: Princeton University Press.

Hidayatullah, Aysha (2014), *Feminist Edges of the Qur'an*, New York: Oxford University Press.

Hidayatullah, Aysha (2016), 'Claims to the Sacred', *Journal of Feminist Studies in Religion* 32, no. 2: 134–8.

Howe, Justine (2017), 'What is Scholarship Good For?', *The Immanent Frame*, 6 December, https://tif.ssrc.org/2017/12/06/what-is-scholarship-good-for/.

Hughes, Aaron W. (2012), 'The Study of Islam Before and After September 11: A Provocation', *Method and Theory in the Study of Religion* 24, nos. 4–5: 314–36.

Johnson, Sylvester (2015), *African American Religions, 1500–2000: Colonialism, Democracy, and Freedom*, New York: Cambridge University Press.

Kandiyoti, Deniz (1988), 'Bargaining with Patriarchy', *Gender and Society* 2, no. 3: 274–90.

Kandiyoti, Deniz (1998), 'Gender, Power, and Contestation: Rethinking Bargaining with Patriarchy', in Cecile Jackson and Ruth Pearson (eds), *Feminist Visions of Development: Gender Analysis and Policy*, London: Routledge, pp. 135–51.

Kelsay, John (2012), 'Islam and the Study of Ethics', *Method and Theory in the Study of Religion* 24, nos. 4–5: 357–70, https://doi.org/10.1163/15700682-12341237.

Khorchide, Mouhanad, and Marco Möller (eds) (2012), *Das Verhältnis zwischen Islamwissenschaft und Islamischer Theologie*, Münster: Agenda Verlag.

Mahmood, Saba (2006), *Politics of Piety*, Princeton, NJ: Princeton University Press.

Mahmood, Saba (2008), 'Feminism, Democracy, and Empire: Islam and the War on Terror', in Joan Wallach Scott (ed.), *Women's Studies on the Edge*, Durham, NC: Duke University Press, pp. 81–114.

Majeed, Debra (2012), 'Amina Wadud and the Promotion of Experience as Authority', in Kecia Ali, Juliane Hammer and Laury Silvers (eds), *A Jihad for Justice: The Work and Life of Amina Wadud*, pp. 59–91, https://www.bu.edu/religion/files/2010/03/A-Jihad-for-Justice-for-Amina-Wadud-2012-1.pdf.

Martin, Richard C. (2012), 'The Uses and Abuses of Criticism in the Study of Islam: A Response to Aaron Hughes', *Method and Theory in the Study of Religion* 24, nos. 4–5: 371–88, https://doi.org/10.1163/15700682–12341238.

Mas, Ruth (2012), 'Why Critique?', *Method and Theory in the Study of Religion* 24, nos. 4–5: 389–407, https://doi.org/10.1163/15700682–12341246.

Rahmaan, YaSiin (2016), 'Feminist Edges of Muslim Feminist Readings of Qur'anic Verses', *Journal of Feminist Studies in Religion* 32, no. 2: 142–8.

Rippin, Andrew (2012), 'Provocation and Its Responses', *Method and Theory in the Study of Religion* 24, nos. 4–5: 408–17, https://doi.org/10.1163/15700682–12341247.

Said, Edward (2003), *Orientalism*, New York: Pantheon.

Seedat, Fatima (2013), 'Islam, Feminism, and Islamic Feminism: Between Inadequacy and Inevitability', *Journal of Feminist Studies in Religion* 29, no. 2: 25–45.

Seedat, Fatima (2016), 'Beyond the Text: Between Islam and Feminism', *Journal of Feminist Studies in Religion* 32, no. 2: 138–42.

Taylor, Ula (2017), *The Promise of Patriarchy: Women and the Nation of Islam*, Chapel Hill: University of North Carolina Press.

Terman, Rochelle (2016), 'Islamophobia, Feminism, and the Politics of Critique', *Theory, Culture & Society* 33, no. 2: 77–102.

Wadud, Amina (2006), *Inside the Gender Jihad*, Oxford: Oneworld.

Wadud, Amina (2016), 'Can One Critique Cancel All Previous Efforts?', *Journal of Feminist Studies in Religion* 32, no. 2: 130–4.

About the Contributors

Shahzad Bashir is Aga Khan Professor of Islamic Humanities at Brown University.

Hadi Enayat is Visiting Lecturer at the Institute for Ismaili Studies, London.

Juliane Hammer is Associate Professor in the Department of Religious Studies at the University of North Carolina, Chapel Hill.

Aaron W. Hughes is Philip S. Bernstein Professor of Jewish Studies at the University of Rochester, NY.

Carool Kersten is Reader in the Study of Islam and the Muslim World at King's College, London.

Susanne Olsson is Professor in the History of Religions at the University of Stockholm.

Jonas Otterbeck is Professor of Islamic Studies at AKU-ISMC in London.

Leif Stenberg is Dean and Professor of Islamic Studies at AKU-ISMC in London.

Philip Wood is Professor of History at AKU-ISMC in London.

Index

EU representative:
Easy Access System Europe
Mustamäe tee 50, 10621 Tallinn, Estonia
Gpsr.requests@easproject.com

www.ingramcontent.com/pod-product-compliance
Lightning Source LLC
Chambersburg PA
CBHW071741270326
41928CB00013B/2753